Business, banking and finance in medieval Montpellier

by

Kathryn L. Reyerson

This is a study of financial techniques and a social history of credit before 1350. During the late thirteenth and early fourteenth centuries, Montpellier was the most important economic center on the Mediterranean coast between Genoa and Barcelona. This work traces the evolution of business partnerships, market transactions, loans, deposit banking and foreign exchange from their first appearance in the documents of the twelfth century through the years of extant notarial evidence from 1293 to 1348.

Proximity to Italy meant that Montpellier benefited from the influence of Italian financial expertise and achieved considerable economic sophistication. The business activities of a cross section of the urban population, including merchants, artisans and agricultural workers, reveal differing investment strategies among local social groups. The use of credit varied from one economic sector to another and led to the elaboration of methods for the recovery of debts. The markets of international trade, local trade, agriculture and real estate responded differently to the changing economic conditions of the early fourteenth century. The interrelationship of medieval commerce and finance is demonstrated in the multifaceted roles of medieval businessmen, who, as commercial bankers, underwrote trade through credit extension in partnerships and in luxury and commodity operations. Business and credit instruments were adapted by Montpelliérains to their specific economic needs. Montpellier served as a fulcrum of trade and finance between the Mediterranean world and northern Europe in the High and Late Middle Ages.

This volume includes an extensive bibliography, an appendix on monetary problems and illustrative transcriptions of Latin commercial and financial instruments.

STUDIES AND TEXTS 75

BUSINESS, BANKING AND FINANCE IN MEDIEVAL MONTPELLIER

by

KATHRYN L. REYERSON

PONTIFICAL INSTITUTE OF MEDIAEVAL STUDIES

CANADIAN CATALOGUING IN PUBLICATION DATA

Reyerson, Kathryn L. (Kathryn Louise), 1945-
Business, banking and finance in medieval Montpellier

(Studies and texts, ISSN 0082-5328 ; 75)
Bibliography: p.
Includes index.
ISBN 0-88844-075-8

1. Montpellier (France) - Economic conditions. 2. Finance - France - Montpellier - History. 3. Credit - France - Montpellier - History. 4. Banks and banking - France - Montpellier - History. I. Pontifical Institute of Mediaeval Studies. II. Title. III. Series: Studies and texts (Pontifical Institute of Mediaeval Studies) ; 75.

HC278.M6R4 1985 330.944′84 C84-099076-6

Pontifical Institute of Mediaeval Studies
59 Queen's Park Crescent East
Toronto, Ontario, Canada M5S 2C4

PRINTED BY UNIVERSA, WETTEREN, BELGIUM

Contents

List of Tables

List of Graphs

Abbreviations

ACA	Archivo de la Corona de Aragon
A. D. Hérault	Archives Départementales de l'Hérault
A. M. Montpellier	Archives Municipales de Montpellier
Annales: ESC	*Annales: Économies, Sociétés, Civilisations*
ARV	Archivo del Reino de Valencia
Cartulaire de Maguelone	*Cartulaire de Maguelone*, ed. Jean Rouquette and A. Villemagne. 5 vols. Montpellier, 1912-1925
Fédération historique	*Bulletin de la Fédération historique du Languedoc Méditerranéen et du Roussillon*
HL	Dom Devic and Dom Vaissète. *Histoire générale de Languedoc*. 14 vols. Toulouse, 1872-1904
Inv. A. M. Montp.	*Archives communales de Montpellier antérieures à 1790, Inventaires et documents*, vols. 1-12
Layettes	A. Teulet, ed. *Layettes du Trésor des Chartes*. 5 vols. Paris
LIM	C. Chabaneau and A. Germain, eds., *Liber Instrumentorum Memorialium. Cartulaire des Guillems de Montpellier*. Montpellier, 1884-1886
Mem. soc. arch. Mplr.	*Mémoires de la société archéologique de Montpellier*
Ordonnances	*Ordonnances des Roys de France de la troisième race*. 23 vols. Paris, 1723-1849
Le Petit Thalamus	*Le Petit Thalamus de Montpellier*, ed. F. Pégat, E. Thomas and Desmazes. Montpellier, 1840
Recueil	*Recueil de mémoires et travaux publié par la société d'histoire du droit et des institutions des anciens pays de droit écrit*
l. t.	*livres tournois*
p. t.	*petits tournois = deniers tournois*
l. melg.	*livres melgoriens*

Preface

The history of banking and credit in medieval Montpellier has not been the subject of a monograph before now.[1] Studies of the financial history of other European towns have proved invaluable as models for this investigation into medieval finance. Classic among such studies is Raymond de Roover's *Money, Banking and Credit in Mediaeval Bruges* (Cambridge, Mass., 1948). De Roover traced the credit operations of the pawnbroker, the money changer and the merchant banker, providing a broad spectrum of urban financial activities. His multiple studies in financial history have made significant contributions to this field. Robert S. Lopez's examinations of the medieval moneyer, the origins of banking activities and the economic exploits of medieval merchants have furnished invaluable technical information for medieval financial history as have the works of Abbott P. Usher, Armando Sapori, André-E. Sayous, Yves Renouard, Philippe Wolff and others.[2] Richard W. Emery's study of Jewish economic activities in Perpignan made an interesting specialized contribution based upon notarial evidence.[3]

For a number of reasons Montpellier is a desirable context in which to explore banking and the financial operations of trade. In the period 1204-1349 Montpellier was first an Aragonese and then a Majorcan enclave within Languedoc.[4] Proximity to Italy meant that Montpellier profited from the influence of Italian commercial expertise and enjoyed a degree of economic sophistication. Montpellier was a typical Mediterranean town in the Middle Ages in that it had a heterogeneous population with numerous agricultural workers as well as local and international merchants, retailers, artisans and legal specialists; yet the absence of an important indigenous cloth industry and its accompanying proletariat sets Montpellier apart from many medieval towns.[5] Montpellier had several urban identities: intellectual with a university of medicine, law and the

[1] This study addresses the issue of private finance. The topics of public finance and taxation in Montpellier were the subject of a lengthy article by Jacques Ellul, "Notes sur les impôts municipaux à Montpellier aux XIIIe et XIVe siècles," *Revue historique de droit français et étranger* 17 (1938), 365-403. The absence of tax lists before the end of the fourteenth century makes research into the fiscal history of Montpellier less fruitful than in towns like Florence and in French towns such as Paris, Albi and Saint-Flour.

[2] The bibliography gives multiple citations for these authors.

[3] R. W. Emery, *The Jews of Perpignan in the Thirteenth Century. An Economic Study Based on Notarial Records* (New York, 1959).

[4] See Introduction, pp. 6-7.

[5] On the lack of a cloth industry, see my article, "Le rôle de Montpellier dans le commerce des draps de laine avant 1350," *Annales du Midi* 94 (1982), 17-40.

arts; commercial as an entrepot of trade between north and south; and financial as a center of banking and foreign exchange. With 30,000 to 40,000 inhabitants by the end of the thirteenth century, Montpellier ranked among the most populous towns of France. Foreigners abounded as temporary visitors, and immigration brought newcomers from central and southern France, Spain and Italy as permanent residents.[6]

Montpellier had a reputation as a financial center in the Middle Ages.[7] The role of financial transactions and, in particular, of money changing, in Montpellier finds its best illustration in the appellation of the eleventh-century pilgrimage oratory Nôtre-Dame-des-Tables because money changers had their focus of business nearby.[8] The financial vocation of Montpellier was facilitated by the proximity of the mint of Melgueil, which can be traced as early as the tenth century.[9] Present in the town were most of the financial functions which historians have identified with medieval banking.[10] In addition to money changing, evidence of foreign exchange, money lending and deposit banking has survived. Furthermore, the interrelationship of medieval commerce and finance is demonstrated in the multifaceted roles of medieval businessmen, who, as commercial bankers in Montpellier and in many economically advanced towns, acted as financiers or underwriters of trade, extending credit through commercial partnerships and in the market operations of the luxury trade and the traffic in commodities.

In this study I will trace the financial history of Montpellier from its beginnings through 1348, a logical *terminus ad quem* in light of changes occurring at the mid-fourteenth century. The mid century represents an economic, demographic and political watershed for Montpellier.[11] The Black Death of 1348 took a massive toll of the local population.[12] The most telling contemporary commentator on the transformation of Montpellier after 1350 was Petrarch, who had been a law student at the university in 1316-1320. Writing in his old age, Petrarch deplored the decadence of Montpellier, bemoaning the incorporation of the old Majorcan citadel into the kingdom of France and evoking the penury of public and private

[6] On the population of Montpellier, see my article, "Patterns of Population Attraction and Mobility: The Case of Montpellier, 1293-1348," *Viator* 10 (1979), 257-281.

[7] See the general study by Louis J. Thomas, *Montpellier, ville marchande: histoire économique et sociale de Montpellier des origines à 1870* (Montpellier, 1936). The presence of Jacques Cœur in Montpellier a century after the end of this study reinforced the financial reputation of the town at the end of the Middle Ages. On Jacques Cœur, see Louise Guiraud, *Recherches et conclusions nouvelles sur le prétendu rôle de Jacques Cœur* (Paris, 1900).

[8] Louise Guiraud, "Recherches topographiques sur Montpellier au moyen âge," *Mem. soc. arch. Mplr.*, 2nd ser., I (1899), 122. See also *Le guide du pèlerin de Saint-Jacques de Compostelle*, 3rd. ed. by Jeanne Vieillard (Mâcon, 1963), p. 2.

[9] See the appendix on "Monetary Problems."

[10] The scholarly debate about the origins of medieval banking will be explored in Chapters 3, 4 and 5.

[11] See the Introduction for the historical background of change.

[12] On one aspect of the effects of the plague, see my article, "Changes in Testamentary Practice at Montpellier on the Eve of the Black Death," *Church History* 47 (1978), 253-269.

affairs, the disappearance of rich merchandise, the diminution in numbers of students and the privation of peace.[13]

The medieval sources of Montpellier are rich. I have explored the charters of the Archives Municipales for information on medieval finance.[14] The local cartularies provided some additional information. Most informative, however, were the notarial registers of the Archives Municipales and the Archives Départementales de l'Hérault. Notarial minutes are among the most well-endowed depositories of debt instruments surviving from the Middle Ages.[15] The earliest extant register in Montpellier dates from 1293-1294. Thirteen registers have been preserved in the period 1293-1348, with a lacuna from 1302 to 1327. After 1348, probably because of the plague, another lacuna in the notarial evidence extends to 1361. The notarial evidence thus reinforces a mid-fourteenth-century end point for this study.

While the notarial evidence is not as abundant as one might wish, the notarial archives of southern France preserve many fewer registers than those of Italian archives.[16] For the late Middle Ages, Philippe Wolff found only two hundred registers in Toulouse.[17] About thirty registers are preserved at Marseille for the thirteenth century, a comparable number at Manosque, one at Grasse and one at Cabasse.[18] Seventeen registers of the thirteenth century survive at Perpignan while several hundred are preserved for the fourteenth century.[19] In spite of the limited number of surviving registers in Montpellier, their data, when combed exhaustively, are sufficiently rich to permit generalizations on many aspects of social and economic life in Montpellier. To supplement the local information, I

[13] *Francisci Petrarchae Florentini Philosophi Oratoris et poetae clarissimi, Opera Omnia*, ed. Henrichus Petri (Basel, 1554), *Rerum senilium*, Liber X: "De mutatione temporum," 960: "Et quanquam de maioribus possem, ut memoria tamen tua, nostrae astipuletur assertioni, de his quae simul ambo vidimus, cupidius tecum loquor, inde igitur simul quoque, nam quid divisim magna aetatis partis gessimus, vicina iam pubertate ad Montem Pessulanum, florentissimum tunc oppidum, iurisque ad studium delati, aliud ibi quadriennium exegimus, cuius tunc potestas, penes maiores Balearice regem erat, exiguum praeter loci angulum, Francorum regi subditum, qui ut semper praepotentium importuna vicinia est, brevi totius oppidi dominium ad se traxit, quae nam vero tunc ibi quoque tranquillitas? quae pax? quae divitiae mercatorum? quae scholarium turba? quae copia magistrorum? quanta ibi nunc horum omnium penuria, publicarumque et privatarum rerum, quanta mutatio, et nos scimus, et cives qui utrumque viderunt tempus sentiunt."

[14] The Bibliography gives details of the archival holdings in Montpellier.

[15] David Herlihy, *Pisa in the Early Renaissance* (New Haven, 1958), Chapter 1, pp. 1-20, provides a good introduction to notarial evidence. The recent work by John H. Pryor, *Business Contracts of Medieval Provence, Selected Notulae from the Cartulary of Giraud Amalric of Marseilles, 1248* (Toronto, 1981), gives very useful background on the notarial contracts of Amalric of Marseille with selected documents for illustration. While earlier than the extant contracts of Montpellier, those of Amalric (1248) show many similarities.

[16] One can compare the immensely wealthy Genoese archives. See R. S. Lopez, "The Unexplored Wealth of the Notarial Archives in Pisa and Lucca," in *Mélanges Louis Halphen* (Paris, 1951), pp. 417-418.

[17] P. Wolff, *Commerces et marchands de Toulouse (vers 1350-vers 1450)* (Paris, 1954), VII.

[18] R. S. Lopez, "The Unexplored Wealth of the Notarial Archives," p. 418.

[19] R. W. Emery, *The Jews of Perpignan*, pp. 1-10. See the inventory of Marcel Robin, *Archives départementales des Pyrénées-Orientales*, I, Série B (Paris, 1868) and the manuscript inventory of Série E.

have consulted published sources from other Mediterranean towns. In an attempt to assess the degree of economic sophistication in Montpellier, I have sought a comparative context to illuminate further the Montpellier findings.

My goal has been to evaluate and refine historians' understanding of the financial reputation of Montpellier through analysis of the financial techniques associated with banking and commercial activities in Montpellier and of the participation of local inhabitants and foreigners in such operations. This work is at one and the same time a history of the emergence and development of business operations in Montpellier and a social history of those activities.[20] I have organized this study around those financial techniques related to business and trade which appear in the surviving evidence. Business partnerships, credit sales, recognitions of debt, commodity futures, deposits, foreign exchange contracts and loans have been probed in depth.

One of the main focuses of this study is on credit in its multiple forms and functions on the Montpellier marketplace, in artisans' industrial activities, in the luxury and commodities trades, in local and foreign financial operations and investments. Given the broad spectrum of the urban population included in the notarial clientele, it has been possible to examine the use of credit by Montpelliérains and foreigners alike: who extended credit, who sought it and under what circumstances. The role of credit in the medieval economy has long been recognized.[21] However, credit activities varied from place to place, and the history of medieval credit can still benefit from the insights of case studies such as this.

I have examined the nature and characteristics of business partnership as a means of investigating the processes of capitalization of commercial and industrial enterprise. The predilection of certain social groups for specific investment mechanisms has been identified. Here, and in the exploration of the other financial techniques of this study, I have sought to distinguish the similarities and differences between practice in Montpellier and in other Mediterranean towns.

The analysis of local market transactions has revealed differences in the use of credit in the luxury trade and in agriculture. Credit practices varied, too, in the wholesale and retail trade and under good economic times and bad.[22] The importance of credit in medieval trade is well illustrated in the Montpellier evidence.

[20] This work does not deal with the history of investment in property nor is it a commercial history of Montpellier. I have dealt with aspects of the history of commerce in articles listed in the Bibliography and I have an extensive study, "Lands, Houses and Real Estate Investment in Montpellier: A Study of the Notarial Property Transactions, 1293-1348," *Studies in Medieval and Renaissance History* 6 (Old ser. 16) (1983), 37-112.

[21] Michael M. Postan, "Credit in Medieval Trade," *Economic History Review* 1 (1928), 234-261. This article has been reprinted in *Medieval Trade and Finance* (Cambridge, 1973), pp. 1-27. Citations will be made to the reprinted edition.

[22] On the question of retail and wholesale trade in the Middle Ages, see the comments of M. M. Postan, "Credit in Medieval Trade," p. 5, and R. L. Reynolds, "Origins of Modern Business Enterprise," *Journal of Economic History* 12 (1953), 356-359.

The widespread use of credit led to the elaboration of methods for the recovery of debts. The repayment of financial obligations was closely related to banking practices in the medieval economy. While the evidence of deposit banking in Montpellier is not as ample as in Flemish and Italian towns, considerable information remains regarding foreign exchange operations and loans. Exploration of these facets of medieval banking in Montpellier again reveals the prevalence of credit in the local and international economy.

A study such as this of financial techniques and practices faces problems given the nature and quantity of the surviving evidence. The cost of credit remains a thorny issue of scholarly debate on which the remaining Montpellier evidence sheds little light.[23] By the same token, the profits of investment were difficult to determine given the omission in the sources of rates of return and of partnership accounts. While the number of cash versus credit transactions can be calculated in the extant documents, it is impossible to assess what proportion of economic operations in Montpellier was based on credit operations.[24] Oral obligations undoubtedly existed. Debtors and creditors may have dispensed with notarial records in favor of charters of obligation exchanged only between them. Other repositories of credit records such as account books do not survive in Montpellier.[25]

The volume of market activity in specific economic sectors cannot be calculated on the basis of the surviving notarial and charter evidence.The same can be said of investment levels. Because of the absence of data on the quantity and quality of merchandise, price series cannot be established with certainty.[26] Instead, the average value of transactions in a particular sector has been plotted as a means of gauging trends within the surviving data.

No study of urban fortune has been possible in the absence of fiscal inventories such as the *estimes* of Toulouse or the remarkable *catasto* of early fifteenth-century Florence.[27] Fiscal surveys date from the late fourteenth century in Mont-

[23] For opposing views on the cost of credit, see Auram L. Udovitch, "Credit as a Means of Investment in Medieval Islamic Trade," *Journal of the American Oriental Society* 87 (1967), 260-264; M. M. Postan, "Credit in Medieval Trade," p. 23; and P. Wolff, *Commerces et marchands de Toulouse*, pp. 366-380.

[24] See n. 21 above. Historians concur in the assessment that it is impossible to ascertain what proportion of economic transactions in the Middle Ages is based on credit operations. M. M. Postan pointed out that the source of this difficulty lies in the fact that most of the surviving medieval economic evidence relates to debts.

[25] On surviving southern French accounts for the Middle Ages, see E. Forestié, ed., *Les livres de comptes des frères Bonis, marchands montalbanais du XIVe siècle*, 2 vols. (Paris and Auch, 1893); P. Mayer, "Le livre-journal de Maître Ugo Teralh, notaire et drapier à Forcalquier," *Notices et extraits des manuscrits de la Bibliothèque Nationale* 36 (1899), 129-170; A. Blanc, *Le Livre de comptes de Jacme Olivier, marchand narbonnais du XIVe siècle* (Paris, 1899).

[26] On the problem of prices in a specific commercial sector, see my article, "Le rôle de Montpellier dans le commerce des draps de laine avant 1350," *Annales du Midi* 94 (1982), 36-38.

[27] See Philippe Wolff, *Les "Estimes" toulousaines des XIVe et XVe siècles* (Toulouse, 1956) and David Herlihy and Christiane Klapisch-Zuber, *Les Toscans et leurs familles. Une étude du catasto florentin de 1427* (Paris, 1978).

pellier.[28] Investment strategies of individual Montpelliérains and of social groups within the town have been explored, but no estimate of the proportion of resources devoted to a particular economic venture has been made. The overall distribution of wealth escapes analysis for the period before 1350.

Despite the shortcomings of the extant data, myriad details which illumine the historian's perception of the financial practices of a medieval urban population have survived. Notarial registers, in particular, are invaluable for the elucidation of economic techniques and structures which form the central concern of this study.[29] While the individual charters and notarial documents are not reliable for the development of statistics or for a study of economic conjuncture, they can inform us on the level of historical orientation regarding financial techniques, their formal basis and practical application.[30]

Several observations are necessary at the beginning of this study, first of all, regarding dates. Notarial dating practice in Montpellier began the year on 25 March, utilizing the Incarnation or *calculus Florentinus* style.[31] As a result, certain of the notarial registers used as evidence in this study extend into two of the modern calendar years. All the dates cited hereafter have been converted to modern usage (*nouveau style*).

Monetary quotations have been made according to the *tournois* system of money of account. In most cases in the evidence the *livre tournois* was reckoned in terms of *deniers tournois* coinage currently in circulation, with the familiar relationship of 1 *livre* = 20 s. = 240 d., which was worth 240 *deniers petits tournois*. An expanded discussion of monetary issues is provided in Appendix 2. However, at the outset of this study it is well to state the following monetary relationships:

> 13 *deniers melgoriens* of Montpellier = 12 *deniers tournois*, so that 1 d. *melg.* = 0.92 d. *t.*
> 8 *deniers parisis* = 10 *deniers tournois*, so that 1 d. *par.* = 1.25 d. t.
> 4 *deniers tournois* = 1 penny *sterling*, up to 1295

It suffices here to alert the reader to the complexity of the medieval monetary situation in a center of commerce and finance such as Montpellier.

[28] A recent École des Chartes thesis dealt with the *compoix* of late-medieval Montpellier: Anne Catherine Marin, "Montpellier à la fin du moyen âge d'après les compoix (1380-1450)," Thèse, École des Chartes, 1980.

[29] Jacques Heers, *L'Occident aux XIVe et XVe siècles, Aspects économiques et sociaux*, 3rd ed. (Paris, 1970), p. 256.

[30] On the problem of the survival and the use of notarial evidence, see also R. W. Emery, *The Jews of Perpignan*, pp. 4-10 and 29.

[31] See the manuscript inventory of the Archives Départementales de l'Hérault for the dating of the registers. On the Florentine style, see A. de Boüard, *Manuel de diplomatique*, 1: 303-304 and R. Dean Ware, "Medieval Chronology: Theory and Practice," in *Medieval Studies, An Introduction*, ed. James M. Powell (Syracuse, 1976), p. 221. The use of the Florentine style in Montpellier is demonstrated in A. D. Hérault, II E 95/377, B. Egidii, f. 318r, when a new year, 1348, is inserted as of 28 March, the first date following the 25th.

This study is an outgrowth of my Yale University dissertation on commerce and society in Montpellier and of my *doctorat d'état* from the Faculté de Droit et des Sciences Économiques de Montpellier on Montpellier as a commercial and financial center.[32] I would like to express my thanks to Robert S. Lopez, André Gouron, Bernard S. Bachrach and James D. Tracy who read and criticized earlier versions of this manuscript. Whatever remaining weaknesses are entirely my responsibility. I am indebted to Danièle Neirinck, archiviste-paléographe, for initiation into the area of financial and banking history. My thanks go to the University of Minnesota for research and travel assistance through the Single-Quarter Leave Program, the Office of International Programs and the McMillan Travel Fund. Without the cooperation of the staffs of the Archives Départementales de l'Hérault and the Archives Municipales de Montpellier and the efforts of Erika Linke and her staff in Interlibrary Loan of Wilson Library at the University of Minnesota, this project would never have come to fruition. Finally, for their unfailing support this book is dedicated to my mother and to the memory of my father.

[32] "Commerce and Society in Montpellier: 1250-1350," 2 vols., Diss. Yale University, 1974, and "Montpellier de 1250 à 1350: Centre commercial et financier," Thèse d'État, Faculté de Droit et des Sciences Économiques – Université de Montpellier I, 1977.

Introduction
The Urban Context

The Lower Languedocian town of Montpellier is located today about ten kilometers distant from the Mediterranean coast of modern France. Here, as elsewhere along the Mediterranean, the gradual deposit of soil and sand has caused a retreat of the sea. Between Montpellier and the sea to the south lie coastal marshlands and a series of inland bays.[1] Approximately five kilometers south is the settlement of Lattes, a port of considerable antiquity which would serve Montpellier before and after the halcyon days of Aigues-Mortes.[2] Montpellier is located in an intermediate zone between the coastal marshlands and the dry region of the *garrigue*, hills of low-level vegetation broken by an occasional sharp peak such as that of Pic Saint Loup. Beyond the *garrigue* are the Cévennes Mountains. To the northeast, through the suburb of Castelnau-le-Lez and the town of Lunel, one reaches Nîmes at about fifty kilometers distance and farther north the Rhône River valley. To the east along the coastal plain lies Mauguio (Melgueil), the last site of the regional count's capital and the location of the mint of *melgorien* coinage. Aigues-Mortes is located to the southeast and was linked with Montpellier by a system of canals and inland bays at the time when it served as the regional port.[3] In the opposite direction to the west along the coastal plain lie Villeneuve-lès-Maguelone, Frontignan, on the coast, Mèze, on the inland bay, the Étang de Thau, and finally Agde, site of a neighboring bishopric and itself a port of some importance.[4] Along a second line inland are found the towns of Montbazin, Villeveyrac, Montagnac and Pézenas. In the valley of the Hérault River to the northwest one finds clustered the towns of Aniane, Gignac and Saint-

[1] For a detailed discussion of Montpellier's geography, see studies by Gaston Galtier, "Les conditions géographiques de Montpellier," in *Mélanges Philippe Arbos* (Clermont-Ferrand, 1953), pp. 237-246 and "Le vignoble et le vin dans le Languedoc oriental de la fin du XIe siècle à la Guerre de Cent Ans," extract of *Études médiévales offertes à M. le Doyen Fliche de l'Institut* (Montpellier, 1951).

[2] Excavations at Lattes in 1964 revealed at least a sixth-century BC origin. In 1965 a port with piles ("pontons sur pilotis et ses pieux d'amarrage") was discovered. Treasure sites containing large amounts of coinage – one of 1900 *oboles massaliotes*, another of 1000 – prove the existence of commerce before the Roman conquest. Lattes served as the port for the Gallic *oppidum* of Substantion. Cf. Jean Baumel, *Histoire d'une seigneurie du Midi de la France*, 1: *Naissance de Montpellier (985-1213)* (Montpellier, 1969), pp. 13-32.

[3] For background on Aigues-Mortes, see the article by Jean Morize, "Aigues-Mortes au XIIIe siècle," *Annales du Midi* 26 (1914), 333ff.

[4] The port of Agde owes its origin to Greek colonization. See Joseph D. Picheire, *Histoire d'Agde* (Lyon, 1960).

Guilhem-le-Désert, and beyond them the region of Lodève. To the north lie Saint-Martin-de-Londres, Ganges and Alès.

Montpellier was a town of medieval foundation which was first mentioned in the documents of the late tenth century.[5] A legend transmitted by Arnaud de Verdale, bishop of Maguelone from 1339 to 1352, relates that in the tenth century two sisters of Saint Fulcrand, bishop of Lodève, donated the *bourgs* of Montpellier and Montpelliéret to the bishop of Maguelone.[6] Unfortunately, there is no proof to substantiate what would be the first mention of Montpellier. However, in 985 there was recorded in the seigneurial cartulary of the Guilhem family, the donation by a Count Bernard of Melgueil of a *mansus*, in which a certain Amalbertus was said to live, to a man designated only as Guillelmus, who is considered the ancestor of the seigneurial family.[7] In this act the unique reference to Montpellier was in connection with the location of the *mansus*, that is to say, *in terminium la Monte pestelario*. A slightly later act in the same cartulary – dated about 990 – was passed in the house of a Guillelmus de Montepistellario, ancestor of the Guilhem family of urban seigneurs who would rule Montpellier until the early thirteenth century.[8]

From 985 to the eleventh century Montpellier had become a thriving town under the Guilhem. It was composed of two quarters: Montpellier under the control of the Guilhem and Montpelliéret belonging to the bishop of Maguelone, whose site was about fifteen kilometers from Montpellier and four hundred meters from the Mediterranean in the Étang de l'Arnel, an inland bay.[9] The count of Melgueil as territorial ruler remained the overlord of the Guilhem. The county of Melgueil passed through marriage to the house of Toulouse in 1172.[10] In 1215 Pope Innocent III confiscated the county from Raymond VI of Toulouse during the

[5] Almost every historian of Montpellier has treated the problem of origins. See Jean-Claude Richard, "Le problème des origines de Montpellier," *Revue archéologique de la Narbonnaise* 2 (1969), 49-62 for the most useful modern view, relying skillfully on archeological data to clarify the distant past. For other approaches see, for example, Bernardin Gaillard, "Sur les origines de Montpellier," *Mémoires de la société archéologique de Montpellier* 2nd series, 9 (1928), 1-9 and Louis J. Thomas, "Note sur l'origine de Montpellier," *Cahiers d'histoire et d'archéologie* 1st series, 2 (1931), 126-135.

[6] Arnaud de Verdale, *Catalogus episcoporum magalonensium*, ed. Alexandre Germain, *Mémoires de la société archéologique de Montpellier* 1st series, 7 (Montpellier, 1881), 441-852.

[7] The text of 985 is no. LXX, pp. 125-126 of the *Liber Instrumentorum Memorialium*, ed. C. Chabaneau and Alexandre Germain (Montpellier, 1884-1886).

[8] The dating of the second act is uncertain, though because of its archaic language it is usually placed at the end of the tenth century. See Gaillard, "Sur les origines," p. 6.

On the Guilhem family, see Archibald R. Lewis, "The Guilhems of Montpellier: A Sociological Appraisal," *Viator* 2 (1971), 159-169; and Martine Dépinay, "Un aspect de l'activité des seigneurs de Montpellier: L'extension territoriale de la seigneurie des origines à la mort de Guilhem VIII (985-1202)," thèse de maîtrise, Faculté des Lettres et des Sciences Humaines de Montpellier, 1971.

[9] The history of Maguelone has been the subject of numerous articles by Alexandre Germain in the *Mémoires de la société archéologique de Montpellier*. The studies by Frédéric Fabrège, *Histoire de Maguelone*, 3 vols. (Paris and Montpellier, 1894-1911) and J. Rouquette, *Histoire du diocèse de Maguelone*, 2 vols (Montpellier, 1921) can be consulted with some interest.

[10] The classic history of Languedoc is by Dom Devic and Dom Vaissète, *Histoire générale de Languedoc*, 15 vols. (Toulouse, 1872-1892). A recent work is that edited by Philippe Wolff, *Histoire de Languedoc* (Toulouse, 1967). See *HL* 6: 348-349, 376-377, 382-383.

Albigensian Crusade and gave it to the bishop of Maguelone who was thereafter the overlord of the lay ruler of Montpellier.[11]

The nucleus of the medieval town, comprised of the seigneur's *bourg*, Montpellier, and the bishop's *bourg*, Montpelliéret, was spread over three hills; from east to west, there was Montpelliéret with an elevation of thirty-seven meters; the hill of Nôtre Dame of Montpellier, forty-nine meters in height, with the most important concentration of population; finally the Peyrou hill, fifty meters high, where the seigneurial settlement would spread and the seigneurs themselves take up residence in the second half of the twelfth century.[12]

Numerous churches, markets, baths and seigneurial châteaux broke the monotony of low houses and narrow streets and moulded the urban inhabitant's horizon as did the rampart of the *Commune Clôture* which surrounded the urban nucleus. In 1196 the last ruler of the Guilhem family, Guilhem VIII, created the defense organization which was to have the responsibility of the construction and administration of the ramparts.[13] The *Commune Clôture* fortifications acquired regional renown and as late as the mid-fourteenth century when Languedocian towns were fortifying against the troubles of the Hundred Years War, they were looked upon as a model by contemporaries.[14]

The *bourg* of Montpellier was from the beginning a more important concentration of population and industry than Montpelliéret, and it was understandable that the *Commune Clôture* included a larger part of Montpellier than of Montpelliéret. The delimitation of parish boundaries between the two *bourgs* can be first established in an act of 1113 in the seigneurial cartulary.[15]

[11] *HL* 6: 622-623. For the transfer of Melgueil, p. 456.

[12] On the topography of Montpellier the best study remains that of Louise Guiraud, "Recherches topographiques sur Montpellier au moyen âge," *Mem. soc. arch. Mplr.* 2nd ser., 1 (1899), 89-335.

[13] For the act of foundation, see A. M. Montpellier, EE 1. 1196. The length of the *Commune Clôture* fortifications is disputed by scholars. M. Vigié, "Des enceintes successives de la ville de Montpellier et de ses fortifications," *Bulletin de la société languedocienne de géographie* 21 (1899), 151, has given a conservative estimate of 1000 meters. The figure of 3762 meters is cited by Jacques Fabre de Morlhon in his informative little pamphlet, *Le Montpellier des Guilhem et des rois d'Aragon* (Montpellier, 1966), p. 10. His information is taken from the entry of *Le Petit Thalamus de Montpellier*, ed. F. Pégat, E. Thomas and Desmazes (Montpellier, 1840), p. 391, for 1374 when the inhabitants made a candle-wick the length of the fortifications, to burn continuously in Nôtre-Dame-des-Tables to ward off epidemic. In this entry, however, reference is made to a larger line of fortifications running through the suburbs of Montpellier, probably too extensive in length for the *Commune Clôture* itself. Using the map drawn to scale by Louise Guiraud, an estimate of about 3000 meters is reasonable.

J. C. Russell, "L'Évolution démographique," p. 350, estimated the surface area within the fortifications at about forty hectares.

[14] It is a generally accepted fact that the Hundred Years War was the great stimulus to the building of ramparts in the later Middle Ages in the south of France. The existing ramparts before the middle of the fourteenth century were either of Gallo-Roman or ninth-century origin, raised or rejuvenated in response to invasions. See André Dupont, *Les cités de la Narbonnaise première depuis les invasions germaniques jusqu'à l'apparition du consulat* (Nîmes, 1942). The influence of the Hundred Years War was signaled in papers of the Congress at Blankenberge, published as *Finances et comptabilité urbaines du XIIIe au XVIe siècle* 1962 , Actes, Handelingen (Brussels, 1964).

[15] See L. Guiraud, "Recherches topographiques," for the topographic details of the following paragraphs.

St.-Firmin, the parish church of Montpellier, and its cemetery were located on a high point of land in the southwestern corner of the first fortifications and were thus well within the *Commune Clôture*. While there was certainly an early nucleus of population and industry around St.-Firmin, of which the drapers and mercers were to be the most famous exponents, more important points of attraction for commerce and industry were the church of Nôtre-Dame-des-Tables, the first seigneurial château and the first town hall still visible in 1361. Nôtre-Dame, an oratory first visited by the pilgrims to Santiago de Compostella in the eleventh century, and the first château, destroyed by a precocious communal revolt in 1141-1143, were situated on the Via Francigena, the main east-west artery crossing Montpellier.

The parish of St.-Denis of Montpelliéret included the area east of the Legassieu gate, running north as far as Boutonnet. It extended from the Blanquerie gate as far as the parish line of St.-Maurice and the Pont Juvenal near Castelnau. The southeastern boundary was represented by the Obilion gate or the gate of Lattes. The border areas of the parish which had administrative or industrial importance were enclosed by the *Commune Clôture*. These included the *Flocaria*, located near the Obilion gate and first mentioned in the seigneurial cartulary in 1127, the *Blancaria*, references to which date from 1127-1139, established near the banks of the Merdanson, and the Salle-Evêque, or bishop of Maguelone's residence. The parish church of St.-Denis with its cemetery remained relatively isolated on a hill at some distance from the *Commune Clôture*.

Inside the walls of the *Commune Clôture* there were relatively few churches: St.-Firmin, Nôtre-Dame-des-Tables, Ste.-Croix, St.-Paul, St.-Mathieu and later St.-Ruf and St.-Benoît. In contrast, the suburbs were crowded with monasteries, convents and hospitals. The inhabitant of Montpellier, like his contemporaries elsewhere, awoke and retired to the sound of church bells.

Town landmarks and urban identity had been forged by the year 1200. In the thirteenth century Montpellier would experience important political changes. The Guilhem family failed to produce a legitimate male heir at the death of Guilhem VIII in 1202. Using the problems of succession as a pretext, the inhabitants of Montpellier established a successful consulate in 1204.[16] They also arranged the marriage of Marie of Montpellier, daughter of Guilhem VIII and his first wife, Eudoxia Comnena, to Peyre II of Aragon. The son of this union, Jacme I, born in

[16] On this era of political transition, see Archibald R. Lewis, "Seigneurial Administration in Twelfth-Century Montpellier," *Speculum* 22 (1947), 562-577 and "The Development of Town Government in Twelfth-Century Montpellier," *Speculum* 22 (1947), 51-67; André Gouron, "Diffusion des consulats méridionaux et expansion du droit romain aux XIIe et XIIIe siècles," *Bibliothèque de l'École des Chartes* 121 (1963), 26-76.

On the origins of consular government in Montpellier, see Bernardin Gaillard, "Origines de la commune de Montpellier," *Bulletin de l'académie des sciences et lettres de Montpellier* (1914), and P. Laborderie-Boulous, "La viguerie de Montpellier au XIIe siècle," *Archives de la ville de Montpellier, Inventaires et documents* 4 (Montpellier, 1920), v-xix.

The classic study of the political history of Montpellier remains that of Alexandre Germain, *Histoire de la commune de Montpellier*, 3 vols. (Montpellier, 1851).

1208, began his long reign at the death of his father at the battle of Muret in 1213. Jacme I and his successors were to be the absentee lords of Montpellier which was incorporated into a Spanish empire.[17]

The expansion of the Spanish Empire of Jacme I facilitated the prosperity of Montpellier. In 1137 the kingdom of Aragon was united with the county of Barcelona. Jacme I brought the Balearic Islands under Aragonese control in 1229-1233 and conquered Valencia in 1238.[18] At his death in 1276, the kingdom was divided between an older son, Peyre, who inherited Aragon and Valencia and a younger son, Jacme II, who received the counties of Roussillon and Cerdagne, the Balearic Islands and the seigneury of Montpellier. This latter ensemble of territories was termed the kingdom of Majorca. Jacme I's Majorcan successors proved less powerful than the kings of Aragon and more vulnerable to French political expansion.[19]

Montpellier escaped direct French political domination until 1349, but it did not fail to experience the effects of French policies in Languedoc after the Treaty of Paris-Meaux in 1229 at the conclusion of the Albigensian Crusade.[20] Paris-Meaux brought part of south-central France and Lower Languedoc into the control of the Capetians. Raymond VII of Toulouse retained territories including the town of Toulouse which passed to his daughter and heir, the wife of Alphonse of Poitiers, upon Raymond's death in 1249. Under Louis IX seats of French justice, administration and military power were established at Carcassonne-Béziers and Beaucaire-Nîmes; these double *sénéchaussées* were within sixty kilometers of Montpellier.[21] By the end of the thirteenth century a French royal

[17] On the political history of Montpellier in the thirteenth and fourteenth centuries, consult Charles de Tourtoulon, *Études sur la maison de Barcelone, Jacme Ier le Conquérant, roi d'Aragon, comte de Barcelone, seigneur de Montpellier, d'après les chroniques et les documents inédits*, 2 vols. (Montpellier, 1863) and Louis J. Thomas, "Montpellier entre la France et l'Aragon pendant la première moitié du XIVe siècle," *Montpeliensia, Mémoires et documents relatifs à Montpellier et à la région montpelliéraine*, 1, fasc. 1 (Montpellier, 1928-1929), pp. 1-56.

[18] C. de Tourtoulon, *Études sur la maison de Barcelone*, pp. 245ff; A. Lecoy de la Marche, *Les relations politiques de la France avec le royaume de Majorque (Iles Baléares, Roussillon, Montpellier*, etc.) (Paris, 1892), 1: 75-78; Robert I. Burns, *The Crusader Kingdom of Valencia* (Cambridge, Mass., 1967), 2: 419; and J. N. Hillgarth, *The Spanish Kingdoms, 1250-1516*. 1: *1250-1410 Precarious Balance* (New York, 1976).

[19] See A. Lecoy de la Marche, *Les relations politiques de la France avec le royaume de Majorque*, 2 vols. (Paris, 1892).

[20] Histories of the Albigensian Crusade and the Capetian conquest are numerous. The entire problem has been re-examined in detail by Michel Roquebert, *L'Épopée cathare. 1198-1212: L'Invasion* (Toulouse, 1970) and *L'Épopée cathare. 1213-1216. Muret ou la dépossession* (Toulouse, 1977). In English the studies of Walter L. Wakefield, *Heresy, Crusade and Inquisition in Southern France, 1100-1250* (London, 1974) and Joseph R. Strayer, *The Albigensian Crusade* (New York, 1971) are useful as background for this period. Also essential are volumes 6, 7 and 8 of Dom Devic and Dom Vaissète, *Histoire générale de Languedoc* (Toulouse-Privat, 1879) and Paul Dognon, *Les institutions politiques et administratives du pays de Languedoc du XIIe siècle aux guerres de religion* (Toulouse, 1895).

[21] Robert Michel, *L'Administration royale dans la sénéchaussée de Beaucaire au temps de Saint Louis* (Paris, 1910).

The first recorded contacts between Montpellier and the king of France occurred in 1214 when inhabitants requested that Philip Augustus extend his protection to the town against the violence of Simon de Montfort's troups. See *HL*, 6: 440-441.

mint had been installed at Sommières, thirty kilometers to the northeast of Montpellier.[22] At about twenty kilometers to the north, near Pic Saint Loup, stood a French royal château, and Aigues-Mortes, the French Mediterranean port, founded by Saint Louis, lay twenty-six kilometers to the east. It would serve as the main outlet for shipping from Montpellier to the Levant.[23]

French encroachment upon the independence of Montpellier was marked by two direct acquisitions and over a century of subtle extension of royal prerogatives. In 1293 Philip IV obtained the episcopal quarter of Montpellier through an exchange with the bishop of Maguelone. The latter was to receive 500 *l. melg.* in annual income assigned on the *baillage* of Sauve and several castellenies in the area of Montpellier.[24] The second stage of acquisition came in 1349 when Philip VI purchased the seigneurial quarter of the town for 120,000 *écus* (150,000 *l. t.*) from the bankrupt Jacme III of Majorca.[25] Long before 1349, however, French courts of justice and French *tournois* coinage dominated the legal and economic sectors of Montpellier.[26]

In spite of dramatic urban and regional political changes, the thirteenth century was an era of economic growth for Montpelliérains, trading east to markets of the Levant, north to the Champagne fairs and south across the Mediterranean to North Africa.[27] Local merchants and foreigners perfected the economic role of Montpellier as a commercial link between the Mediterranean world and the north of Europe. Northern woolen cloths were exported through Montpellier to points south and east. Spices, silks, leather, pharmaceutical goods and other exotic items were imported and shipped north or re-exported within the western Mediterranean basin. Locally, artisans' industries prospered. The dyeing of fine imported northern cloths and of Mediterranean silks became a specialty of Montpellier in the twelfth and thirteenth centuries.[28]

The medieval formula for financial and commercial achievement operated most successfully in areas where the political structure was fragmented to the

[22] On the history of mints in the area of Montpellier, see Marc Bompaire, "L'Atelier monétaire royal de Montpellier et la circulation monétaire en Bas Languedoc jusqu'au milieu du XVe siècle," Thèse, École des Chartes, 1980.

[23] On Aigues-Mortes, see Jean Combes, "Origine et passé d'Aigues-Mortes," *Revue d'histoire économique et sociale* 50 (1972), 304-326.

[24] A. Lecoy de la Marche, *Les relations politiques de la France avec le royaume de Majorque*, 1: 311ff., discussed the incidents leading to the purchase of Montpelliéret. See also *HL*, 9: 167-170. A. Germain, *Histoire de la commune de Montpellier*, 2: 354, published the document of sale as did Jean Rouquette, ed., *Cartulaire de Maguelone* (Montpellier, 1920-1921), 3: 506.

[25] Louis J. Thomas, "Montpellier entre la France et l'Aragon," pp. 1-56 and *HL*, 9: 550-559.

[26] On *tournois* coinage, see Appendix 2, "Monetary Problems." On jurisdiction, see Chapter 4, "Deposit Banking and the Recovery of Debts."

[27] The old work by Alexandre Germain, *Histoire du commerce de Montpellier*, 2 vols. (Montpellier, 1861), remains a classic in commercial history.

[28] Reyerson, "Le rôle de Montpellier dans le commerce des draps de laine," pp. 19-21 and my article, "Medieval Silks in Montpellier: The Silk Market ca. 1250-ca. 1350," *The Journal of European Economic History* 11 (1982), 122-123.

level of the city-state.[29] Montpellier almost attained that degree of political independence under non-resident Aragonese and Majorcan rulers. Except for Italian towns where urban development was in advance of the rest of western Europe, there were few towns as economically important, as politically independent and as cosmopolitan as Montpellier. Its trades and professions showed an early creativity of which the *Commune Clôture* defense organization of 1196 and the *Consuetudines* of 1204 were the results.[30]

At the end of the thirteenth century Montpellier was a large town by medieval standards.[31] The jurisdictional and political divisions between the two *bourgs* of Montpellier and Montpelliéret remained, but the urban environment was united by busy market areas, fortifications and suburban expansion. After the Angevin conquest of Marseille in 1262 and the economic decline of the great Provençal port, Montpellier was the most important Mediterranean town between Genoa and Barcelona.[32] Yet, the seeds of classic fourteenth-century crisis were visible in Montpellier from the late thirteenth century.

Bad harvests, famine and epidemic affected the economic equilibrium of Montpellier in the first half of the fourteenth century. The town chronicle noted climatic disturbances suggesting a changing weather pattern.[33] Droughts alternated with floods. Imports of food stuffs were necessary in years of poor agricultural yields.[34]

Commercial upheavals coincided with the subsistence crisis. Montpellier suffered from the shrinking trade opportunities caused by crusader losses in Syria at the end of the thirteenth century and by the disruption of the Mongol Empire in the fourteenth.[35] In the last decades of this study, the town was under increasing fiscal pressure from the French king.[36] The dynamic Jewish community of the twelfth and thirteenth centuries fell victim to royal exploitation and usury legislation.[37] Social unrest in reaction to economic problems and taxation

[29] Italy offers the best examples of this process. See Yves Renouard, *Les hommes d'affaires italiens du moyen âge* (Paris, 1949; rev. ed., 1968) and Daniel Waley, *The Italian City Republics* (New York, 1969).

[30] The best version of the 1204 *Consuetudines* is found in *Les Layettes du Trésor des Chartes*, ed. A. Teulet (Paris, 1863), 1: 255-266.

[31] Josiah Cox Russell, "L'Évolution démographique de Montpellier au moyen âge," in *Annales du Midi* 74 (1962), 345-360, treated the problem of population size. See also my discussion of population estimates in "Patterns of Population. Attraction and Mobility," p. 257, n. 2.

[32] E. Baratier, *Histoire du commerce de Marseille* (Paris, 1951), 2: 207-219, discussed the ill effects of Angevin domination.

[33] *Le Petit Thalamus, Chronique romane*, pp. 343-346. For a description of famines and epidemics, see Elizabeth Carpentier, "Autour de la peste noire: famines et épidémies dans l'histoire du XIVe siècle," *Annales: ESC* 17 (1962), 1062-1092 and Marie-Josèphe Larenaudie, "Les famines en Languedoc au XIVe siècle," *Annales du Midi* 64 (1952), 27-39.

[34] *Le Petit Thalamus, Chronique romane*, p. 347.

[35] On these events and their bad effects, see my article, "Montpellier and the Byzantine Empire: Commercial Interaction in the Mediterranean World before 1350," *Byzantion* 48 (1978), 456-476.

[36] See my article, "Les opérations de crédit dans la coutume et dans la vie des affaires à Montpellier au moyen âge: le problème de l'usure," in *Diritto comune e diritti locali nella storia dell'Europa*, Atti del Convegno di Varenna (12-15 June 1979) (Milan, 1980), pp. 189-209.

[37] *Ibid.*, pp. 201-209.

punctuated the 1320s and 1330s.[38] The economic apogee of Montpellier was over long before the plague and the Hundred Years War created new problems at the mid century.[39]

[38] Jean Combes, "Finances municipales et oppositions sociales à Montpellier au commencement du XIVe siècle," *Fédération historique* (Montpellier, 1972), 99-120. Jan Rogozinski has recently examined these incidents of social unrest in detail in *Power, Caste, and Law. Social Conflict in Fourteenth-Century Montpellier* (Cambridge, Mass., 1982).

[39] The town would again enjoy prominence at the end of the Ancien Régime as a *ville d'intendance*, an administrative center, a general orientation which still characterizes Montpellier today.

1

Investment in Business Partnerships

Techniques of business partnership were essential to the growth of international maritime trade, the most spectacular component of the commercial revolution of the Middle Ages.[1] Partnerships were also vital to the operations of regional and local commerce, finance and industry. They served multiple economic functions: furthering the expansion of trade and industry as commercial loans, providing vehicles for speculative investment of capital, stimulating the recruitment of labor and allowing the division of financial responsibilities and the sharing of business risks.[2]

Partnership skills spread from Italy throughout western Mediterranean Europe in the twelfth and thirteenth centuries.[3] Partnerships fell into two main categories

[1] On the history of commercial contracts, see the bibliographical comments in R. S. Lopez and I. W. Raymond, *Medieval Trade in the Mediterranean World* (New York, 1955), pp. 156-158. For examples of medieval partnerships, one can consult R. Doehaerd, *Les relations commerciales entre Gênes, la Belgique et l'Outrement*. Still useful in the field of Mediterranean commercial techniques in the Middle Ages are Wilhelm Heyd, *Histoire du commerce du Levant au moyen âge*, 2 vols. (Leipzig, 1885-1886; revised edition, Amsterdam, 1959) and Adolf Schaube, *Handelsgeschichte der romanischen Völker des Mittelmeergebiets bis zum Ende der Kreuzzüge* (Munich and Berlin, 1906). On the development of commercial techniques in Montpellier, see André-E. Sayous and Jean Combes, "Les commerçants et les capitalistes de Montpellier aux XIIIe et XIVe siècles," *Revue historique* 65 (1940), 341-377, and my dissertation, "Commerce and Society in Montpellier," 1, Chapter 2.

[2] Michael M. Postan, "Partnership in English Medieval Commerce," reprinted in *Medieval Trade and Finance* (Cambridge, 1973), pp. 66-71, discussed the functions of medieval partnerships.

See also the comments of Rosalind K. Berlow, "The Sailing of the 'Saint Esprit'," *Journal of Economic History* 39 (1979), 348. Berlow compares the interpretations of Max Weber and Werner Sombart.

[3] Medieval land partnerships bore similarities to the Roman *societas* which may be defined as "a union of property, skill or labor, or any combination of these for a common purpose or exploitation." See W. W. Buckland, *A Manual of Roman Private Law*, 2nd. ed. (Cambridge, 1953), p. 294. Continuity of *societas* partnerships from the Roman period to the Middle Ages is impossible to prove, but it is interesting to note that medieval civil lawyers consulted the *Corpus Iuris Civilis* of Justinian in their discussion of contemporary *societates*. See John H. Pryor, "The Origins of the *Commenda* Contract," *Speculum* 52 (1977), 5-37. Pryor cited the example of Panormitanus utilizing the *Corpus Iuris Civilis*. Lopez and Raymond, *Medieval Trade*, p. 185, noted the absence of a thorough study of medieval *societas* partnerships, a lacuna which persists today.

The origins of the *commenda* contract, a partnership used in both land and maritime trade, have given rise to much historical controversy. John H. Pryor, *ibid.*, has supplied a recent revision of interpretations. There were multiple precedents for the medieval *commenda* of which the Babylonian *tapputin* was the most ancient. Pryor retained for serious consideration only those contracts capable of

according to their orientation to land trade and industry or to maritime commerce.[4] In Italy land partnerships were generally termed *compagnia* and *societas terrae* while *commenda*, *collegantia*, *societas maris*, *accomendatio*, to name the most common terms, were applied originally to maritime contracts. In Genoa the bilateral *commenda* was called a *societas maris*.[5] In Montpellier the terms *comanda* and *societas* were used in both land and maritime activities.

Besides the geographic orientation of the economic activity, the distinctions among these contracts were based upon the distribution of investments, profits and risks and upon the duration of the contractual agreement. In the classic *commenda* contract, the sedentary investor provided the initial capital and bore all the financial risk.[6] He was rewarded with three-fourths of the profits while the traveling partner furnished labor and marketing expertise and derived one-fourth of the profits as reward. The *compagnia*, in contrast, was characterized by joint, unlimited liability; investing and working partners shared profits and losses.[7] The *societas terrae* resembled the *commenda* in that investors sustained losses of capital while working partners derived no benefits if the enterprise was without profits. In general, the *compagnia* and the *societas* were of longer duration than the maritime *commenda*, which was in force for only one voyage.

The *commenda* and *societas* contracts of the Middle Ages were business operations of great flexibility which generally escaped the condemnation of usury by canon lawyers and theologians, who took a negative view of the simple loan contract.[8] The unilateral land-based *commenda* was considered the most questionable of partnership engagements in that it resembled a loan.[9] *Societas* contracts were less vulnerable to categorizations of moral illegitimacy owing to their shared investments, profits and losses. The maritime *commenda* was exonerated from usurious connotations because of the large element of risk

plausible influence on the development of the *commenda*; these included the Roman *nauticum fenus* and *societas*, the Jewish *'isqa*, the Byzantine *chreokoinonia* and the Muslim *qirad*. After a careful examination of each of these contracts, Pryor concluded that all but the *nauticum fenus* exerted probable influence on the *commenda*, each to a different degree. The *qirad* resembled the *commenda* in the area of liability, the *'isqa* in that of division of profits. The *chreokoinonia* was of direct influence in fusing concepts of partnership and debt, while the *societas* may well have provided the original model, transmitted and partially transformed through the centuries.

[4] For a discussion of terminology, see Lopez and Raymond, *Medieval Trade*, pp. 174-176 and 185-187.

[5] On Genoese contracts, see, for example, Mario Chiaudano, *Contratti commerciali genovesi del secolo XII (contributo alla storia dell' accomandatio e della societas)* (Turin, 1925); and R. L. Reynolds, "Gli studi americani sulla storia genovese," *Giornale storico e letterario della Liguria* ser. 3, 14 (1938), 1-24. See also Hilmar C. Krueger, "Genoese Merchants, Their Associations and Investments, 1155 to 1230," *Studi in onore di Amintore Fanfani* (Milan, 1962), 1: 423-426.

[6] Lopez and Raymond, *Medieval Trade*, p. 175.

[7] *Ibid.*, pp. 185-186.

[8] On those contracts escaping censure, see T. P. McLaughlin, "The Teaching of the Canonists on Usury (XII, XIII and XIV Centuries)," *Medieval Studies* 1 (1939), 120-144.

[9] On problems encountered by the Venetian *commenda*, called a *colleganza*, see F. C. Lane, "Investment and Usury in Medieval Venice," *Explorations in Entrepreneurial History* 2nd ser., 2 (1964), 3-15.

involved in any overseas venture.[10] Interest or profits, which might be impressive in the maritime *commenda*, could be justified on the basis of risk.

*
**

Given the demonstrated Italian influence on political and legal developments in southern France, and the precocious emergence of business partnerships in Italian hands, it is reasonable to look to Italy for the initial inspiration of partnership techniques in Montpellier.[11] Merchants of Montpellier were traced in Genoa in the 1150s, shortly after a treaty between the two towns restricted the navigation of Montpelliérains to the western Mediterranean basin.[12] At the mid century the Genoese were using primitive *commenda* contracts in their shipments of saffron, pepper, sugar, dye stuffs, lacquer, nuts and iron to southern France.[13] Montpelliérains in Genoa were exposed to the commercial mechanisms of the Genoese.[14] By the end of the twelfth century, Montpelliérains operating out of Genoa were accepting early forms of *commenda* investments for trade between Genoa and Spain, Sicily and Naples.[15] The question remains whether they used these commercial techniques at home in this period.

While a Genoese influence on the development of Montpellier's business techniques should be presumed, logically, in view of the strong ties between the two cities in the mid and late twelfth century, the lack of surviving commercial documents from Montpellier until the late thirteenth century makes it impossible to find hard and fast proofs of it.[16] A comparison between Genoese *commenda*

[10] Pirates of Barcelona and Majorca joined Italians in harassing the maritime commerce of merchants of Montpellier. For an example, see A. D. Hérault, II E 95/369, J. Holanie, f. 18v.

[11] On political and legal influence from Italy, see A. Gouron, "Diffusion des consulats méridionaux et expansion du droit romain aux XIIe et XIIIe siècles," *Bibliothèque de l'École des Chartes* 121 (1963), 26-76.

It is Venice which preserves the earliest medieval commercial contracts. See Gino Luzzatto, "Les activités économiques du patriciat vénitien (X^e-XIVe siècles)," *Annales d'histoire économique et sociale* 9 (1937), 25-26. It is from twelfth-century Genoa, however, that the first notarial registers preserving commercial contracts come. See the edition of the oldest surviving register, Mario Chiaudano and Mattia Moresco, eds., *Il cartolare di Giovanni Scriba*, 2 vols. (Turin, 1935).

[12] On Genoese twelfth-century expansion in southern France, see André Dupont, *Les relations commerciales entre les cités maritimes de Languedoc et les cités méditerranéennes d'Espagne et d'Italie* (Nîmes, 1942), and Reyerson, "Commerce and Society in Montpellier," 1: 57-67.

[13] See *Il cartolare di Giovanni Scriba*, ed. M. Chiaudano and M. Moresco (Turin, 1935), 2 vols. See 1, acts CXLIV, CCCXXXVII, CDXXXIII, CDXCIV and 2, acts XVI, CMXLV, DCCCXLVII, MLXXIV, MCLII, MLX, MLXXX, MXCVII.

[14] A.-E. Sayous and J. Combes, "Les commerçants et les capitalistes de Montpellier aux XIIIe et XIVe siècles," *Revue historique* 65 (1940), 352, noted this fact. See the discussion at the end of this chapter regarding their interpretations.

[15] M. W. Hall, H. G. Krueger, and R. L. Reynolds, eds., *Guglielmo Cassinese (1190-1192)* (Genoa, Turin, 1938), 2 vols. See vol. 1, acts 784, 785, 872; vol. 2, acts 1118 and 1461. See also Mario Chiaudano, ed., *Oberto Scriba de Mercato (1186)* (Turin, 1940), acts 307 and 328.

[16] The argument for Genoese influence finds its strongest support in the early contacts between the Ligurian and Languedocian towns and in the similarities of the *comanda* and *commenda* contracts. Twelfth-century contracts of sea loan and ship shares of Genoa find no parallel later in Montpellier. On these latter commercial techniques, see Eugene H. Byrne, *Genoese Shipping in the Twelfth and*

contracts and the later *comanda* contracts of Montpellier reveals a similarity of detail with some slight difference in terminology.

By the early thirteenth century, the oldest extant commercial contracts of nearby Marseille throw some light on the activity of Montpellier merchants there.[17] In the years 1227-1237 they traded between Marseille and North Africa, using *commenda* partnerships.[18] By 1248 they had expanded their efforts out of Marseille and were exporting European cloths to the Levant, especially to Saint-Jean-d'Acre, in response to the economic stimulus of the Seventh Crusade.[19] *Commenda* and *societas* partnerships as well as sea loans were employed.

From at least 1248 on, Montpellier was the site of business operations for numerous Italian merchants from Piacenza, Siena, Lucca, Pisa, Pistoia, Florence, and, of course, Genoa.[20] In spite of the restriction of Italian activities in France to Nîmes and Aigues-Mortes by Philip III in 1278, and the departure of the Italian community from Montpellier, exile was only temporary as further examples of Italian presence remain from the end of the thirteenth century.[21] At home and abroad by the dates of the first extant notarial register (1293-1294), Montpelliérains had a long history of exposure to Italian business techniques.

Thirteenth Centuries (Cambridge, Mass., 1930) and Calvin B. Hoover, "The Sea Loan in Genoa in the Twelfth Century," *Quarterly Journal of Economics* 40 (1926), 495-529.

Merchants of Montpellier were familiar with such contracts in Marseille half a century later. For examples of contracts that combined elements of the sea loan and the sea exchange, see Louis Blancard, *Documents inédits sur le commerce de Marseille au moyen âge* (Marseille, 1885), 2, acts 145, 185 and 469. See A.-E. Sayous and J. Combes, "Les commerçants et les capitalistes," p. 359.

[17] The oldest surviving commercial partnerships of the south of France are preserved in Marseille. See the edition, Louis Blancard, ed., *Documents inédits sur le commerce de Marseille au moyen âge*, 2 vols. (Marseille, 1885).

[18] L. Blancard, *Documents inédits sur le commerce de Marseille*, 1, acts 16, 25, 34, 42, 48, 65, 82 and 86.

[19] L. Blancard, *Documents inédits sur le commerce de Marseille*, 2, acts 31, 55, 183, 236, 547 and 561 as an illustration. These six contracts were concluded among Montpelliérains exclusively. On the development of commercial techniques in Marseille, see John H. Pryor, *Business Contracts of Medieval Provence. Selected Notulae from the Cartulary of Giraud Amalric of Marseilles, 1248* (Toronto, 1981). On contracts of Marseille, see also André-E. Sayous, "Les transferts de risques, les associations commerciales et la lettre de change à Marseille pendant le XIVe siècle," *Revue d'histoire du droit* 14 (1935), 469-494, and "Le capitalisme commercial et financier dans les pays chrétiens de la Méditerranée occidentale depuis la première Croisade jusqu'à la fin du moyen âge," *Vierteljahrschrift für Sozial-und-Wirtschaftsgeschichte* 29 (1936), 270-295.

[20] References to Italian activities in Montpellier are scattered. See Pierre Racine, "À Marseille en 1248: l'activité des hommes d'affaires de Plaisance," *Annales du Midi* 78 (1966), 221-233. On the Sienese, see A. Germain, *Histoire de la commune de Montpellier*, 2: 42-43; also *Inv. A. M. Montpellier*, I, *Grand Chartier*, Arm. F., Cass. 5, acts 2800 and 2810. On the Lucchese, see A. Germain, *Histoire de la commune de Montpellier*, pp. 42-43, n. 6. See also Thomas W. Blomquist, "Trade and Commerce in Thirteenth-Century Lucca," Diss. University of Minnesota, 1966; and Florence Edler de Roover, "The Silk Trade of Lucca during the Thirteenth and Fourteenth Centuries," Diss. University of Chicago (1930), p. 163. See also my study "Medieval Silks in Montpellier." On merchants of Pistoia and Florence in Montpellier, see Sven Stelling-Michaud, "Le transport international des manuscrits juridiques bolonais entre 1265 et 1320," *Mélanges Antony Babel* (Geneva, 1963), 1: 114-115.

[21] *Ordonnances*, IV, 669: February 1278. See also A. Germain, *Histoire du commerce de Montpellier*, 1: 277-284 and A. M. Montpellier, *Grand Thalamus*, f. 61r-61v. See also J. Pagézy, *Mémoires sur le port d'Aigues-Mortes* (Paris, 1879, 1886), 1: 373-388.

Land and maritime *comanda* and *societas* contracts have survived in the notarial evidence of Montpellier.[22] It is useful to examine them in separate categories of maritime versus land and *comanda* versus *societas* to elucidate similarities as well as distinctions. *Comanda* and *societas* contracts directed to maritime trade generally included the geographic destination of the traveling partner or partners whose task it was to sell western merchandise abroad and return with the proceeds, usually in the form of foreign merchandise. By the end of the thirteenth century, with the fall of the crusader port of Acre in 1291, the Levant trade of Montpellier was re-oriented toward Cyprus and the Byzantine Empire. From 1327 to 1343, when maritime contracts survive, Cyprus and

22 COMMERCIAL PARTNERSHIPS

Notarial Register	Year	Total	Maritime		Land	
			Comanda	*Societas*	*Comanda*	*Societas*
AM II 1	1293-1294	9	2		3	4
AM II 2	1301-1302	4	1			3
AD II E 95/368	1327-1328	15	6		8	1
AD II E 95/369	1333	21	14		7	
AD II E 95/373	1333	0				
AD II E 95/370	1336	4	2		1	1
AD II E 95/374	1337-1342	9	4		3	2
AD II E 95/375	1339-1340	16	6	1	7	2
AD II E 95/371	1342	22	14		5	3
AM II 3	1342-1343	1	1			
AD II E 95/372	1343-1344	17	7	1	5	4
AD II E 95/376	1342-1346	2			1	1
AD II E 95/377	1347-1348	4			1	3
Totals		124	57	2	41	24

a. In addition to contracts establishing partnerships, this chart reflects mentions of partnerships in documents such as specific acquittals of account where details were provided. Not included were general references to *comanda* and *societas* engagements in blanket acquittals of legal responsibility.

b. Source: all extant notarial registers before 1350 housed in the Archives Municipales de Montpellier (AM) and the Archives Départementales de l'Hérault (AD).

Romania were the most frequent destinations of commercial investments.[23] Armenia and Alexandria were also recorded as sailing goals.[24] However, Montpelliérains did not neglect the western Mediterranean in this period. North Africa remained a target of Montpellier commercial enterprise, although no local contracts cite such a destination.[25] Sicily, Sardinia, southern Italy, on the one hand, and Barcelona, Valencia, Majorca and southern Spain, on the other, were noted in the local business partnerships.[26]

In the local maritime *comanda* a sedentary investor extended credit in the form of cash or goods to a traveling partner who contributed his labor and marketing skill to the partnership. In the notarial contract the traveler established a recognition of debt *in comanda* or *causa comande* for the investment.[27] The traveling partner generally acknowledged the receipt of instructions regarding the geographic destination of the venture and the means of transportation. There were few restrictions or suggestions regarding the conduct of trade or business. With a carte blanche in marketing procedures, the traveler's objective was to dispose of his merchandise and to buy new goods which he would bring back to Montpellier. The financial risks of the maritime *comanda* were generally borne by the investor, but the traveler's remuneration was dependent on profits from his trade.[28]

The Montpellier maritime *comanda* lasted, as in Genoa, only for the duration of the voyage. Upon his return home the traveling partner settled accounts with the investor, first restoring the investor's initial capital contribution. Then, whatever profits existed were to be divided in the proportion of three-fourths to the

[23] See my article, "Montpellier and the Byzantine Empire: Commercial Interaction in the Mediterranean World before 1350," *Byzantion* 48 (1978), 464, n. 36. The two maritime *societas* contracts were directed to Majorca and Barcelona (A. D. Hérault, II E 95/375, P. de Pena, f. 114: 1339) and to Sardinia (II E 95/372, J. Holanie, f. 12r: 1343).

[24] Raymundus de Conchis, *burgensis* of Montpellier, was in Alexandria with fellow Montpellier merchants in 1264. See J. Combes, "Quelques remarques sur les bourgeois de Montpellier au moyen âge," in *Recueil, Mélanges Pierre Tisset* (Montpellier, 1970), p. 98, and E. Bonnet, "Les séjours à Montpellier de Jacques le Conquérant roi d'Aragon," *Mem. soc. arch. Mplr.* 2nd ser, 9 (1927), 58, n. 2.

The presence of Montpelliérains at Famagousta and in Armenia was attested in documents of Marseille in the last quarter of the thirteenth century. See E. Baratier, *Histoire du commerce de Marseille* (Paris, 1951), 2: 210-213.

[25] E. Baratier, 2: 103, noted voyages to Alger and to Collo in which Montpelliérains and Marseillais participated in the years 1330-1350.

[26] See Reyerson, "Commerce and Society," 2: Appendix V, table on "*Commenda* and *Societas* Contracts," pp. 236-248.

[27] On the legal particularities of the Montpellier maritime *comanda*, see the discussion by P. Bouges, "La pratique contractuelle à Montpellier de la fin du XIIIe siècle à la fin du XVe," Thèse d'État, Faculté de Droit et des Sciences Économiques – Université de Montpellier – 1, 1972, 1: 141-168.

[28] See Appendix 1, "Documents," A. D. Hérault, II E 95/372, J. Holanie, f. 52v, for the formula on risks: "eundo tamen et reddeundo ad periculum et ad resegne vestrum et ad fortunam Dei, ignis, maris, et malarum gentium." The formula given by P. Bouges, "La pratique contractuelle," 2: 71, n. 137, varies slightly. Common sharing of risks was rare in the Montpellier documents. See P. Bouges, p. 168, A. D. Hérault II E 95/369, J. Holanie, f. 69r and A. M. Montpellier, II 2, ff. 14r and 111r. On the question of risk, see Erich Mäschke, "La Mentalité des marchands européens au moyen âge," *Revue d'histoire économique et sociale* 42 (1964), 457-484.

investor, one-fourth to the traveler.[29] The *Petit Thalamus* of Montpellier preserves an undated statute (certainly thirteenth or fourteenth century) relating to *comanda* and *societas* contracts.[30] Full accounting for the investments and profits of a trip by sea, or on land, was required. The failure of the traveling partner to submit his accounts could lead, upon the request of the investing partner, to the intervention of the court of Montpellier enforcing restitution of what was due the investor.[31]

Formal acquittals of the traveling partner by the investor before the notary are preserved at the conclusion of some partnership contracts.[32] Acquittals of maritime *comanda* obligations involving Muslim lands, the crusader states and the Byzantine Empire were recorded anywhere from six months to a year after the establishment of the original contract. The probable minimum interval of travel round trip from Aigues-Mortes to the Levant ports was about six months if stopovers in ports of call and necessary delays for the sale of merchandise and the purchase of goods of eastern origin are taken into account.[33] Merchants of Montpellier traveled on boats commanded by Italian and Spanish captains and on boats of Languedocian ownership.[34]

Merchants, changers and members of the retail/wholesale trades were the principal local investors in terms of numbers and capital in the maritime *comanda* and *societas* contracts as Table 1 shows.[35] The important participation of foreign-

[29] In most Montpellier contracts the division of profits was one-fourth/three-fourths. However, exceptions can be found. For a division of one-third/two-thirds, see A. D. Hérault, II E 95/369, J. Holanie, f. 24v.

[30] See *Le Petit Thalamus*, p. 132. Municipal legislation was frequent in the first half of the thirteenth century regarding debts and contracts.

[31] According to a statute of 1212, only those credits and debits pertaining to the particular partnership, in the case of a *societas*, could be invoked in a settlement. See *Layettes*, 1: 380-381, for the statutes of 1212. See especially article 2. Statutes of 1223, *Layettes*, 2: 4-10, provide additional information about representation among associates and about liability.

[32] For example, A. D. Hérault, II E 95/369, J. Holanie, f. 36r.

[33] Two acts of 1343 permit the calculation of travel time. In mid-April the "Saint-Clemens," a ship captained by a Montpelliérain, had been the subject of *comanda* contracts destined for *Romania*. (A. D. Hérault, II, E 95/372, J. Holanie, f. 13r). On 17 October 1343, a second act (II E 95/372, J. Holanie, f. 94v) recorded the arrangements for discharging the cargo of the "Saint-Clemens" which was expected to arrive in Aigues-Mortes from *Romania* at any time. The trip lasted about six months. Most acquittals of commercial obligations occurred a year after the date of the original contract regulating travel, often on the occasion of the establishment of another contract. The shortest interval between establishment and acquittal was again six months.

[34] See the table, "*Commenda* Contracts," included in Appendix V of Reyerson, "Commerce and Society in Montpellier," 2: 236-248.

[35] This finding differs from that of Hilmar Krueger for mid-twelfth-century Genoa and that of Rosalind Berlow for mid-thirteenth-century Marseille. See H. Krueger, "Genoese Merchants, Their Partnerships and Investments, 1155-1164," *Studi in Onore di Armando Sapori* (Milan, 1957), 1: 259-271, and R. Berlow, "The Sailing of the 'Saint-Esprit'," *The Journal of Economic History* 39 (1979), 345-362. Both historians found that most investors in maritime *commenda* contracts were not of merchant background and invested only modest capital. Krueger found, however, that merchants, though they accounted for only 6.6% of the investors, made up 40.4% of the capital contributions.

The categories used in this table and in subsequent tables have emerged from identifications of clients made by the notaries. It has seemed useful to scrutinize separately the activities of the specialized personnel of international commerce and finance. Thus, merchants, changers and moneyers, and retail/wholesalers have been assigned different categories. Included in the last group were apothe-

ers in such investments is not surprising in a cosmopolitan center such as Montpellier. Especially noteworthy, however, is the fact that the average foreign investment was almost twice that of the merchant and changer and more than twice that of the retail/wholesaler. Merchants of Narbonne, a nearby town with which Montpellier cooperated in trading ventures, were the most common foreign investors. Other foreigners from Barcelona, Perpignan and Millau also passed maritime contracts in Montpellier.[36] The level of average investment of women reflects the participation of daughters of merchants and retail/wholesalers in this type of investment.[37]

The dividing line between the maritime *comanda* with multiple investors and the maritime *societas* with investments from the sedentary and traveling partners was not sharply drawn in the Montpellier contracts.[38] One of the two surviving maritime *societas* contracts followed the traditional format with risks shared by both partners.[39] The other contract, which I have chosen to consider as a *societas* because of investments from sedentary partners and the traveler, although the contract failed to carry a specific term and spoke rather of engagements *causa mercandi*, allotted risks proportionate to the investments of the partners.[40] The

---

caries, mercers, drapers, silk merchants, linen merchants, grain merchants, pepperers and furriers. The urban elite included *burgenses* and *milites*, *domini* and *domicelli* of the town and the immediate region of Montpellier. The university faculty, doctors, lawyers, jurists and paralegal personnel have been assigned a separate category of "Professions/Education." The financial activities of the Jews have left considerable trace at the end of the thirteenth and in the early fourteenth century of Montpellier. The credit operations of officers of the royal administrations of the king of Majorca and the king of France in Montpellier have been considered separately as have the activities of the clergy. The role of women in financial and business affairs has been concentrated in one category to assess their impact upon economic life. In specific instances, the social and professional background of women participating in credit and investment activities has been examined.

Large numbers of the urban population undoubtedly fell into the categories of "Artisan/Service," "Food Trades" and "Agriculture." The artisans/service category groups artisans of local industry and a host of individuals involved in service functions within the town. Among these inhabitants were ironmongers, blacksmiths, barbers, innkeepers, brokers, transporters, cordmakers, beltmakers, coffermakers, shoemakers, precious metalworkers, artists, wood merchants, tailors, knifemakers, silk cloth workers, silver cloth workers, raw wool bleachers, animal merchants and wine merchants. The food trades, vital to the existence of any large town, were given a separate category. The importance of the agricultural population of a medieval town is at times underappreciated by twentieth-century observers; within this category were included cultivators, gardeners and fishermen.

Finally, the category of foreigners included all individuals whom notaries identified as inhabitants of localities other than that of Montpellier. Again, in specific instances, as with the category of women, that of foreigners will be delimited according to geographic proximity of origin when necessary. The markets of Montpellier attracted numerous foreign merchants from Italy and Spain and from regions of central and northern France.

[36] A. D. Hérault, II E 95/368, J. Holanie, ff. 12r, 15v, 35v: Narbonne; f. 78v: Barcelona; II E 95/372, J. Holanie, f. 148v: Perpignan, II E 95/369, J. Holanie, f. 72r: Millau. Moreover, the one ecclesiastic among the maritime *comanda* investors was a cleric from the diocese of Beauvais. See A. D. Hérault, II E 95/371, J. Holanie, f. 110r.

[37] See n. 57 below.

[38] See A. D. Hérault, II E 95/372, J. Holanie, f. 52v, for an example of a maritime *comanda* with two investors.

[39] A. D. Hérault, II E 95/375, P. de Pena, f. 114v.

[40] A. D. Hérault, II E 95/372, J. Holanie, f. 12r.

TABLE 1: MARITIME *COMANDA* AND *SOCIETAS* INVESTORS
OF THE MONTPELLIER NOTARIAL EVIDENCE (1293-1348)
WITH INVESTMENTS QUOTED IN LIVRES TOURNOIS OF APRIL 1330

	No. of Acts	% Total Acts	Capital	% Total Capital	Average Cap. per Investment
Merchants	30	50.8%	7328.6	48.8%	244.3
Changers/ Moneyers	6	10.2%	1533	10.2%	255.5
Retail/ Wholesale	12	20.3%	2446.3	16.3%	203.9
Nobles/ *Burgenses*	–	–	–	–	–
Professions/ Education	1	1.7%	37.5	.2%	37.5
Jews	–	–	–	–	–
Royal Administration	–	–	–	–	–
Ecclesiastics	1	1.7%	77.75	.5%	77.75
Women	2	3.4%	375.2	2.5%	187.6
Artisans/ Service	–	–	–	–	–
Food Trades	–	–	–	–	–
Agriculture	–	–	–	–	–
Foreigners	7	11.9%	3231.83	21.5%	461.7
Unidentified					
Local	–	–	–	–	–
Other	–	–	–	–	–

* Given the limited number of maritime *societates*, their data have been included in this table.

comanda with several investors assigned risks to the investors. Profit arrangements in both cases were variable. Although the *comanda* generally had a three-fourths/one-fourth division of profits, a fixed sum might also be assigned the traveler as remuneration.[41] The maritime *societas* might divide profits proportionately along with the risks or assign a percentage division such as one-fourth to the traveler.[42] In the maritime *comanda* with multiple investors, merchants and retail/wholesalers could include investments from widows and children of

[41] For example, A. D. Hérault, II E 95/372, J. Holanie, f. 13r.

[42] For one-fourth of the profits to the traveler, see n. 39 above. For a proportional division, n. 40.

former associates in their own undertakings.[43] Finally, in one of the extant maritime *societates*, the contractual arrangement was for three years; in the second *societas*, one voyage was envisioned, as was the case with the *comanda* contracts.[44]

TABLE 2: MARITIME *COMANDA* AND *SOCIETAS* TRAVELERS OF THE MONTPELLIER NOTARIAL EVIDENCE (1293-1348)

	Acts	% Total
Merchants	27	45.8 %
Changers/ Moneyers	1	1.7 %
Retail/ Wholesale	10	16.9 %
Nobles/ *Burgenses*	–	–
Professions/ Education	–	–
Jews	–	–
Royal Administration	–	–
Ecclesiastics	–	–
Women	–	–
Artisans/ Service	–	–
Food Trades	–	–
Agriculture	–	–
Foreigners	19	32.2 %
Unidentified		
Local	2	3.4 %
Other	–	–

The maritime *comanda* could involve several traveling partners who were frequently young merchants of Montpellier or foreigners drawn from Narbonne, from the Massif Central and the Cévennes, mountainous regions which sent many inhabitants to Montpellier in search of business careers.[45] Table 2 gives the distribution of traveling partners among social and occupational groups. Business

[43] See n. 41 above.

[44] See nn. 39 and 40 above.

[45] See my article, "Patterns of Population Attraction and Mobility," pp. 275-276, on in-migration from these regions.

practice reveals the use of the maritime *comanda* as a vehicle for merchant apprenticeship and for investment credit. The traveling partner received the capital necessary to launch or expand a career providing that he made shrewd use of the opportunity.

The activities of the Magalassio family, merchants whose activities would not seem radically atypical of Montpellier, can further illuminate the contractual relationship of the maritime *comanda*. Jacobus de Magalassio, a Montpellier merchant, was involved in seven extant *comanda* engagements in the late 1330s and 1340s.[46] In these years Magalassio provided the capital in *comanda* investments, at times alone, at times in cooperation with other merchants, for trade throughout the Mediterranean basin, to Sicily, to Cyprus, to *Romania*. His share of cash or merchandise in each engagement ranged from about 100 to 500 *l. t.*[47] His traveling partners included merchants of Narbonne, Alès, Aurillac, Béziers and Montpellier. During this period his nephew, Petrus de Magalassio, participated in international trade as a traveling merchant. On 20 September 1343, after stating before a notary that he was over twenty years old and without a curator, Petrus accepted *comanda* contracts from his uncle and two other merchants of Montpellier to sell approximately 645 *l. t.* worth of cloth in Cyprus.[48] Petrus was fulfilling the normal apprenticeship as an international merchant, financed with *comanda* credit. His share in these ventures was to be one-fourth of the profits. Another nephew of Jacobus de Magalassio, one Petrus de Monteleone, son of a sister of Jacobus, died in Famagousta, Cyprus in the early 1340s while traveling with *comanda* investments. Jacobus was instrumental in straightening out the commitments resulting from this untimely death.[49] Only ten years earlier, Jacobus himself had traveled in the Levant as the representative of another Montpellier merchant.[50] The passage from traveler to investor may have been a subtle one with a possible intermediate stage where the traveler invested his own funds.[51] In general, younger members of the merchant class were traveling partners; older members were investing partners.

46 A. D. Hérault, II E 95/375, P. de Pena, ff. 2r and 76v; II E 95/371, J. Holanie, ff. 71r, 113v and 115v; II E 95/372, J. Holanie *et al.*, ff. 52v and 84r.

47 On 16 September 1339, Magalassio confided the equivalent of 214 *l. t.* invested in French wool cloth to an inhabitant of Montpellier, in-migrant from Aurillac, for a trip to Cyprus (A. D. Hérault, II E 95/375, P. de Pena, f. 76v). In 1341 he invested the equivalent of 390 *l. t.* (1561 l. in money of 4 October 1341) in another trip to Cyprus, this time by a merchant of Narbonne (II E 95/371, J. Holanie, f. 15v). In 1342 Magalassio joined other merchants of Montpellier and Narbonne in furnishing a total equivalent to 484 *l. t.* good money in cloth of Chalons and cloth of Narbonne to a Narbonnais traveler for sale in Cyprus (II E 95/371, J. Holanie, ff. 111v-112v). In 1343 de Magalassio cooperated with yet another Narbonnais to invest the equivalent of 389 *l. t.* in French cloths and local cloths for a trip to Sicily (II E 95/372, J. Holanie, f. 52v).

48 A. D. Hérault, II E 95/372, J. Holanie et al., ff. 84r, 84v and 87r.

49 A. D. Hérault, II E 95/371, J. Holanie, ff. 111v-112v. Jacobus de Magalassio had an investment in this venture, too.

50 A. D. Hérault, II E 95/369, J. Holanie, f. 80v. As early as 1331, Magalassio was also investing in trade. See II E 95/371, J. Holanie, ff. 71r-v.

51 R. Berlow, "The Sailing of the 'Saint Esprit'," pp. 348 and 357-360, found considerable interchangeability of traveling and investing partners in mid-thirteenth-century Marseille.

Jacobus de Magalassio invested either cash capital or cloths in his *comanda* partnerships. However, in one instance in the *comanda* between Jacobus and his nephew, Petrus de Magalassio, the 492 *l. t.* investment by Jacobus included exchange contract debts due him by another Montpellier merchant, Petrus de Lauzis.[52] The negotiability of commercial obligations is revealed in this investment, the only of its kind extant, in which an exchange credit provided the capital for a commercial undertaking. The short terms of debt associated with money exchanges may have facilitated the arrangements of this *comanda*. Conversely, the transfer of outstanding *comanda* credits would serve as a means of debt repayment.[53]

It was to the advantage of the traveling merchant to contract multiple *comanda* partnerships before making a voyage to the Levant. This tactic permitted a maximization of effort and a diversification of commitment. An example of the accumulation of *comanda* engagements was provided by Petrus Guersii in 1333. Guersii recorded four *comanda* contracts prior to a voyage to Cyprus.[54] His financiers included two merchants of Montpellier, a money changer and an inhabitant of Millau. Their combined investments, concentrated in wool cloths but including other merchandise, totaled 439 *l. t.* According to the terms of the *comanda* contracts, Guersii was to receive one-fourth of the profit in each case. The traveling partner of a *comanda* might enter into several contracts and negotiate some of his own goods, thereby increasing his profits while limiting his expenses. His share of profits, although not as great as the investor's, was certainly not negligible.[55]

In addition to the *comanda* investments made by merchants, changers and members of the retail/wholesale trades, the participation of women in commercial partnerships deserves note. For example, in 1301, Johanna and Blanca, daughters of the deceased merchant, Philippus de Orlhaco, entrusted 260 *l. t.* in French linen cloths in *comanda* to their brother, Bertrandus, with a fifty-fifty division of profits, perhaps out of respect for the family relationship.[56] This merchandise was to be sold in Cyprus and Armenia. In another exception to the general rule, losses in this contractual relationship were also to be shared equally. To raise the capital for this investment the sisters had gone into debt for 300 *l. t.* to a merchant of Montpellier; 250 *l. t.* were owed through a recognition of debt for the purchase of linen cloth and 50 *l. t.* were borrowed from the merchant, B. Garrigas, as a loan.[57] The destination of the 40 *l. t.* remaining after the *comanda* investment of 260 *l. t.* was never referred to in these documents. At the same time, in payment of their debts to the merchant, the sisters surrendered to him a

[52] A. D. Hérault, II E 95/372, J. Holanie et al., f. 84r.

[53] See Chapter 4, "Deposit Banking and the Recovery of Debts."

[54] A. D. Hérault, II E 95/369, J. Holanie, ff. 72r, 74r, 75v, 77r.

[55] On the polemic among historians regarding the traveler's share of the profits, see R. Berlow, "The Sailing of the 'Saint Esprit'," pp. 348 and 360.

[56] A. M. Montpellier, II 2, J. Grimaudi, f. 14r.

[57] A. M. Montpellier, II 2, J. Grimaudi, f. 13v.

credit obligation which they held on a Montpellier Jew, Crescas den Mascip.[58] This obligation had been established on the occasion of the sale of a house to den Mascip with conditional tenure, *in precaria*. Such a sequence of involvements is revealing of the interrelation between commercial and real estate credit transactions. Assets of real property had been converted into liquid capital for maritime commercial investment.[59]

Maritime *comanda* and *societas* partnerships were the cornerstones of the international luxury trade in Montpellier. Also vital to the urban economy were the land contracts. The local land *comanda* contracts were similar in most respects to the maritime *comanda*.[60] However, three distinctions are worthy of note. In one example of the land *comanda*, the working or traveling partner contributed funds or goods to the venture, making the contract a bilateral *comanda*. A second difference concerned the duration of the contract which, in the case of the land contract, was a set period, often several years. In two contracts of 1327 and 1339, eight years was the contractual period.[61] The third distinction related to the direction of investment in the land *comanda* to overland trade or to local industrial or business activities. Among the destinations of Montpellier land *comanda* contracts were Avignon, Toulouse, the Languedocian fairs at Pézenas and Villeveyrac, and Burgundy.[62] In numerous contracts there was no mention of a geographic destination, and it may be assumed that those contracts were addressed to the local context.[63]

Tables 3 and 4 provide a breakdown of the investing and working participants of the land *comanda* contracts and their financial contributions. Among investors, the merchant class was less prominent here than in the maritime *comanda* contracts. Women used this type of investment in numbers equal to those of the retail/wholesalers, but the former's investments were, on the average, somewhat

[58] *Ibid.*

[59] There is considerable historical controversy over the origin of commercial capital. Henri Pirenne viewed trade as the generating force of additional capital, in short *sui generis*. See, for example, his article, "The Stages in the Social History of Capitalism," *American Historical Review* 19 (1913), 494-515. In this stance, he was opposed to Werner Sombart who viewed land rents as the original source of capital. The latter dated the rise of capitalism from the sixteenth century. See *Der Moderne Kapitalismus*, 2nd ed. I (Munich, 1916). See the recent discussion of the formation of capital in Flanders by David Nicholas, "Structures du peuplement, fonctions urbaines et formation du capital dans la Flandre médiévale," *Annales: ESC* 33, no. 3 (1978), 501-527. See also Jacques Heers, "The 'Feudal' Economy and Capitalism: Words, Ideas and Reality," *Journal of European Economic History* 3 (1974), 609-653.

On these arrangements, see also Salomon Kahn, "Documents inédits sur les Juifs de Montpellier au moyen âge," *Revue des études juives* 28 (1894), 122, and A.-E. Sayous and J. Combes, "Les commerçants et les capitalistes," p. 363. The same kind of practice was recorded, that is, the conversion of capital from real estate into commercial investment, in a land *comanda* (A. D. Hérault, II E 95/368, J. Holanie, ff. 59r-59v). See A.-E. Sayous and J. Combes, *ibid.*, pp. 367-368.

[60] See n. 22 above for their distribution.

[61] For example, A. D. Hérault, II E 95/368, J. Holanie, f. 13r and II E 95/374, G. Nogareti, f. 30vR.

[62] See the table, "Commenda Contracts," in my dissertation, "Commerce and Society in Montpellier," 2: Appendix V, pp. 249-260.

[63] For example, A. D. Hérault, II E 95/368, J. Holanie, f. 9v.

smaller. A broader cross-section of the local population was involved in the land *comanda* than in the maritime *comanda* partnerships.[64] Foreigners were comparatively few in number in the land contracts, but their average investments were high. Overall, the average capital per investment in the land *comanda* contracts among the most frequently participating social and occupational groups compares favorably with that of the maritime contracts of Table 1.

TABLE 3: LAND *COMANDA* INVESTORS OF THE MONTPELLIER NOTARIAL EVIDENCE (1293-1348) WITH INVESTMENTS QUOTED IN LIVRES TOURNOIS OF APRIL 1330

	No. of Acts	% Total Acts	Capital	% Total Capital	Average Cap. per Investment
Merchants	6	14.6%	812	18.7%	135.3
Changers/ Moneyers	1	2.4%	514.8	11.9%	514.8
Retail/ Wholesale	9	21.95%	599	13.8%	66.6
Nobles/ *Burgenses*	1	2.4%	500	11.5%	500
Professions/ Education	2	4.9%	65.9	1.5%	32.95
Jews	1	2.4%	32.75	.8%	32.75
Royal Administration	–	–	–	–	–
Ecclesiastics	1	2.4%	15	.3%	15
Women	10	24.4%	746.5	17.2%	74.7
Artisans/ Service	5	12.9%	91	2.1%	18.2
Food Trades	–	–	–	–	–
Agriculture	–	–	–	–	–
Foreigners	4	9.8%	960.15	22.1%	240.0
Unidentified					
Local	1	2.4%	5.5	.1%	5.5
Other	–	–	–	–	–
TOTALS	41	–	4342.6	–	–

[64] In one of the few surviving examples of the participation of a *burgensis* of Montpellier in active trade, the *burgensis* Johannes Crespini received 500 *l. melg.* worth of ginger and other goods from merchants of Saint-Antonin. Crespini was to travel to Burgundy to trade. See A. M. Montpellier, II 1, J. Grimaudi, f. 45r. See Tables 5 and 6 for the participation of these groups. Important retail/ wholesalers such as furriers used these contracts to further their trade (A. D. Hérault, II E 95/371, J. Holanie, f. 140r).

TABLE 4: LAND *COMANDA* WORKERS OF THE MONTPELLIER NOTARIAL EVIDENCE (1293-1348) WITH INVESTMENTS QUOTED IN LIVRES TOURNOIS OF APRIL 1330

	No. of Acts	% Total Acts	Capital	% Total Capital
Merchants	4	9.8%	–	–
Changers/ Moneyers	2	4.9%	–	–
Retail/ Wholesale	9	21.95%	170.5 (1 act)	3.9%
Nobles/ *Burgenses*	1	2.4%	–	–
Professions/ Education	–	–	–	–
Jews	1	2.4%	–	–
Royal Administration	–	–	–	–
Ecclesiastics	–	–	–	–
Women	1	2.4%	–	–
Artisans/ Service	10	24.4%	–	–
Food Trades	–	–	–	–
Agriculture	4	9.8%	–	–
Foreigners	7	17.1%	–	–
Unidentified				
Local	2	4.9%	–	–
Other	–	–	–	–
TOTALS	41	–	–	–

Among the junior partners or workers in this type of investment, the important representation of retail/wholesalers and of artisans is not surprising since the land *comanda* seems to have operated here as in Venice as a form of business loan. In Venice the local form of land *commenda*, the *colleganza*, had become in essence a loan by the fourteenth century.[65] Its profit potential was at first controlled, and it was later condemned as usurious by municipal statute in 1351.[66] No comparable

[65] See n. 9 above.

[66] R. C. Mueller, "Les prêteurs juifs de Venise au moyen âge," p. 1230, noted that the local *colleganza* contracts were declared illicit in 1351. On credit instruments in Venice, see also R. C. Mueller, *The Procuratori di San Marco and the Venetian Credit Market: A Study of the Development of Credit and Banking in the Trecento* (New York, 1977).

legislation is extant for Montpellier. Here shoemakers, a glassblower, a tailor, an innkeeper and agricultural workers accepted this type of financing openly for their business endeavors.[67]

In the only contract of *comanda* partnership noted for the Jews of Montpellier, a father-in-law, Samuel de Mauguio, provided the equivalent of 32.75 *l. t.* in *comanda* to his son-in-law in 1289; the latter received an acquittal at the conclusion of the partnership with his father-in-law on 17 December 1293.[68] The probable object of this local enterprise was the financing of a lending business. Another related document detailed a series of small debts by local inhabitants in an accounting of principal and profits, which were not specified.[69] The lack of more ample evidence (the Jews were present in only one extant *societas* as well) regarding the use of business partnerships by the Jews of Montpellier, and, in particular, their absence from any maritime commercial endeavors is similar to the situation which R. W. Emery found in studying the Jews of Perpignan.[70]

While little evidence of Jewish partnership has survived, women took an active role in land partnership investments in Montpellier. The relative frequence of women investors in land-based *comanda* contracts can be compared with their infrequent investments in maritime ventures.[71] Women of humble background used the land *comanda* investment. The widow of a cultivator financed her son-in-law in this fashion.[72] The widow of a fisherman financed a grain merchant's commerce.[73] A merchant's widow also utilized this form of investment of funds.[74] Only one example of a woman accepting a *comanda* partnership as the junior or working partner has survived. In 1327 a Franciscan, Jacobus de Asperis, provided 15 *l. t.* in *comanda* to the widow of a tailor, presumably for use in a trade.[75] Here, as in many of the extant land *comanda* engagements, the contract transferring funds from an investor to a partner did not specify the economic context of the investment.

[67] It should be noted that many land *comanda* contracts did not carry any specification of commercial intent. For example in 1333 a *canabasserius* gave a mercer 40 *l. t.* without details of trade. See A. D. Hérault, II E 95/369, J. Holanie, f. 100v. See also the *comanda* of 1334 granted by a shoemaker of 50 *l. t.* to the son of a furrier (acquittal in A. D. Hérault, II E 95/371, J. Holanie, f. 43v).

[68] A. M. Montpellier, II 1, J. Grimaudi, f. 49r. See the transcription of the act in Salomon Kahn, "Documents inédits sur les Juifs de Montpellier au moyen âge," *Revue des études juives* 22 (1891), 276.

[69] See *ibid.*, for the transcription of this act.

[70] The *societas*, also transcribed *ibid.*, pp. 278-279 is found in A. M. Montpellier, II, 1, J. Grimaudi, f. 76v. Another act which Kahn, p. 278, terms an act of association, II, 1, f. 64v, was an agreement between brothers envisioning a common front in legal defense. On Perpignan Jews, see R. W. Emery, *The Jews of Perpignan*, p. 32.

[71] Most women invested in land-based as opposed to maritime *comanda* contracts. Compare Tables 1 and 3.

[72] A. D. Hérault, II E 95/369, J. Holanie, f. 90v.

[73] Acquittal in A. D. Hérault, II E 95/369, J. Holanie, f. 43r.

[74] See also A. D. Hérault, II E 95/369, J. Holanie, ff. 52v and 95v for the *comanda* contract of the widow of a merchant.

[75] A. D. Hérault, II E 95/368, J. Holanie, f. 36v.

The transfer of partnership credits could be used as a means of repayment of other obligations. On 26 May 1333, Agatha, the widow of a fisherman, Jacobus de Portabus, acquitted her *comanda* partner, a grain merchant, for the payment of 10 *l. t.* of a debt of 50 *l. t.* outstanding from their contractual relationship.[76] She assigned the remaining 40 *l. t.* of the debt to a merchant of Montpellier, to whom she was indebted and who acknowledged receipt of 15 *l. t.* as a first installment of repayment. The transfer of *comanda* credit obligations by a partner to a third party was a form of negotiability of credit instruments.[77]

The inhabitants of Montpellier were capable of ingenious use of the existing legal forms of the *comanda* and the *societas* for their own best advantage. The arrangements between partners would vary according to the specific circumstances as would the duration and the details of the association. On occasion, *comanda* and *societas* would be present in the same contractual agreement. For example, on 31 July 1343, a glassblower provided 55 *l. t.* in grain *in comanda* to a grain merchant.[78] The grain merchant stated that he would market the merchandise on land or on water but not on the sea, along with 140 *l. t.* of his own which he placed *in societate* with the glassblower. Risks were to be shared proportionately with the profits. In addition, one-third of the profits were assigned to the grain merchant as salary. Accounts were to be rendered the following summer at the Feast of Saint John the Baptist (24 June). The combination of *comanda* and *societas* contracts permitted personal arrangements regarding risks and profits which fulfilled the financial needs of the participants.[79]

In Montpellier as elsewhere there were basic differences between the *comanda* and the *societas*. The sharing of capital investment, however unequally, by the partners characterized the *societas*, in contrast to the *comanda*. In the *societas* the division of profits was generally assigned at a fixed percentage at the outset, but, occasionally, as just above, the profits and risks might be proportional to the investments of each partner.[80] An alternative form of *societas* involved contributions of capital and work from both associates.[81] More frequently, the partner contributing less capital would furnish his work as well, for which he

[76] A. D. Hérault, II E 95/369, J. Holanie, f. 43r.

[77] See Chapter 4, "Deposit Banking and the Recovery of Debts."

[78] A. D. Hérault, II E 95/372, J. Holanie et al., f. 66v.

[79] On the issue of ambiguity in types of partnership, see P. Bouges, "La pratique contractuelle," 1: 190 and A. D. Hérault, II E 95/371, J. Holanie, f. 34r. See also A. D. Hérault, II E 95/368, J. Holanie, f. 69r.

[80] See A. D. Hérault, II E 95/372, J. Holanie et al., f. 12r. P. Bouges, "La pratique contractuelle," 1: 185, maintained that no proportional divisions were practiced: "Nous n'avons pas rencontré à Montpellier de répartition du bénéfice au prorata des apports en capital social, alors qu'au contraire cette règle est très générale pour les sociétés en nom collectif italiennes à partir de la fin du XIIIe siècle et tout au long du XIVe siècle." Here again, his sampling of notarial registers forced him to overlook an example to the contrary, as it led him to declare, p. 182, that there were no maritime *societates*, a statement that is not strictly accurate as Table 1 reveals. On the concept of liability in the Montpellier *societas*, see P. Bouges, 1: 177-181.

[81] P. Bouges, "La pratique contractuelle," 1: 181; examples can be found in A. D. Hérault, II E 95/372, J. Holanie et al., f. 133v: a *societas* among barber surgeons; and II E 95/377, B. Egidii, f. 31r: a *societas* among painters.

would be remunerated. Nevertheless, capital investment may have earned in these contracts a better return than labor.[82]

Similarities between the *societas* and the land-based *comanda* are worthy of note. The *societas* might last for a period of years; two to six years was a common term of partnership.[83] The *societas* resembled the land-based *comanda* in that it was used frequently by the retail/wholesalers and artisans for the financing of local business activities.

Tables 5 and 6 give the breakdown of participants in the land *societas* contracts of Montpellier. On the whole the participation of the local population as major partners was broadly based, although the frequency of employment of this type of contractual agreement was not as common as that of the land *comanda*. High individual investments were made by merchants, by Martha de Cabanis, mother of the Cabanis brothers, and by a foreigner from Ganges. Junior partners were widely distributed across social and occupational lines. Their capital investments were considerably smaller than those of the major partners.

In the extant *societas* contracts it was common to find family ties. The practice of leaving inheritances undivided and the existence of *frayresque* partnerships have left their trace in the Montpellier evidence.[84] In one example, the sons of a draper, Bernardus Roardi, agreed in a *societas* contract to hold all their goods and possessions in common for life, including the dowries of their wives.[85]

As in the maritime *comanda* contracts, the *societas* partnership might serve to launch the younger generation in a business career. In 1301 the *canabasserius* Berengarius de Sumena formed two *societas* partnerships in which he was the working junior partner. First of all, on 17 August 1301, he furnished 27 *l. t.* to the capital of the partnership with an uncle who provided a capital of 1100 *l. t.* to the venture.[86] Using these funds Berengarius was to trade in Montpellier and elsewhere on land for two years. At the end of this period, 250 *l. t.* of the profit was to be his, the rest his uncle's. On 4 October 1301, Berengarius acquired additional funds through a *societas* established with another *canabasserius* in which Berengarius contributed 300 *l. t.* in linen or canvas and his partner 200 *l. t.* with an equal division of profit.[87] This partnership, to last until 1 August 1303,

[82] P. Bouges, "La pratique contractuelle," 1: 187, remarked that the situation in Montpellier with less remuneration going to labor contrasted with that of Toulouse where a shortage of labor heightened its value. P. Wolff, *Commerces et marchands de Toulouse*, pp. 491-492, whose work Bouges cited, was, of course, dealing with the period after the Black Death when massive demographic change had occurred. In Montpellier in the first half of the fourteenth century, labor was still plentiful. On demography, see my article, "Patterns of Population Attraction and Mobility," p. 257, n. 2. The actual profits of *societates* are generally impossible to determine.

[83] For an instance of six years, see A. D. Hérault, II E 95/375, P. de Pena, f. 35v.

[84] On this type of institution in Provence, see Roger Aubenas, "La famille dans l'ancienne Provence," *Annales d'histoire économique et sociale* 8 (1936), 523-541. For an Italian comparison, see the Venetian *fraterna*: Lopez and Raymond, *Medieval Trade*, pp. 186-188 and F. C. Lane, "Family Partnerships and Joint Ventures," *Journal of Economic History* 4 (1944), 178-196.

[85] A. D. Hérault, II E 95/372, J. Holanie et al., f. 80v.

[86] A. M. Montpellier, II 2, J. Grimaudi, f. 26r.

[87] A. M. Montpellier, II 2, J. Grimaudi, f. 38v.

involved trade in Montpellier, in Burgundy and elsewhere on land. The first *societas* of Berengarius may well have financed the second, obeying the ageless maxim, it takes money to make money.

The *societas* was given application in Montpellier outside the realms of trade and industry in art. Artists used *societates* to finance their artistic endeavors.[88] For

TABLE 5: LAND *SOCIETAS* MAJOR PARTNERS OF THE MONTPELLIER NOTARIAL EVIDENCE (1293-1348) WITH INVESTMENTS QUOTED IN LIVRES TOURNOIS OF APRIL 1330

		No. of Acts	% Total Acts	Capital[1]	% Total[2] Capital	Average Capital per Investment
Merchants	(2)	3	12.5%	1890	19.7%	945
Changers/ Moneyers		1	4.2%	100	1.0%	100
Retail/ Wholesale	(8)	11	45.8%	3008.5	31.4%	376.1
Nobles/ *Burgenses*		–	–	–	–	–
Professions/ Education		–	–	–	–	–
Jews		1	4.2%	91	.9%	91
Royal Administration		–	–	–	–	–
Ecclesiastics		–	–	–	–	–
Women		1	4.2%	1340	13.98%	1340
Artisans/ Service	(1)	5	20.8%	297	3.1%	297
Food Trades		–	–	–	–	–
Agriculture		–	–	–	–	–
Foreigners		1	4.2%	892.5	9.3%	892.5
Unidentified Local		1	4.2%	–	–	–
Other		–	–	–	–	–
TOTALS		24	–	7619	79.5%	–

[1] Figures in parentheses indicate the number of acts for which data was available and upon which calculations of capital and average capital per investment were based. In some cases no data remained.

[2] The total capital of the *societates* contributed by major and junior partners, was used as the basis of these calculations.

[88] On the artists of Montpellier, the old article by J. Renouvier and A. Ricard, "Des maîtres de

TABLE 6: LAND *SOCIETAS* JUNIOR PARTNERS OF THE MONTPELLIER EVIDENCE WITH INVESTMENTS QUOTED IN LIVRES TOURNOIS OF APRIL 1330

		No. of Acts	% Total Acts	Capital	% Total Capital	Average Capital per Investment
Merchants		3	12.5%	300	3.1%	100
Changers/ Moneyers		–	–	–	–	–
Retail/ Wholesale	(6)	9	37.5%	1121.9	11.7%	186.98
Nobles/ *Burgenses*		–	–	–	–	–
Professions/ Education		1	4.2%	–	–	–
Jews		1	4.2%	91	.9%	91
Royal Administration		–	–	–	–	–
Ecclesiastics		–	–	–	–	–
Women		1	4.2%	223.25	2.3%	223.25
Artisans/ Service	(3)	7	29.2%	228.2	2.4%	76.1
Food Trades		–	–	–	–	–
Agriculture		–	–	–	–	–
Foreigners		–	–	–	–	–
Unidentified						
Local		2	8.3%	–	–	–
Other		–	–	–	–	–
TOTALS		24	–	1964.35	20.5%	–

* See notes 1 and 2 of Table 7.

example, in 1347, a painter of Prato, inhabitant of Montpellier, pooled resources with two immigrant painters from Florence for a period of three years.[89] They were to divide expenses equally with the exception of arrangements for their atelier. One Florentine was responsible for one-fourth of these atelier expenses while the other two partners were to divide the remaining costs. Profits were to

pierre et des autres artistes gothiques de Montpellier," *Mem. soc. arch. Mplr.* 1st ser, 2 (1854), 135-350, has never been surpassed.

[89] A. D. Hérault, II E 95/377, B. Egidii, f. 31r. See, for other examples, ff. 12r, 111v and 126v.

be shared in the same proportions. Such a partnership permitted the installation of these painters; their association may also have brought a fruitful enlargement of artistic contacts and of a potential clientele.

Business association among Montpelliérains and among foreigners with a Montpellier base is further suggested by numerous mentions of associates (*socii*) in a wide variety of notarial contracts, recognitions of debt, transport contracts and *comanda* contracts themselves. Associates such as the Cabanis brothers, whose activities included cloth exports to the Levant, sales of Lucchese silks in Montpellier and shipments of saffran to Champagne, conducted their affairs with the aid of subordinate associates, agents and procurators.[90] The same business network was characteristic of the Alamandini family whose ventures encompassed the apothecary trade and the changers' profession.[91] It may well be that many associations were never formalized by written contracts. However, a substantial, if inestimable, portion of international and local trade and industry was carried on through this form of association of a few colleagues or family members.[92] The elaborate organization of partnerships of the Tuscan towns, with extensive use of branches and agents, was not duplicated in Montpellier. Not only the famous Florentine companies, the Bardi and the Peruzzi, but the Sienese Bonsignori and the Lucchese Ricciardi had such structures.[93] The Montpellier associations involved fewer associates. Moreover, there remains no trace in Montpellier of the sophisticated investment possibilities of the Italian companies, no *sopra corpo* or outside investments, no companies with shareholders.[94]

In the *societas* and *comanda* contracts utilized by participants in international trade and by members of other social and occupational categories, including artisans, the service trades and agricultural workers, capital was generated through the extension of credit and positioned through the pooling of resources. Such cooperative efforts provided valuable incentives for young merchants and artisans while furnishing established business persons with mechanisms of investment to increase their fortunes.

[90] A. D. Hérault, II E 95/374, G. Nogareti, *passim*. John H. Pryor, *Business Contracts*, p. 151, described the procurator thus: "In private law a procurator might be a general administrator of property or a representative in legal cases." The procurator's mandate might be general or specific. See also his Glossary, p. 273, for definitions of procuration.

[91] On the Alamandini, see A. M. Montpellier, II 1, J. Grimaudi, ff. 5v, 15r, 15v, 24v, and A. D. Hérault, II E 95/372, J. Holanie et al., f. 85r. See also Renée Doehaerd, *Les relations commerciales entre Gênes, la Belgique et l'Outremont*, 3, act 1669: 10 May 1309, for an exchange contract passed in Genoa.

[92] Thomas W. Blomquist, "Trade and Commerce in Thirteenth-Century Lucca," pp. 20-21, suggested that partnership agreements might have been drawn up privately and stored at company headquarters. He found no surviving partnership contracts for the large Lucchese companies. Only associations directed to a "lower level of economic activity" seem to have been preserved.

[93] On the Bardi and the Peruzzi, see, Armando Sapori, *La crisi delle compagnie mercantili dei Bardi e dei Peruzzi* (Florence, 1926); on the Lucchese, see, for example, Richard W. Kaeuper, *Bankers to the Crown: The Riccardi of Lucca and Edward I* (Princeton, 1973).

[94] On late medieval Italian techniques, see Raymond de Roover, *The Medici Bank* (New York, 1948) and *The Rise and Decline of the Medici Bank, 1397-1494* (Cambridge, Mass., 1963). On Italian business practice in general, see also Armando Sapori, *Le marchand italien au moyen âge* (Paris, 1952).

GRAPH 1: AVERAGE *COMANDA* AND *SOCIETAS* CONTRACTS (MARITIME)

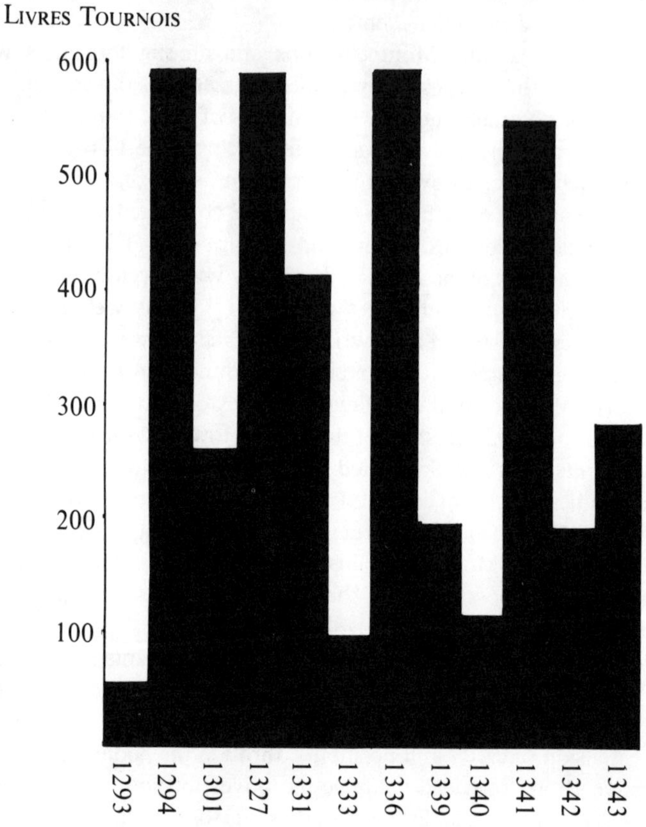

Personnel and organization of business partnerships shed light on the business and financial climate of medieval Montpellier. Exploration of the levels of investment in Montpellier partnerships can further an understanding of business practice. Graphs 1, 2 and 3 show the average investment per transaction in a given year in the types of contracts examined above.[95] The most consistent information comes from Graph 1, giving average investments in maritime *comanda* and *societas* engagements. Although on a year to year basis the variation in level of average investment was greater than one to six throughout the period under study, in years when information was available, a level of 500-600 *l. t.* frequently was attained. Individual contracts could involve much larger commitments of funds. An acquittal of 3 June 1342 preserved details of the largest

[95] Graphs 1, 2 and 3 have been developed along the lines of monetary conversion described in Appendix 2, "Monetary Problems." In Graph 1, the figure for 1301 represents a single record. Single records were found in 1336 and 1346 in Graph 2 and in 1327 and 1336 in Graph 3.

extant maritime *comanda* investment.[96] On 5 May 1341, the equivalent of 1701 *l. t.* of 1330 had been confided by merchants of Montpellier to a compatriot and to a merchant of Nîmes for a trip to *Romania* (the Byzantine Empire). Several other extant maritime *comanda* acts provided evidence of investments worth over 1000 *l. t.*[97] Small sums were also found in this type of investment. On 20 July 1342, a local draper supplied another draper with the equivalent of 8 *l. t.* that was invested in local wool cloths for a trip to Cyprus.[98]

GRAPH 2: AVERAGE *COMANDA* CONTRACTS (LAND)

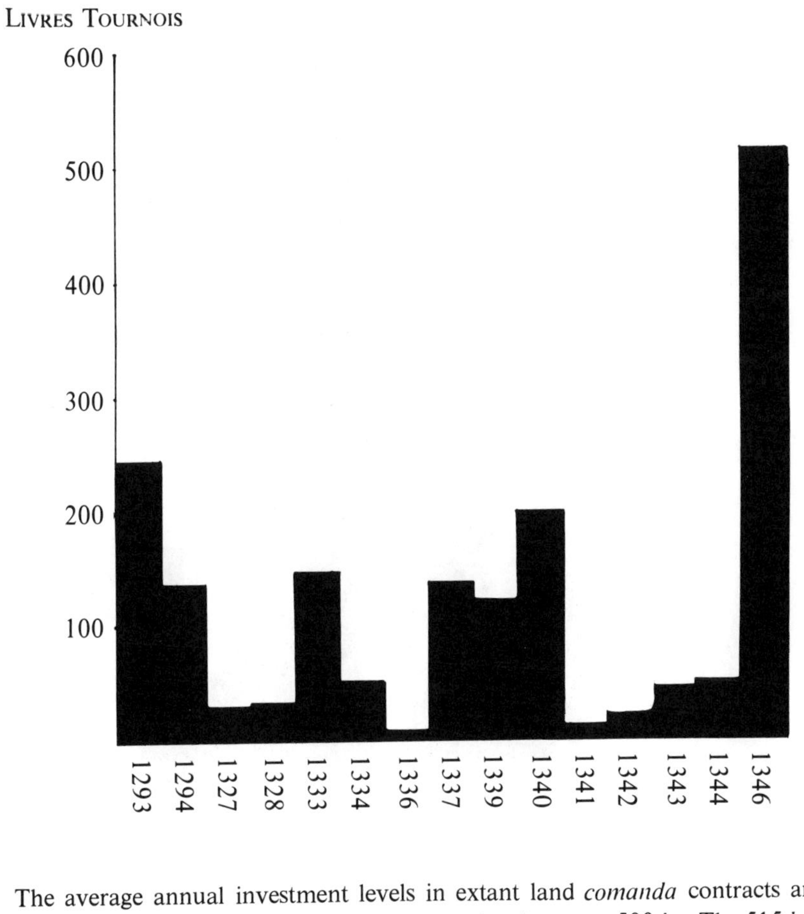

The average annual investment levels in extant land *comanda* contracts are given in Graph 2. Only in 1346 did the average level surpass 500 *l. t.* The 515 *l. t.*

96 A. D. Hérault, II E 95/371, J. Holanie, f. 46v.
97 See, for example, A. D. Hérault, II E 95/368, J. Holanie, ff. 15v and 35v.
98 A. D. Hérault, II E 95/371, J. Holanie, f. 102r.

of this year was the largest extant individual land *comanda* contract.[99] Small investments of less than 5 *l. t.* were not uncommon.[100] While land *comanda* partnerships were utilized in the financing of overland trade, this technique could also be used in local artisans' activities.

GRAPH 3: AVERAGE *SOCIETAS* CONTRACTS (LAND)

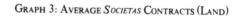

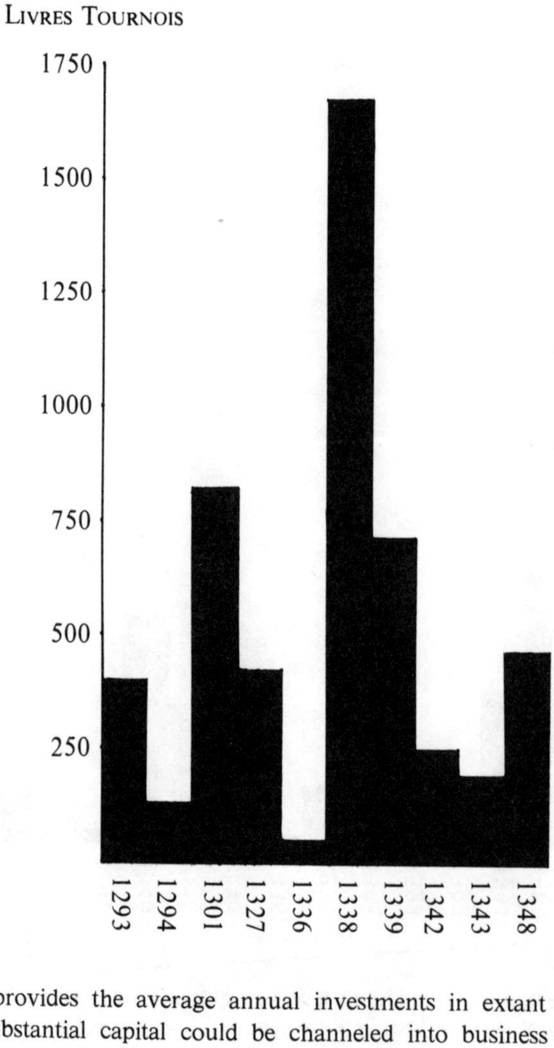

Graph 3 provides the average annual investments in extant land *societas* contracts. Substantial capital could be channeled into business through this

[99] The exceptional year of 1346 is due to the passage of a land *comanda* between two changers for the large sum of 515 *l. t.* in the good money of 1330 (A. D. Hérault, II E 95/377, B. Egidii, f. 101v).

[100] See, for example, A. D. Hérault, II E 95/371, J. Holanie, f. 22r.

method. The largest *societas* of record was established on 18 March 1338, between Jacobus de Cabanis, merchant of Montpellier and major partner, and Petrus del Euser, merchant and working partner.[101] The engagement was to last for four years. Jacobus, acting with the consent of his mother, Martha, his curator, furnished 1340 *l. t.*, Petrus 670 *l. t.* Damage to the act prohibits precision regarding all its clauses; however, these sums seem to have been invested in a variety of merchandise for the purpose of trade. Martha de Cabanis, one of the few women recorded in large *societates*, utilized a wide range of credit techniques in the family business.[102] As a rule, capital investment in *societas* contracts was substantially larger than in land-based *comanda* contracts. It was also larger, on the average, than that of maritime *comanda* engagements.

Within each of the partnership categories analyzed above, there was a wide range of capital investment.[103] In no category was a specific partnership technique the monopoly of one occupational group within Montpellier. The prevalence of merchants, changers and members of the retail/wholesale trades as investors in maritime contracts can be contrasted with the broader base of participation of social and occupational groups in land-oriented investments. Maritime trade was a more speculative form of investment than overland trade and local artisans' activities, although all investments carried some risks. Although the evidence is scanty at best, the profit levels of these partnership investments and the salaries of traveling partners and workers must be addressed.

Within the Montpellier evidence more information is available regarding the retainers of traveling partners and the division of profits between investors and traveling partners than concerning the actual level of return on specific investments. The extant acquittals at the conclusion of partnerships rarely provided any details about the profits of the venture. Most acquittals merely recorded the investing partner's satisfaction with the accounting provided by the traveling partner.

In the maritime *comanda* contracts, the share of profits due the traveling partners was generally one-fourth of the whole. Fixed retainers were sometimes substituted for such a percentage. In April 1342 and April 1343 two associated drapers of Montpellier, Guillelmus Bertholomei and Andreas Tilholi, supplied *comanda* capital to traveling partners for trips to the Byzantine Empire.[104] In the first contract 1013 *l. t.* capital was provided with a remuneration of 50 *l. t.* to the

[101] A. D. Hérault, II E 95/374, G. Nogareti, f. 12rR.

[102] See, for example, A. D. Hérault, II E 95/374, G. Nogareti, f. 18rR. Martha provided a capital of 550 *l. t.* (1100 *l. t.* of 10 February 1339) and a local *canabasserius*, a capital of 170 *l.*; the latter was to use these sums in his trade, deriving 200 *l.* salary with the profits divided evenly. Here labor seems relatively well remunerated.

[103] In spite of the economic problems which are apparent in certain years of the history of Montpellier in the period under study, investment in business partnerships such as that of the maritime *comanda* continued to attain levels consistent with those of the early fourteenth century in the 1340s. On fourteenth-century problems in general see Édouard Perroy, "À l'origine d'une économie contractée: les crises du XIVe siècle," *Annales: ESC* 4 (1949), 167-182.

[104] A. D. Hérault, II E 95/371, J. Holanie, f. 13v and II E 95/372, J. Holanie et al., f. 13r.

traveling partners; in the second *comanda* the capital was 625 *l. t.* and the remuneration 50 *l. t.* to one traveler.[105] The circumstances surrounding these contracts differed somewhat. In 1342 the travelers were a local draper and an immigrant from the region of Cahors. In 1343 after his partner died, the draper traveled alone. In the 1343 investment of 625 *l. t.*, although the contract was termed a *comanda*, contributions from the daughter and the widow of the deceased Cahorsin represented approximately ten percent of the whole capital. The retainers of the travelers came to five percent in the investment of 1013 *l. t.* and six percent in that of 625 *l. t.* The circumstances of the two contracts may account for this slight variation. In both instances no further division of profits was included in the travelers' share. If the retainers of five and six percent of the initial capital investment are interpreted to represent the equivalent of the normal share of profits in a *comanda*, i.e., one-fourth, then the overall returns anticipated by the investors in these contracts were twenty and twenty-four percent respectively.

Other maritime *comanda* contracts recorded remuneration levels for the traveling partner as low as three percent.[106] Whatever the theoretical level of remuneration and profit, it is much more difficult to calculate the actual, realized profits from commercial ventures. Two acquittals of *comanda* contracts did provide the sums of money returned to investing partners by travelers and quoted, as well, the levels of initial capital investment. Interpretation of the profit level was hampered in both instances, however, by the problems of currency manipulations. The margin of return on one contract was either four percent or thirty percent according to the currency conversion date used.[107] In the second case the profits were enormous. On an initial investment of 25 *l. t.* current on 1 September 1337, 230 gold *denarii al pabalho* or *pavillons d'or* were returned on 29 January 1340.[108] The acquittal stated that one gold *denarius* was worth 30 *s.* yielding a total of 345 *l. t.* current money. The day of the acquittal, 29 January 1340, was also the date of a reminting of *tournois* coins.[109] According to whether calculations are based on the new or old precious metal value of those coins, the gold *denarii* were worth either 138 *l. t.* or 231.2 *l. t.* in the currency standard of April 1330, yielding profits of 550% or 920%. In both of the above acquittals, the presumption would be that the sums quoted represented three-fourths of the actual profits or the theoretical share due the investing partners.

[105] The sums involved were converted to the currency standard of April 1330.

[106] A. D. Hérault, II E 95/371, J. Holanie, f. 112v.

[107] A. D. Hérault, II E 95/375, P. de Pena, f. 119r. According to whether the precious metal value of coins is considered at the level of 29 January 1340 or at the preceding level, the initial investment of the equivalent of 89.4 *l.* in June 1337 yielded either 92.8 *l. t.* or 116 *l. t.* on 29 January 1340, representing a gain of either four percent or thirty percent.

[108] A. D. Hérault, II E 95/375, P. de Pena, f. 118v. On the value of a *pavillon d'or*, see Natalis de Wailly, "Mémoire sur les variations de la livre tournois depuis le règne de Saint Louis jusqu'à l'établissement de la monnaie décimale," *Mémoires de l'Académie des inscriptions et belles lettres* 21 (1857), 238.

[109] See Appendix 2, Table of Currency Conversion.

The profits from *societas* partnerships were structured somewhat differently from those of maritime *comanda* contracts. No acquittals providing actual cash figures of profits survive. The level of remuneration of junior or working partners varied substantially. In one *societas* described earlier, a nephew contributed 2.4% of the initial capital and was to receive the profits equal to 22.2% of the total investment.[110] The drapers Tilholi and Bertholomei supplied two furriers with a *comanda* of 375 *l. t.* and entered into a *societas* of 100 *l. t.* in which they contributed 50 *l. t.* and the furriers contributed 50 *l. t.*[111] This complex partnership was to run for two years and three months. The furriers expected a remuneration of 100 *l. t.* for their labor and one-fourth of the profits of the *comanda*, or 21.1% of the combined capital of the *societas* and the *comanda* plus one-fourth of the *comanda* profits. Their capital contribution to the whole represented 10.5%. The anticipated profits in *comanda* and *societas* partnerships were substantial.

Actual profits confirmed the theoretical expectations of this type of investment. By the fourteenth century profit levels of at least twenty percent were projected in maritime investments and, in fact, potential profits of considerably greater size were probably anticipated.

Historians have grappled with the general problem of investment profits from trade. Jacques Bernard estimated that "sea adventuring" yielded a return from thirty to forty percent.[112] David Herlihy, in examining the *commenda* contracts of Pisa, suggested that merchants could have expected about a twenty percent return on their investments.[113] Pisa's trade after the battle of La Meloria in 1284 was directed primarily to the western Mediterranean.[114] The level of profits from Mediterranean commerce as a whole undoubtedly declined overall from the twelfth to the fourteenth centuries, making spectacular profit the exception and not the rule.[115] It is probable, however, that the profit levels on maritime commercial investments were the highest in the successful venture to the eastern Mediterranean where risks and speculation were high, where records of piracy and the problems of recovery of merchandise have been preserved.[116] Montpelliérains' profits from investment in business partnerships would seem competitive with those of other Mediterranean traders. It is time to place the investment partnerships of Montpellier overall in a broader Mediterranean context.

Historians' efforts to distinguish among techniques of business partnership first with regard to Italian towns produced two broad geographic categories: maritime

[110] A. M. Montpellier, II 2, J. Grimaudi, f. 26r. The profits of the junior partner might be enhanced by provisions for food, clothes and expenses. See II 1, J. Grimaudi, f. 91v.

[111] A. D. Hérault, II E 95/371, J. Holanie, f. 34r.

[112] Jacques Bernard, "Trade and Finance in the Middle Ages, 900-1500," in *The Fontana Economic History of Europe*, ed. Carlo Cippola, 1: *The Middle Ages* (London and Glasgow, 1972), p. 308.

[113] David Herlihy, *Pisa in the Early Renaissance*, pp. 163-164.

[114] *Ibid.*, pp. 162-186.

[115] Benjamin Z. Kedar, *Merchants in Crisis* (New Haven and London, 1976), pp. 23-25 and 62-65.

[116] See n. 10 above.

towns and towns of the interior. Yves Renouard contrasted the practices of towns of the Tuscan interior where a reliance on long-term association and family-oriented partnerships prevailed with the Genoese model of short-term maritime partnerships.[117] The inland partnerships had a great diversity of business focus, with investments in trade, industry and banking. Merchants of inland towns developed complex organizations with branches of business agents located in commercially strategic markets across western Europe.[118] The Genoese partnerships linked an investor with a merchant adventurer for the length of one maritime voyage.[119] Speculative and potentially dangerous, these latter business ventures could be directed to the frontiers of European commerce.[120] The methods of the port of Genoa reflected a spirit of economic individualism which sparked, among other offshoots, a precocious growth of ingenious insurance arrangements.[121] In contrast to the Tuscan towns and Genoa, Venice provided a variation on the theme of commercial dynamism; the intervention of the state and the existence of a state fleet led to a more traditional and sedentary approach to commerce with concerted use of agency and representation.[122]

Forty years ago in a collaborative article on merchants and capitalists in Montpellier, André-E. Sayous and Jean Combes maintained that the local economy of Montpellier long remained that of an inland town but that in the late thirteenth and fourteenth centuries Montpellier developed a "morphological uniqueness" which led to the adoption on the part of Montpelliérains of the *comanda* contract as the main form of local commercial association.[123] With the exception of *comanda* use, Sayous and Combes argued that Montpellier failed to acquire the characteristics of a maritime town. Sayous' and Combes' conclusions and subsequent study by Combes led the 1955 International Congress of Historical Sciences in Rome to describe Montpellier, along with Marseille and Toulouse, as centers where partnerships, and business techniques in general, remained traditional and archaic, where the *commenda* persisted into the fourteenth century as the normal form of association in contrast to more complex

[117] See André-E. Sayous, "Les transformations des méthodes commerciales dans l'Italie médiévale," *Annales d'histoire économique et sociale* 1 (1929), 161-176, and Yves Renouard, *Les hommes d'affaires italiens du moyen âge* (Paris, 1948, 1968).

[118] Y. Renouard, *Les hommes d'affaires*, pp. 152-216.

[119] *Ibid.*, pp. 123-139.

[120] See, for example, Robert S. Lopez, "L'extrême frontière du commerce de l'Europe médiévale," *Le Moyen Age* 69 (4th ser., 18) (1963), 479-490 and "Nouveaux documents sur les marchands italiens en Chine à l'époque mongole," *Comptes rendus, Académie des inscriptions et belles-lettres* (1977), 445-458.

[121] See the discussion of the development of insurance contracts in R. S. Lopez and I. W. Raymond, *Medieval Trade*, pp. 255-256, and the comments by Y. Renouard, *Les hommes d'affaires*, pp. 133-135.

[122] Y. Renouard, *Les hommes d'affaires*, pp. 140-151. On Venetian commercial techniques in a general historical background, see Frederic C. Lane, *Venice, A Maritime Republic* (Baltimore and London, 1973). For a more technical discussion of specific issues, see F. C. Lane, *Venice and History* (Baltimore, 1966).

[123] A.-E. Sayous and J. Combes, "Les commerçants et les capitalistes," pp. 366 and 376.

Italian forms of partnership.[124] The Sayous-Combes evaluation of partnership techniques in Montpellier, based as it was on samplings of a widely spaced chronological nature in the remaining notarial evidence, bears reconsideration from the standpoint of the above detailed examination of surviving contracts in all the extant notarial registers.

The assessment by Sayous and Combes of the importance of the *comanda* contract in Montpellier cannot be questioned. However, their arguments regarding the limited use of the *societas* by Montpelliérains would profit from some refinement and nuance given the amount of capital concentrated by Montpelliérains in the formal contractual association as well as the numbers of *socii*, perhaps more informally joined, in the documents.[125] *Societas* contracts directed to overland trade and to local industry are sufficiently numerous to sustain the contention that this type of commercial method was commonly in use. Furthermore, although the surviving maritime *societates* were few, the capital input in these contracts was substantial.[126]

The "morphological uniqueness" of Montpellier must be considered in the context of Mediterranean French practices in maritime trade and in local business activities. The use of business partnerships in inland towns of southern France has been amply demonstrated by contemporary historians such as Philippe Wolff, Étienne Fournial and Paul-Louis Malausséna.[127] In the areas of the Toulousain, the Forez and eastern Provence, partnership investments were directed to overland trade and local industrial and artisans' activities. While linked to the interior, Montpellier must be distinguished from these regions because of the interest of its inhabitants in maritime commercial investments.

Within southern France, Montpellier enjoyed early and important relations with Marseille.[128] Marseille's advantage in the possession of a fine maritime port was overshadowed by the negative repercussions of Angevin political ambitions on the activities of Marseillais merchants.[129] The commercial expansion of Mont-

[124] M. Mollat, P. Johansen, M. Postan, A. Sapori, C. Verlinden, "L'Économie européenne aux deux derniers siècles du moyen âge," *Relazioni del X Congresso internazionale di Scienze Storiche, Storia del Medioevo* (Florence, 1955), 3: 767 ff.

[125] Transactions relating to the grain trade and to the cloth trade were especially rich in mentions of associates. See, for examples, the table, "Grain Trade," in my dissertation, "Commerce and Society in Montpellier," 2: 169-194.

[126] The maritime *societas* contracts, A. D. Hérault, II E 95/375, P. de Pena, f. 114v and II E 95/372, J. Holanie et al., f. 12r involved 428 *l. t.* and 245 *l. t.* respectively. On the *societas* see the comments of A.-E. Sayous and J. Combes, "Les commerçants et les capitalistes," p. 135.

[127] P. Wolff, *Commerces et marchands*, pp. 483-513, E. Fournial, *Les villes et l'économie d'échange en Forez*, p. 666, and P.-L. Malausséna, *La vie en Provence orientale*, pp. 233-245. Fournial found no extant contracts, although he maintains that *commenda* and *societas* associations were frequent. Malausséna found only land-based contracts *ad medium lucrum*. P. Wolff found considerable variety in the partnerships of Toulouse.

[128] On the thirteenth-century relations between Montpellier and Marseille, see Jean Combes, "Les relations commerciales entre Marseille et Montpellier au XIIIe siècle," *Congrès de civilisation et culture provençales* (Avignon, 1961), pp. 42-46.

[129] E. Baratier, *Histoire du commerce de Marseille*, 2: 207-219. See also Régine Pernoud, *Histoire du commerce de Marseille*, 1: 346-360.

pellier and Marseille had been based on the use of the maritime *commenda* emphasizing short-term association and the assumption of risks by investing partners. In neither Montpellier nor Marseille were local merchants organized into branch companies with numerous associates. Rather, familial associations or alliances between a few colleagues in the same occupation characterized business arrangements. In this regard the image of Genoa is more easily invoked than that of inland Tuscan towns.[130] An intermediate form which is more strictly Languedocian (or Provençal for Marseille) may ultimately be the most accurate characterization.

Genoese influence on Montpellier and Marseille was significant in the expansive phase of European commerce of the twelfth century. After the decline in Genoese hegemony over the southern French coast, contacts continued but were probably less close. The technical framework of commercial enterprise in both Montpellier and Marseille retained aspects of earlier Genoese influence. Consistent with the influence of Genoese individualism, inhabitants of Montpellier elaborated their own approach to changing economic and political conditions in the fourteenth century. A certain flexibility characterized the investment arrangements and the sharing of risks, losses and profits. Hybrid contractual agreements employing both the *societas* and the *comanda* forms were introduced. The role of Montpellier as an entrepot of Mediterranean goods in transit to northern France and to northern Europe placed demands on the business techniques of Montpelliérains which differed from the exigencies of the Italian business communities in both inland and maritime towns.

Inhabitants of Montpellier borrowed and imitated Italian and especially Genoese models; they did not initiate technological change. Rather than succumbing to archaism, the dimensions of the commerce of Montpellier (and of Marseille) remained more modest than those of the Italian ports, or even of Barcelona, and, as a result, partnerships were less complex and business organization simpler. Advanced capitalistic structures had no use whereas the basic contracts of partnership in maritime trade, overland trade and industry resembled those of the great Italian ports.

The business partnerships of Montpellier reveal the variety of local economic activities, as well as the interrelationship of those activities. While specializations abound – retail/wholesalers, changers and merchants utilizing maritime *comanda* investments exporting wool cloth and linen throughout the Mediterranean, or land-based investments which were trade-related, with, for example, drapers investing in drapery trade – evidence of cross-fertilization also existed. A shoemaker and a furrier collaborated, as did a glassmaker and a grain merchant, and a changer and a hotelkeeper. Merchants invested in ironwork, and a spice merchant and a pepperer shared their expertise. The specialists of trade and finance, the merchants and the changers, used the *comanda* and the *societas*, but

[130] On familial partnerships in twelfth-century Genoa, see H. Krueger, "Genoese Merchants ... 1155-1164," p. 267.

so did agricultural workers and a barrelmaker. Furthermore, credit obligations from other economic sectors might be utilized for investment in business partnerships. Thus, real estate credits and credits from exchange contracts were used as capital for investment in the Levant trade. By the same token, *comanda* credits could serve to liquidate outstanding debts. Finally, the Jews of Montpellier seemed to have financed some of their lending business with land *comanda* partnerships. Montpelliérains adapted the existing contractual framework to their own financial needs. Engagements went from the temporary in the maritime *comanda* to the total pooling of resources in a *societas* which resembled a Provençal *frayresque* or a Venetian *fraterna*. Through the business partnerships of Montpellier the economic nervous system of the town was revealed. Commercial, industrial and agricultural sectors emerged. They can be explored further by examination of the Montpellier markets in luxuries and in commodities.

2

Credit in the Market Place

Market transactions in Montpellier bring to light several credit operations in use in medieval trade.[1] By far the most commonly recorded credit practice was the recognizance, entailing a purchase agreement with the formal establishment of a recognition of debt. This recognition might be employed in conjunction with a down payment sales contract. Full credit sales contracts, infrequently noted, could be used with a promise of future delivery of merchandise. Further, recognizances with obligations unspecified and acquittals for payments of undescribed debts illustrate the prevalence of credit operations in Montpellier business practice.

The medieval market did not distinguish retail and wholesale functions.[2] Market transactions in Montpellier varied greatly in size and value. Inhabitants of Montpellier often engaged in both very large and very small purchases and sales, even though they were specialists in a particular sector of activity. Some of the transactions treated in this chapter were intended for consumption while large credit transactions assisted in the building of commercial inventories and in the movement of goods. If market trends allowed cheap purchase and expensive resale, capital could be generated from profits.[3]

[1] As P. Wolff, *Commerces et marchands de Toulouse*, p. 355, pointed out, the notarial registers probably did not contain all the credit operations in the medieval economy; some obligations may have passed from hand to hand without recourse to a notary. M. Postan, "Credit in Medieval Trade," p. 5, stated that there was no way of estimating the volume of facts preserved by the extant records of medieval credit transactions.

[2] Some economists today might have difficulty admitting the aptness of modern distinctions between retail and wholesale trade within the medieval economy. There were certain differences to be sure. In the Middle Ages the wholesale seller had to find a market for his goods whereas today the buyer seeks out the seller at merchandising marts. On the nature of the medieval economy, see Gabriel le Bras, "Conceptions of Economy and Society," *Cambridge Economic History* 3 (Cambridge, 1963), 554-575; Raymond de Roover, "The Organization of Trade," *Cambridge Economic History* 3 (Cambridge, 1963), 42-118, and Robert L. Reynolds, "Origins of Modern Business Entreprise: Medieval Italy," *Journal of Economic History* 12 (1952), 350-365.

[3] "E scarso compere et largo venga," was the motto of Francesco di Balduccio Pegolotti. See the edition of his merchants' manual by Allan Evans, ed., *La pratica della mercatura* (Cambridge, Mass., 1936). On merchant mentality, see Benjamin Kedar, *Merchants in Crisis* and Erich Mäschke, "La mentalité des marchands européens au moyen âge," *Revue d'histoire économique et sociale* 42 (1964), 457-484.

A great variety of merchandise was bought and sold on full credit in Montpellier: luxury items such as silks and spices; woolen, cotton and linen cloths; building materials such as wood and stones; raw materials such as wool and hemp; necessities such as salt and wax, food products including grain, grapes, meat, fish, beans, barley, lentils; products of industrial use such as alum and dyes; and a host of other items including law books and paper.[4] For some of these items only a few records remain; for others, over a hundred acts might be noted.

In the basic recognition of debt the debtor-contractant confessed owing to the creditor a specific sum of money quoted in real coins or in money of account, for particular goods, which might be briefly described in qualitative, but rarely in quantitative, terms.[5] The receipt of this merchandise *causa emptionis* was acknowledged by the debtor. The projected terms of payment then followed. The debt was often guaranteed by the debtor with the obligation of person and goods.[6] The debtor frequently submitted to the jurisdiction of the *Cour du Petit Scel*, a specialized commecial court of the king of France, operative in Montpellier from the thirteenth century.[7] Such a submission procured for the creditor a theoretical legal recourse in the case of default on the debt. Roman law renunciations on the debtor's part might be included in the contract.[8] Additional features were at times included in these obligations. A third party, termed a *fidejussor* or a *fidejutrix* (literally an oath swearer) might be associated with the debtor as a guarantor of good faith and as surety for the debt.[9] The *fidejussor* obligated his person and possessions and promised solidarity with the debtor in joint responsibility for the whole debt.[10]

The essential obligation of the debtor was the payment of the purchase price of the goods.[11] In addition to the provisions of a guarantor in debt contracts, penalties such as double indemnity for non-performance might be included in the original instrument.[12] The degree of abbreviation of the notarial minutes may

[4] See Reyerson, "Commerce and Society in Montpellier," 2: Appendix I, "Distribution of Notarial Acts," pp. 116 and 121-123.

[5] Philippe Bouges, "La pratique contractuelle à Montpellier de la fin du XIIIe siècle à la fin du XVe," Thèse, Université de Montpellier-I, 1972, 2 vols., has studied the legal aspects of the history of contracts from a sampling of notarial registers over two centuries. For practical examples of these formulae and the following, see A. D. Hérault, II E 95/369, J. Holanie, f. 40r, II E 95/372, J. Holanie et al., f. 140r and Appendix I, "Documents" below.

[6] See P. Bouges, "La pratique contractuelle," 1: 62-66.

[7] A. Gouron, "L'Origine du Tribunal du Petit Scel," and A. Gouron and J. Hilaire, "Les sceaux rigoureux du Midi."

[8] On renunciations, see Peter Riesenberg, "Roman Law, Renunciations, and Business in the Twelfth and Thirteenth Centuries," in *Essays in Medieval Life and Thought presented in Honor of Austin P. Evans* (New York, 1955), 207-225; and Edmondo Meynial, "Des renonciations au moyen âge et dans notre ancien droit," *Nouvelle revue de droit français et étranger* 24 (Paris, 1900), 108-142; 25 (1901), 241-277.

[9] For example, A. D. Hérault, II E 95/372, J. Holanie et al., ff. 19v and 47r. See also P. Bouges, "La pratique contractuelle," 1: 66.

[10] For background on the institution of *fidejussor*, see Mireille Castaing-Sicard, *Les contrats dans le très ancien droit toulousain* (Toulouse, 1959), pp. 379-403.

[11] P. Bouges, "La pratique contractuelle," 1: 72.

[12] On double damages, see A. Berger, *Encyclopedic Dictionary*, p. 446, "duplum."

account for the seeming omission of this protection in some acts; late or non-payment penalties were guarantees which a creditor might logically, but may not always, have demanded. The satisfaction of the buyer was implicit in the establishment of the debt instrument.

The term of credit in recognizances was generally *de die in diem* (on demand), that is, at the request of the creditor.[13] It is difficult to imagine the use of this practice without some discretionary period in which the debtor could secure the necessary funds. When specific dates of payment were scheduled, they coincided with the main religious festivals of the medieval calendar: Easter, the feast of Saint John the Baptist (24 June), the Ascension of the Virgin (15 August), the feast of Saint Michael (Michaelmas, 29 September), All Saints' Day (1 November) and Christmas. Credit terms of three to six months were common.

At the end of many recognizances the notary inserted an interlineated notice of cancellation.[14] A concise form merely stated that the act was cancelled. Greater detail regarding the original participants and the sum due might be included. Three hundred eighty-six general and specific acquittals have survived as separate acts.[15] It is thus not a certainty that cancellations of debts were noted after the original debt contracts.

In general, the recognizance served as a formal obligation of indebtedness and as a receipt for goods. In contrast, the credit sales instrument was used most frequently in circumstances where down payments were made. It functioned as a sales receipt of funds. Credit sales in trade employed a somewhat different vocabulary with the verb to sell, *vendere*.[16] The seller set down the terms of the contract which usually included a brief identification of the goods sold. The price, often the universal price, less frequently the price per item, was quoted, and the receipt of a certain portion of it was acknowledged by the seller.[17] Provision for the payment of the remainder was described. Promises to pay and to deliver goods could be included in the act. Guarantees similar to those in the recognizances followed. When the sales contract concerned goods, the seller, in some cases, extended protection to the buyer against hidden flaws in the merchandise.[18] Roman law renunciations of legal action might be mentioned.[19] In down payment sales cancellations of the obligation with the receipt of full payment were recorded, on occasion, in an interlineated notice.

[13] On the phrase "on demand" (*de die in diem*), see P. Wolff, *Commerces et marchands de Toulouse*, pp. 363-365.

[14] On cancellation, see D. Herlihy, *Pisa in the Early Renaissance*, 5. In Montpellier many acquittals, for which the original contracts were recorded elsewhere, have also been noted in the notarial registers.

[15] There remain 386 specified and unspecified acquittals. In addition there are 137 extant unspecified obligations.

[16] See for example, A. D. Hérault, II E 95/368, J. Holanie, f. 97v.

[17] P. Bouges, "La pratique contractuelle," 1: 72-73. For example, see A. D. Hérault, II E 95/368, J. Holanie, ff. 39r-39v, 43v.

[18] P. Bouges, "La pratique contractuelle," 1: 71.

[19] See n. 8 above.

The full credit sales contract, rare in the extant evidence, was used in situations where neither the merchandise nor the payment had been received.[20] It was, in short, both an agreement to sell and an obligation to buy. The circumstances under which payment would be made and delivery of the goods effectuated were described. The employment of the instruments of recognition of debt and sale can be explored first in the long distance luxury trade and then in the agricultural market.

The traffic in spices, silks and cloths belonged to an international commercial network of which Montpellier was a part. Foreign merchants and merchants of Montpellier shared in the spice trade, which relied on connections with the Levant for supplies of pepper, sugar, pharmaceutical products, cinnamon, ginger and other goods.[21] Ties with Spain, especially Catalonia, furthered the provisioning of the Montpellier market in saffron. Foreigners from a variety of southern French, Italian and Spanish towns – Genoa, Pavia, Narbonne, Perpignan, Lerida, Montblanch, Puigcerda, Barcelona and Cardona – sold spices on the Montpellier market, often to clients from Paris or Avignon, and shipped goods to these places as well as to the Champagne fairs. Spices were in demand farther north as well, in the Low Countries and in England.[22] Members of the local retail/wholesale trades were also represented in this commerce, but in many fewer numbers. Full credit recognizances were the only type of contract to be recorded in the thirty-five extant contracts of the spice trade.

The silk trade presents the same profile of credit transactions as the spice trade. Montpellier merchants, mercers, and silk merchants as sellers dominated the traffic in silks (fifty-seven acts) and mercery of Lucca (sixty-eight contracts) such as damasks and brocades, products of the Lucchese silk finishing industry.[23] An important local clientele of silk merchants and mercers and foreigners from Cahors, Toulouse and Castille, in particular, bought silks and mercery. The Cabanis brothers, Montpellier merchants who specialized in sales of mercery of Lucca, recorded over sixty credit transactions regarding these goods in the notarial register of Guillelmus Nogareti.[24] Six of these transactions were recognitions of debt with down payments from the Cabanis clients; the remaining were full credit recognizances.[25]

[20] See for example, A. D. Hérault, II E 95/368, J. Holanie, f. 60r.

[21] See Reyerson, "Commerce and Society in Montpellier," 1: 165-176. I discussed the spice trade of Montpellier in a paper, "The Medieval Spice Trade before 1350: One Index of Mediterranean Commerce from the Perspective of Montpellier," October 1976 Northern Great Plains History Conference, University of Wisconsin, La Crosse, Wisconsin. See Reyerson, "Commerce and Society in Montpellier," 2: Appendix IV, pp. 145-150 for a synoptic table of spice transactions.

[22] *Ibid.*, Appendix V, pp. 261-267, for transport contracts regarding the shipment of spices to northern France.

[23] On the silk trade in Montpellier, see my article, "Medieval Silks in Montpellier: The Silk Market ca. 1250-ca. 1350," *Journal of European Economic History* 11 (1982), 117-140.

[24] The Cabanis' transactions were recorded in A. D. Hérault, II E 95/374, G. Nogareti. See also, Reyerson, "Commerce and Society in Montpellier," 2: Appendix IV, pp. 151-168, for synoptic tables of silk and mercery transactions.

[25] See A. D. Hérault, II E 95/374, G. Nogareti, ff. 22v, 23r, 29r, 36r, 31rR bis and 44vR.

Besides these most prominent merchants, the silk trade could count Jews, women and artisans as participants, using full credit recognizances in the purchase of silk.[26] Wives and daughters of mercers and of silk industry personnel also accepted this credit arrangement when they were selling silks.[27] Two recognizances of the silk trade noted partial payments and indebtedness for the remainder.[28]

In three cases of 1293-1294 the purchase of silk was to be paid off in the skilled labor of silk finishing. A merchant of Montpellier and a merchant of Alès bought silk on recognizance, promising to reimburse the sum due in kind through the finishing of silk cloths in the respective fashions of Montpellier and Alès.[29] In the third instance a local dyer agreed to repay his debt for silks through silk dyeing.[30] This interlocking of commerce and industry in credit operations permitted artisans of the silk finishing industry to obtain raw materials on credit and to repay those purchases with the products of their labor.

Montpellier did not possess a well-developed urban cloth industry during this period. However, the trade in woolen cloths was active here. Woolen cloth from northern Europe appeared on the Montpellier market and was a frequent object of export to the eastern and western Mediterranean basins. My study of the cloth trade revealed a more varied set of participants in the cloth trade than in the commerce in spices and in silks, more exclusive products of the medieval luxury trade.[31] Dominant among cloth sellers in the extant evidence were the retail/wholesale trades, especially the drapers, and merchants of Montpellier, followed in number by foreign merchants from southern France. Full credit recognizances characterized the vast majority of the one hundred forty transactions in cloth. No full credit sales or down payment sales were noted. A large foreign clientele also from the South was attracted to Montpellier from near and far in search of cloths of northern France and products of the regional Languedocian cloth industry.[32]

The commerce in leather and skins had regional and international overtones in Montpellier. Merchants, leather merchants and furriers were the principal selling agents on the local market. They also dominated the export of leather, the shipments of cordouan to northern France.[33] Bleaching and finishing of skins formed a part of the local industrial activities for which purchases of skins and

[26] See A. M. Montpellier, II 1, J. Grimaudi, ff. 7r, 21r, 27r, 28v, 50v, 47v, for credit purchases by Jews.

[27] See Reyerson, "Commerce and Society in Montpellier," 2: Appendix IV, pp. 151-168.

[28] A. D. Hérault, II E 95/370, J. Holanie, f. 31r and II E 95/371, J. Holanie, f. 105v.

[29] A. M. Montpellier, II 1, J. Grimaudi, ff. 63r and 64r.

[30] A. M. Montpellier, II 1, J. Grimaudi, f. 21r.

On regulations of the Montpellier dyeing industry, see *LIM*, act XCIV and *Le Petit Thalamus*, pp. 137-139. See also *Layettes*, 1, articles 109 and 110, pp. 263-264.

[31] See my article, "Le rôle de Montpellier dans le commerce des draps de laine avant 1350," *Annales du Midi* 94 (1982), 17-40.

[32] *Ibid.*

[33] On the leather trade in Montpellier, see Reyerson, "Commerce and Society in Montpellier," 1: 197-203.

pelts were made. With the exception of two down payment sales contracts and two full credit sales for future delivery of skins over time, participants used the full credit recognizance in thirty-six contracts to buy and sell this merchandise. Again, the procurement by artisans of the leather industry of those raw materials necessary to their trade was a feature of this sector of commerce.[34]

With the proviso that the terms "retail" and "wholesale" were not part of the terminology of the Montpellier acts, the transactions in spices, silks, mercery, cloth and skins can be examined at these two levels, according to whether or not goods were purchased in quantity sufficient for more than personal use. The silk trade and the spice trade were predominantly wholesale, if judgment is based on the size of indebtedness. A sale of ginger in 1293 involved over 586 *l. t.*[35] A sale of over 396 *l. t.* in mercery of Lucca was recorded in 1341.[36] In both trades smaller transactions occurred, but the participants were professionals purchasing the goods of their business, not private individuals supplying their family and personal needs.

Within the cloth trade, both the wholesale and retail markets can be studied. Recognizances for small purchases of a retail nature have a different economic implication from those of wholesale purchases for large amounts of goods on credit. Small credit recognizances belong to the realm of consumer or distress credit and may reflect an insufficiency of cash in the hands of the purchasers or, more generally, problems of coinage supply and circulation. Difficult financial straits could force some individuals to buy on credit; but the purchase on credit in itself implies that the buyer had some credibility as a credit risk. Purchases of a wholesale nature, in international trade as in local artisans' activities, may have relieved problems of cash flow. However, wholesale recognizances were sufficiently numerous in Montpellier and elsewhere in medieval Europe to lend support to the hypothesis that they were part of normal business practice.

The forty-six cloth trade transactions of the 1327-1328 register of Johannes Holanie were the most numerous of any recorded in one register. They provide the historian with a glimpse of the retail trade in cloth. Twenty-four of the forty-six transactions involved purchases of 5 *l. t.* or less.[37] Members of the regional nobility, villagers from the surrounding territory and inhabitants of small towns such as Frontignan, approximately twenty kilometers from Montpellier, made up the clientele for cloth in these purchases.[38] An inexpensive cloth such as *burel* cost about 6 *s. t./canne*, that is, per two meters in length.[39] Medium quality cloth such as the Carcassonne *mesclat*, one of the products of the Languedocian cloth

[34] Compare the findings of P.-L. Malausséna, *La vie en Provence orientale*, p. 177; artisans of Grasse bought raw materials on credit for their work in the leather industry.

[35] A. M. Montpellier, II 1, J. Grimaudi, f. 2r.

[36] A. D. Hérault, II E 95/374, G. Nogareti, f. 41vR.

[37] See for example, A. D. Hérault, II E 95/368, J. Holanie, f. 70v.

[38] For example, A. D. Hérault, II E 95/368, J. Holanie, ff. 82r and 83r.

[39] On the *canne* of Montpellier, see P. Guilhiermoz, "De l'équivalence des anciennes mesures," *Bibliothèque de l'École des Chartes* 74 (1913), 288.

industry, came to about 17 *s. t./canne*.[40] The largest of these retail purchases would have been at most sixteen meters of cloth, a modest allotment for the clothing of several adults and children. Another feature of the cloth transactions of these years was the prevalence of price quotations in real coins, as opposed to money of account; thus *réaux*, *agneaux* and *gros tournois* appeared in the sums due.[41]

The general economic conditions of the time may have accentuated the regional inhabitants' need to rely upon credit in order to obtain the necessities of life. For Montpellier and for western Europe as a whole, the fourteenth century contained many years of economic difficulty.[42] The beginnings of a sporadically recurring subsistence crisis in Montpellier can be traced to the late thirteenth century. By the early fourteenth century natural disasters, earthquakes, floods and droughts accentuated an already declining agricultural production.[43] Mediterranean commerce was plagued with uncertainty for Montpellier merchants. The loss of crusading colonies on the Syrian coast, in which Montpelliérains had trading contacts and, in some instances, privileges shrank the outlets of Near Eastern and Oriental trade. Venetian-Genoese military rivalry and persistent piracy on the part of the Catalans and the Majorcans contributed to the insecurities.[44] From the 1330s the breakup of the Mongol Empire in Central Asia made far-eastern links in the luxury trade networks more precarious.[45] Closer to home, rising fiscal demands of the French crown and devaluations of French royal coinage plagued economic activities.[46] Poor harvests characterized the yields of the late 1320s and early 1330s in the region of Montpellier.[47] Finally, social unrest reflecting the difficult conditions was recorded in Montpellier in the 1320s and early 1330s.[48]

Set in this general social and economic context the cloth recognizances of the years 1327-1328 may be seen to reflect the economic turmoil of the era. From a twentieth-century perspective it is impossible to reconstruct with certainty the economic priorities of medieval inhabitants. Yet, the need to eat and the need to be clothed must rank among the most basic of those priorities. When credit was

[40] On the Languedocian cloth industry, the best treatment is that of Philippe Wolff, "Esquisse d'une histoire de la draperie en Languedoc du XIIe au début du XVIIe siècle," in *Produzione, commercio e consumo dei panni di lana (nei secoli XII-XVIII)*, a cura di Marco Spallanzani (Florence, 1976), pp.435-462.

[41] See for example, A. D. Hérault, II E 95/368, J. Holanie, ff. 70r, 82r and 93v.

[42] On fourteenth-century crisis, see Edouard Perroy, "À l'origine d'une économie contractée: les crises du XIVe siècle," *Annales: ESC* 4 (1949), 167-182.

[43] See the records of "La chronique romane" in *Le Petit Thalamus*, pp. 336-339, 343-347.

[44] On piracy, see Ch. 1 "Investment in Business Partnerships," n. 10.

[45] See Introduction.

[46] On French taxation in this period see John Bell Henneman, *Royal Taxation in Fourteenth Century France. The Development of War Financing, 1322-1356* (Princeton, 1971).

[47] See Elisabeth Carpentier, "Autour de la peste noire: famines et épidemies dans l'histoire du XIVe siècle," *Annales: ESC* 18 (1962), 1062-1092 and Marie-Josèphe Larenaudie, "Les famines en Languedoc au XIVe siècle," *Annales du Midi* 64 (1952), 27-39. See also *Le Petit Thalamus*, pp. 343-346.

[48] See Jean Combes, "Finances municipales et oppositions sociales à Montpellier au commencement du XIVe siècle," *Fédération historique, XLVIe congrès, Privas, 1971* (Montpellier, 1972), pp. 99-120.

used to procure a product necessary for survival, it became distress or consumer credit. Not only were greater numbers of small cloth purchases made on credit, but the debts due were specified in circulating gold coins and silver coins of relatively good precious metal content. Sellers must have been able to drive good bargains. In 1326 French coinage experienced a massive debasement.[49] Real coin quotations for cloth prices provided the seller with greater certainty regarding the precious metal content of the coins in which payment of the debt was to be made. Repayment in *deniers tournois*, calculated from quotations in money of account, was thereby avoided. In the early 1340s when *deniers tournois* were again thoroughly debased, cloth price quotations would reflect the monetary situation in another fashion. Rather than quotations in real coins, prices were quoted simply in "current money" (*monete currente*).[50]

The cloth transactions of 1327-1328 also recorded purchases by artisans of the cloth industry who had recourse to credit, as did their counterparts in the silk and leather industries, to obtain the raw materials of their trade. For example, on 16 September 1327, a cloth cutter obtained a cloth of Toulouse for 4 *agneaux* on credit with a recognizance in favor of Boninus de Meldeo of Novara, an inhabitant of Montpellier.[51] In another comparable case, on 3 August 1327, a shirtmaker bought nine pieces of *biffe* cloth (a Languedocian product) for 6 *agneaux* from Meldeo.[52] The importer-wholesaler Meldeo occupied an unusual position in Montpellier as an enterprising merchant who acted at times as a French royal official. In 1327 he was the king's commissioner for the levy of customs taxes on cloth exports at Lattes and in 1336 tax commissioner in Montpellier for the Italians of *Outremont*.[53] His specialization in Toulousain and Carcassonnais cloths set him apart from the majority of cloth merchants who tended to sell either local cloths or French cloths. How Meldeo obtained the cloths which he sold cannot be determined from the 1327-1328 notarial register.[54]

Records of large credit purchases of a wholesale nature were preserved for the cloth trade and for the traffic in silks, spices, skins and furs. Foreigners were involved as both buyers and sellers with merchants of Montpellier in these transactions. In addition to promises of repayment in Montpellier, the satisfaction of debts might be scheduled for two to three months hence in a town other than Montpellier. There is evidence at the end of the thirteenth century for the arrangement of repayments at the Champagne fairs for spices, silks and cloths purchased by Montpelliérains and merchants of the Lot region and of Paris in

[49] See E. Fournial, *Histoire monétaire*, pp. 91-95 and my Appendix 2 "Monetary Problems."

[50] See for example, A. D. Hérault, II E 95/371, J. Holanie, f. 106v.

[51] A. D. Hérault, II E 95/368, J. Holanie, f. 46r.

[52] A. D. Hérault, II E 95/368, J. Holanie, f. 19r. Meldeo generally accepted recognizances in real money rather than in money of account.

[53] A. D. Hérault, II E 95/368, J. Holanie, f. 16r and II E 95/370, J. Holanie, f. 107v.

[54] Meldeo was engaged in other kinds of economic endeavors as well. He participated in the grain trade, in land acquisitions, in pursuits of debts and in money exchanges. See A. D. Hérault, II E 95/368, J. Holanie, ff. 24r, 39r, 41r, 41v, 44r, 44v, 47r, 47v, 82r, 138v; II E 95/369, J. Holanie, ff. 29v, 32r, 82v; II E 95/370, J. Holanie, ff. 92v and 93v.

Montpellier. Thus, in October 1293, the Crusolis brothers stated that they would reimburse merchants of Cajarc at the Lagny fairs for 253 *l. t.* of cloth bought in Montpellier.[55] In the fourteenth century debt settlements might be scheduled for the growing Languedocian fairs of Pézenas, Montagnac and Villeveyrac.[56] Southern French merchants from towns such as Toulouse favored these tactics of reimbursement.[57] Medieval fairs served as convenient clearinghouses for merchant debts.

Credit operations increased the numbers of transactions in which medieval merchants might engage without expanding their commitment of liquid capital. Trade was stimulated thereby. The problems of cash payments necessitating the transport of gold and silver coins or of bullion were avoided. Credit transactions with deferrals of payment to a later time in another place helped minimize the need of changing money in this era of multiple local coinages. With the exception of years like 1327-1328, credit operations in trade left their trace in the wholesale sector of the traffic in spices, silks, furs, skins and cloth which formed part of regional and international commercial networks.

Operations on the Montpellier market in the products of agriculture and animal husbandry displayed a different distribution of credit transactions than did activities of the luxury trade. The agricultural sector employed greater use of down payment sales, full credit sales and futures than did the luxury trade. There is evidence of the full credit recognizance, but the recognizance could also take a slightly altered form in the purchase of futures. The debtor drew up an obligation for the delivery of the product. The receipt of all or part of the purchase price was acknowledged in advance. The recognizance could be combined with the down payment sales contract for future delivery of commodities and with the exchange of animals where one beast was of greater value than the other.[58] The trader of the less expensive beast would establish a recognizance in favor of the other participant to cover the remaining cost of the latter's animal. The full credit sales contract might be used with the promise of future delivery of merchandise. Down payment sales without recognizance appeared most often in the agricultural market. Cash sales contracts, serving, like the down payment sale, as a receipt of payment, in this case full payment, occurred in transactions of the agricultural trade.[59]

With links to the luxury trade in raw materials and to the rural economy, the wool market in Montpellier provides a transition from the credit techniques of the

[55] A. M. Montpellier, II 1, J. Grimaudi, f. 17r. See also ff. 15r, 34v, 51v.

[56] On the Languedocian fairs, see Jean Combes, "Les foires en Languedoc au moyen âge," *Annales: ESC* 13 (1958), 231-259.

[57] A. D. Hérault, II E 95/374, G. Nogareti, ff. 36v, 5rR and 22rR.

[58] Compare the comments of P.-L. Malausséna, *La vie en Provence orientale*, p. 48. In Provence and elsewhere in the south of France, the credit sale was common in the rural world. On the Forez, see E. Fournial, *Les villes et l'économie d'échange en Forez*, pp. 703-704. Fournial found evidence of credit transactions in the grain trade, the wine trade, other food stuffs, horses, cows, cloths, and in real estate and service.

[59] For example, see A. D. Hérault, II E 95/375, P. de Pena, f. 115r.

luxury trade to those of agriculture and animal husbandry. The salt marshes to the west of Montpellier near the Montagne de Sête were a grazing ground for local sheep and for sheep of the Montagne Noire region in winter transhumance.[60] Sheep and goats of the dry *garrigue* land north of Montpellier were led to summer pasturage in the Cévennes.[61] Montpellier was a market for regional wool and for wool imported from as far away as Burgundy. The emergence of an important regional cloth industry in Languedoc can be dated from the thirteenth century.[62] Centers such as Narbonne produced good quality wool cloths, the renowned "blancs de Narbonne." [63] Carcassonne, Toulouse and Limoux became sites of the cloth industry. There is also evidence of a rural or semi-rural cloth industry in the immediate region of Montpellier.[64]

With industrial-commercial and agricultural connections, the extant wool transactions were distinguished from the wholesale activities of the sectors of regional and long-distance trade examined earlier in the pattern of credit practices which survives. Of the twenty-eight transactions for which there are extant records, three were full credit sales with the promise of future delivery of wool; nine were down payment sales with the future delivery of wool scheduled for the next or spring cuttings. The remaining transactions included full credit recognizances, acquittals, cash sales and a transfer of debt. The wool trade presented a greater admixture of transactions of credit and cash and deferred delivery of goods than did the sectors of trade considered earlier. The buyer enjoyed a choice of clippings from the best animals of a particular flock of sheep in some instances.[65] The purchase of future wool clips was a common feature of the medieval wool trade. As P.-L. Malausséna noted, in a discussion of the prepayment futures in wool which he found in Provençal records, there was an element of speculation involved in these transactions.[66] The participants involved in buying and selling wool in Montpellier came from the social and occupational categories which were preeminent in the regional and long-distance luxury trade. Merchants, wholesalers and foreigners were the most numerous clients and sellers of wool.

[60] For a discussion of regional geography cf. Gaston Galtier, "Les conditions géographiques de Montpellier," in *Mélanges Philippe Arbos* (Clermont-Ferrand, 1953), pp. 237-246 and *Le vignoble du Languedoc méditerranéen et du Roussillon, Étude comparative d'un vignoble de masse*, 3 vols. (Montpellier, 1960). See also R. Dugrand, "La garrigue montpelliéraine," *Bulletin de la société languedocienne de géographie* 2nd ser., 34 (1963), 3-266. Although the last works focus on the modern period, they provide a useful geographical introduction to the region of Montpellier.

[61] Pasturage paths still exist today. Although their origin lies in the distant past, they were given a special judicial statute under the Intendants in the seventeenth century. See J.-B. Gèze, *Les drailles du Département de l'Hérault* (Montpellier, 1926), a publication of the Office Agricole Départemental de l'Hérault, for a discussion of the location of the *drailles* or pasturage paths. See also a report by the Service Vicinal on the *drailles*, preserved in A. D. Hérault, 2 S 39.

[62] See Reyerson, "Le rôle de Montpellier dans le commerce des draps de laine avant 1350," *Annales du Midi* 94 (1982), 17-40.

[63] See n. 40 above.

[64] See n. 62 above.

[65] See, for example, A. D. Hérault, II E 95/374, G. Nogareti, f. 17rR.

[66] P.-L. Malausséna, *La vie en Provence orientale*, p. 174.

Sheep were not the only animals implicated in market transactions in Montpellier. There was an active trade in animals of burden and transportation: asses, mules and horses.[67] The volume of animal sales, one hundred twenty-four transactions, establishes Montpellier as a center of regional and perhaps long-distance animal traffic. This contention is supported by the high participation of foreigners, regional inhabitants and individuals from more distant areas among sellers and their representation among buyers. Innkeepers, accounting for most of the artisans' and service trades' participation, had access to animals of transport since they kept stables to accommodate foreign merchants and professional transporters in transit.[68] The number of agricultural workers among buyers and sellers was dictated by the needs of their work.[69] Further, the broad representation of other social and professional groups reflects the dependence of the economy on animals for overland transport of all kinds.[70] Asses and mules commanded a higher price than horses in this market since practical considerations of care, hardiness and suitability for transport favored the mule and the ass over the horse.[71]

Of the extant transactions involving animals, one hundred were full credit recognizances, sixteen were down payment sales followed by recognizances, five were acquittals, two were certifications of possession and one was a cash sale. In addition to these acts, twenty-three exchanges of animals have been preserved, with recognizances established for the greater value of one of the two animals involved. The persistence of exchanges in the rural sector recalls an early stage of economic development when barter was an important feature of market transactions. Such practices were not inconsistent with the more limited use of credit and the greater use of cash characterizing transactions in agriculture and animal husbandry.

There were no extant records of the above animals being sold for meat. However, twenty down payment sales and one full credit sale for the delivery of animal parts, generally heads and stomachs of sheep and lambs by butchers to cooked meat sellers (*cabasserii*), were preserved.[72] In these acts the delivery period extended over the months from Easter of one year to Lent of the following year.[73] The meat trade reflected the religious calendar in this respect. Five other

[67] See table "Trade in Animals of Burden and Transport," in Reyerson, "Commerce and Society in Montpellier," 2: Appendix IV, pp. 216-234. Twenty-three acts relating to this trade involved exchanges.

[68] Concerning medieval overland transport, see Robert S. Lopez, "The Evolution of Land Transport in the Middle Ages," *Past and Present* 9 (1956), 17-29.

[69] See, for example, A. D. Hérault, II E 95/377, B. Egidii, ff. 30v and 56v.

[70] See Jean Combes, "Transports terrestres à travers la France centrale à la fin du XIVe siècle et au commencement du XVe," *Fédération historique, XXIXe congrès* (Mende, 1955), 3-7.

[71] There were more recognizances in favor of those exchanging mules and asses than horses. See Reyerson, "Commerce and Society in Montpellier," 2: Appendix IV, pp. 216-234.

[72] On the meat trade in Montpellier, see Reyerson, "Commerce and Society in Montpellier," 1: 225-231.

[73] See, for example, A. M. Montpellier, II 1, J. Grimaudi, f. 47v, for a merchant's sale of lambs. See A. D. Hérault, II E 95/368, J. Holanie, f. 82v, for a butcher's sale to a *cabasserius*.

recognizances were noted for the sale of salted meat and one for the sale of two pigs.[74]

Further important dimensions of the agricultural market include the commodity transactions in grapes and grain. In contrast to the grape monoculture of the present day in the region of Montpellier, a polyculture including cereals existed in the Middle Ages.[75] However, the importance of vineyards should not be minimized in the medieval economy. One hundred twelve transactions in grapes have been identified in the extant notarial registers.[76]

The notary Johannes Holanie recorded the largest number of grape transactions in all of his surviving registers in the year 1327 for which thirty-four acts have been preserved.[77] Analysis of these thirty-four transactions reveals the use of both cash and credit. The credit sales contract was employed when down payments or full payments were made. Nineteen of the thirty-four acts were down payment credit sales; twelve were cash sales for future delivery of merchandise; two were debts in kind (in grapes) and one was an acquittal for a debt in kind. Holanie signaled the extraction of a copy of one down payment sale, of one paid sale and of the one acquittal.[78] Three paid sales and one recognizance were later cancelled through interlineated notes.[79] On one occasion a separate recognizance was drafted in conjunction with a down payment sale.[80] For most of the parties appearing before Holanie, the notarial document was clearly sufficient proof of the economic agreement.

The dates of contraction of cash sales and of down payment sales are given below:

	Feb.	Mar.	Apr.	July	Aug.	Sept.
down payment			1	2	11	5
cash	2	1		4	3	2

While cash sales occurred over the five-month period, down payment sales appear to have been common just before harvest. The cash sales were futures involving prepayments with promises of delivery of the grapes at harvest.

At times a specified quantity of grapes was sold in these transactions; at other times the whole yield of a vineyard was at issue.[81] Whole yields in 1327-

[74] For a salted meat sale, see A. D. Hérault, II E 95/368, J. Holanie f. 48r. For the pigs, II E 95/370, J. Holanie, f. 130v.

[75] For background on the effects of climate on the agriculture of Languedoc, see Emmanuel LeRoy Ladurie, *Les paysans du Languedoc* (Paris, 1966), especially 1: 17-19.

[76] See Reyerson, "Commerce and Society in Montpellier," 2: Appendix IV, pp. 195-209, for a synoptic table of grape transactions.

[77] A. D. Hérault, II E 95/368, J. Holanie.

[78] See A. D. Hérault, II E 95/368, J. Holanie, ff. 9r, 24v and 58r.

[79] A. D. Hérault, II E 95/368, J. Holanie, ff. 37r, 39v, 41r and 124v.

[80] A. D. Hérault, II E 95/368, J. Holanie, f. 34v.

[81] See for a whole yield, A. D. Hérault, II E 95/368, J. Holanie, f. 35r; for 16 *saumate*, f. 40r.

An operation utilized in the years 1327-1328 by various inhabitants was the grape future. The total harvest of a vineyard, an unpredictable future yield, was sold for a pre-determined price. A down payment was made at the time of the establishment of the bargain, with the buyer promising payment

1328 were noted in eight down payment sales, three cash sales and in one recognizance. Cash and down payment arrangements contained elements of speculation since harvest conditions were not entirely predictable. The total price in seven of the down payment sales was set at the market price on a specific date: at harvest, on the delivery of the grapes or at the feast of St. Gilles (1 September).[82]

The price of grapes undoubtedly varied according to growing conditions, the fertility of the land, the type and quality of the vine, and the exposure to sunshine, but it is feasible to compare the prices per *saumata* of unidentified grapes in cash and credit sales. The documents of 1327-1328 show lower prices per *saumata* in cash sales (8.3 s. t., 8.7 s. t., 9 s. t., 10 s. t., 12 s. t., and 13 s. t.) than in credit sales (12 s. t., 12.3 s. t., 12.5 s. t., 13 s. t., and 13.3 s. t.). In those cases where the type of grapes was mentioned (black, white or *mitadenc*) the information was not sufficiently full in categories of cash and credit to permit comparisons.[83] However, the size of down payments varied according to the specific type of grapes. A variety called *mitadenc* or *mitadenque* commanded higher down payments per *saumata* (5 s. t. to 7.8 s. t.) than did grapes of undescribed type (3.75 s. t. to 5 s. t.). In sum, credit sales appear somewhat more expensive with the size of the down payment in grape futures dependent on the type of grapes purchased.

The largest number of extant grape transactions was recorded by the notary Bernardus Egidii in the years 1347-1348.[84] Again, as in the Holanie register of 1327-1328, the mixture of cash and credit agreements was noted. Thirteen acts were cash sales, fifteen were down payment sales, one was an acquittal and eight were debts in grapes. Some variations in formulae emerged in the Egidii register. The eight recognizances for debts in grapes provide a case in point. Six of these acts were commitments of specific quantities of grapes for a "just price." [85] The two remaining acts recorded the engagement of a specific quantity of grapes for a stated price. The formulae used by Egidii placed emphasis on the indebtedness of the producer or grape owner similar to that of the promise of delivery included in a down payment sale. The "just price" recalls the terms of price at harvest or on the delivery day in the acts of Holanie; the implication of all these terms was the market price.[86]

---

of the remainder of the price upon the delivery of the grapes. For example, on 27 August 1327, a tailor sold to a pepperer the total harvest of two vineyards at 12s./*saumata*, a relatively good price (f. 35r). The down payment was 100s. The remainder paid would depend on the size of the harvest. One vineyard often yielded twelve to eighteen *saumate* in these years. The advantage of this type of transaction lay in the receipt of cash before the grape harvest at a time when reserves may have been running low, especially for the agricultural population.

[82] See for example, A. D. Hérault, II E 95/368, J. Holanie, f. 18r.

[83] See for example, A. D. Hérault, II E 95/368, J. Holanie, f. 30v for *mitadenque*, f. 5r for black and white. One act (f. 2v) made a distinction between wine grapes and dark red (black) grapes. It is legitimate to suppose that some of the production of the local vineyards was for the table not the glass.

[84] A. D. Hérault, II E 95/377, B. Egidii.

[85] See for example, A. D. Hérault, II E 95/377, B. Egidii, f. 66v.

[86] On the medieval just price, see John W. Baldwin, *The Medieval Theories of the Just Price. Romanists, Canonists and Theologians in the Twelfth and Thirteenth Centuries. Transactions of the*

TABLE 1: SELLERS IN TRANSACTIONS IN GRAPES OF THE MONTPELLIER NOTARIAL EVIDENCE (1293-1348) (112 acts)

	No. of Acts	% Total Acts
Merchants	5	4.5%
Changers/ Moneyers	1	0.9%
Retail/ Wholesale	15	13.4%
Nobles/ *Burgenses*	2	1.8%
Professions/ Education	2	1.8%
Jews	–	–
Royal Administration	1	0.9%
Ecclesiastics	1	0.9%
Women	7	6.3%
Artisans/ Service	20	17.9%
Food Trades	3	2.7%
Agriculture	51	45.5%
Foreigners	2	1.8%
Unidentified		
Local	1	0.9%
Other	1	0.9%

With the exception of the Jews of Montpellier, all social and occupational groups were represented as grape sellers and most were present as buyers, as shown in Tables 1 and 2. As might be expected, agricultural workers dominated the sellers' category while few were recorded as grape buyers. Inhabitants connected with the luxury trade (merchants, changers, retail/wholesalers) were more heavily represented as buyers. Some export of the wine of Montpellier to

American Philosophical Society, n.s. 49 (Philadelphia, 1959). See also, Raymond de Roover, "The Concept of the Just Price: Theory and Economic Policy," *Journal of Economic History* 18 (1958), 418-434; Kenneth S. Cahn, "The Roman and Frankish Roots of the Just Price of Medieval Canon Law," *Studies in Medieval and Renaissance History* 6 (1969), 3-52; and Samuel Hollander, "On the Interpretation of the Just Price," *Kyklos* 18 (1965), 615-634. The most convincing arguments regarding the just price in the Middle Ages interpret it as the market price. On the just price in Montpellier, see *Layettes*, 1: 259, art. 39 of the 1204 *consuetudines*.

Paris, to Avignon and, in the case of spiced wine, perhaps to England, may have stimulated the interest of inhabitants involved in international commerce.[87]

TABLE 2: BUYERS IN TRANSACTIONS IN GRAPES OF THE MONTPELLIER NOTARIAL EVIDENCE (1293-1348) (112 acts)

	No. of Acts	% Total Acts
Merchants	14	12.5%
Changers/ Moneyers	13	11.6%
Retail/ Wholesale	27	24.1%
Nobles/ *Burgenses*	1	0.9%
Professions/ Education	4	3.6%
Jews	–	–
Royal Administration	–	–
Ecclesiastics	–	–
Women	13	11.6%
Artisans/ Service	28	25.0%
Food Trades	7	6.3%
Agriculture	4	3.6%
Foreigners	–	–
Unidentified		
Local	1	0.9%
Other	–	–

Women engaged in the grape trade as buyers and sellers. Their social and economic background reflected the overall representation of the population. Women buyers came from backgrounds associated with the occupations of

[87] See Reyerson, "Commerce and Society in Montpellier: 1293-1348," 1: 232-240. For background on medieval wines, the reader should consult Roger Dion, *Histoire de la vigne et du vin en France des origines au XIXe siècle* (Paris, 1959). Also useful is Georges Duby, ed., *Histoire de la France rurale* (Paris, 1975), 1: 454-473. Medieval wine was of mediocre alcoholic content and could not be preserved over many years. On the spiced and perfumed wines of Montpellier production, see R. Dion, p. 315.

On medieval wine see also *Le vin au moyen âge: production et producteurs, Actes du IIe congrès des Médiévistes, Grenoble 1971* (Grenoble 1978).

merchant, money changer, shirtmaker, butcher, cultivator, baker, stone mason, ironsmith and wood merchant. Five women of cultivator background represented the largest number of any category. The seven women recorded as grape sellers had backgrounds of royal servant, silk artisan, commercial broker, silk merchant, baker and notary.

The sale of grape futures in down payment transactions offered the owners of vineyards a possibility to acquire cash just before the grape harvest, at a time when reserves may have been low, especially for agricultural workers. For agricultural workers, artisans and other inhabitants in need of cash for consumption, selling grape futures may have permitted the purchase of grain stuffs during the difficult months preceding the next harvest.[88]

A further perspective on credit in the agricultural economy can be obtained through the extant transactions of the grain trade.[89] Within the context of natural disasters and climatic difficulties of the fourteenth century, regional harvests were adequate for the needs of the population of Montpellier in years of good yield. Grain exports from Lower Languedoc were recorded in some years of the first half of the fourteenth century.[90] However, imports of grain were necessary to supplement the local production in years of poor harvests. Such a period existed in the late 1320s and early 1330s, relenting in intensity at the end of the decade only to resume in earnest in the mid 1340s.[91] In 1333, famine raged in Montpellier, young men were weakened by a poor diet of raw herbs and people were dying in the streets, according to the town chronicle, which further stated that no grain was to be had from Lombardy or Sicily because of a Genoese war, or from Catalonia. Some provisions were forthcoming from Burgundy and the Comtat Venaissin.

Of the one hundred and ninety acts relating to transactions in grain noted, one hundred and sixty were recognizances, two were cessions of rights in grain, one a cession of debt regarding grain, six were acquittals for payment, two were down payment sales, two were credit sales, three were cash sales, one was a composition over grain, and thirteen transactions were debts in grain futures similar to those noted in grape transactions.[92] Eighty-three percent of the extant records regarding grain were preserved in the Holanie registers of 1327-1328 with fifty-three acts and of 1333 with one hundred and five acts.[93]

[88] On peasant credit and futures, see P.-L. Malausséna, *La vie en Provence orientale*, pp. 118-120.

[89] On grain, see Reyerson, "Commerce and Society in Montpellier," 1: 212-224.

[90] See Henri Bresc, "Marchands de Narbonne et du Midi en Sicile (1300-1460)," *Fédération historique, Narbonne au moyen âge* (Montpellier, 1973), pp. 93-99 and E. Baratier, "Marseille et Narbonne au xivᵉ siècle d'après les sources marseillaises," *ibid.*, pp. 85-92.

[91] See n. 47 above. See also *Inv. A. M. Montp.*, 11, *Documents comptables*, no. 96, *Livre de dépenses de l'Hôpital Saint-Lazare*, 1346-1347, f. 54ff which details a large number of sales of imported grain.

[92] Dealing in futures was of questionable morality in the eyes of the scholastics. See Frederic C. Lane, "Investment and Usury in Medieval Venice," *Explorations in Entrepreneurial History* 2nd ser., 2 (1964), 3-15, for comments on the Venetian stance on futures and usury in general.

[93] A. D. Hérault, II E 95/368, J. Holanie and II E 95/369, J. Holanie.

The Holanie register of 1327-1328 contains acts which reveal two stages of the marketing of grain. Grain imports necessary in these years were in the hands of merchants of Montpellier with connections in international trade. They recorded transactions in Byzantine grain, sold on recognizance to grain merchants (*ordearii*) of Montpellier in amounts ranging from 10.5 *l. t.* to 63.5 *l. t.*[94] The grain merchants then retailed the product in smaller quantities in credit transactions before the notary.

Table 3: Buyers in Transactions in Grain of the Montpellier Notarial Evidence (1293-1348) (190 acts)

	No. of Acts	% Total Acts
Merchants	22	11.6%
Changers/ Moneyers	2	1.1%
Retail/ Wholesale	9	4.7%
Nobles/ *Burgenses*	1	1.0%
Professions/ Education	1	1.0%
Jews	–	–
Royal Administration	–	–
Ecclesiastics	7	3.7%
Women	2	1.1%
Artisans/ Service	6	3.2%
Food Trades	3	1.6%
Agriculture	6	3.2%
Foreigners	25	13.2%
Unidentified		
Local	2	1.1%
Other	–	–
Grain Merchants	104	54.7%

The size of transactions in the grain trade varied greatly according to agricultural and market conditions. When grain was scarce in 1333, the Bardi

[94] A. D. Hérault, II E 95/368, J. Holanie, ff. 18v, 23r and 30v for examples.

Society of Florence was noted in two sales of 10,000 *sestarii* of wheat for 3,000 *l. t.* each to grain merchants of Montpellier. These were exceptionally large transactions for the Montpellier market.[95] By the same token, credit purchases by agricultural workers and regional villagers were high in years of poor harvest.

A group of specialized professionals, the grain merchants, dominated the grain trade, as Tables 3 and 4 show. Foreigners, especially Italians, and merchants of Montpellier were active in the international trade in grain. The broad-based participation of most social and occupational groups reflects here, as in grape transactions, the wide distribution of landholding among the urban population.

TABLE 4: SELLERS IN TRANSACTIONS IN GRAIN OF THE MONTPELLIER NOTARIAL EVIDENCE (1293-1348) (190 acts)

	No. of Acts	% Total Acts
Merchants	6	3.2%
Changers/ Moneyers	2	1.1%
Retail/ Wholesale	7	3.7%
Nobles/ *Burgenses*	4	2.1%
Professions/ Education	3	1.6%
Jews	–	–
Royal Administration	–	–
Ecclesiastics	1	1.0%
Women	11	5.8%
Artisans/ Service	13	6.8%
Food Trades	2	1.1%
Agriculture	27	14.2%
Foreigners	95	50.0%
Unidentified		
Local	–	–
Other	–	–
Grain Merchants	19	10.0%

[95] A. D. Hérault, II E 95/369, J. Holanie, ff. 52v and 84v.

The years of 1347-1348 were again part of a period of agricultural problems. The notary Egidii used formulae in the grain transactions which differed from those employed by Holanie earlier and recorded debts in wheat and grain mixtures.[96] The seller of grain acknowledged receipt of a "just price" and promised to deliver the grain at a specific date.[97] The quantities involved in these sales were not mentioned. These debts in grain were drawn up in April and May of 1347 with the debtors promising conveyance of the grain in the mid or late summer after harvest. The likelihood of prepayments yielding some kind of discount may have offset the obvious speculative risks involved for the buyer of grain.

In conclusion, comparisons of the agricultural market with the luxury market are in order. The market in agricultural products and in animal husbandry was distinguished from the luxury trade in Montpellier in the types of credit techniques employed. The down payment sale with promise of future delivery of goods appeared in the grain, grape, wool and meat trades. The wholesale food trade showed evidence of the full credit recognizance. Cash sales also occurred within the agricultural economy. When credit and cash transactions admitted of comparison, as in the grape trade, the Montpellier evidence suggests that higher prices were the rule when credit was employed. Credit costs may well have varied from the retail to the wholesale sphere in keeping with the difference between consumer credit on the one hand and commercial and investment credit on the other. A somewhat broader distribution of credit participants across social and occupational groups characterized the market in agricultural products and animal husbandry. Women using credit in trade reflected in their backgrounds the broad based participation of the urban population as a whole in such transactions.

If the surviving transactions in the grape and grain trades are considered on a year-to-year basis, the general economic circumstances would seem to be echoed by the prevalence of credit in times of crisis. Credit transactions in agriculture were more common in 1327, 1333 and 1347, when agricultural yields were low and economic conditions difficult. Only the retail cloth trade, among luxury transactions, left evidence of the same responsiveness of the population to crisis. Basic clothing was almost as much of a necessity as food.

Those engaged in the luxury trades and in agricultural occupations made extensive use of credit instruments, but in differing combinations and intensities. The presence of animal exchanges and the recorded employment of cash in the rural commodities market suggest a more conservative approach to market transactions; the predominance of credit in the luxury trade points to a more sophisticated level of economic technique as might be expected. However, there were no barriers between these spheres. Their interrelation was evident in the

[96] See A. D. Hérault, II E 95/377, B. Egidii.

[97] For example, on 6 April 1347, two cultivators of Montpellier recognized owing a wine merchant two *sestarii* of good wheat to be paid after the next feast of Saint John the Baptist (24 June). They acknowledged receipt of a "just price," unspecified in the documents. See A. D. Hérault, II E 95/377, B. Egidii, f. 36v.

activities of the Montpellier merchants who participated in the grain trade along with specialized grain merchants and foreigners when local shortages created a demand for regional and international imports.

The market in luxury goods in Montpellier – spices, silks, skins, furs and cloths – was characterized by extensive use of the full credit recognizance, relieving participants of the necessity of raising large amounts of cash capital to launch commercial ventures and facilitating cash flow. Merchants and retail/wholesalers along with foreigners dominated the credit transactions of the luxury trade. When artisans' activities associated with the luxury trade are considered, the participation of the urban population was broader. Wholesale credit was consistently present in good economic times and in bad. Retail credit in a sector such as the cloth trade was visible in eras of crisis. Under normal circumstances retailer and consumer avoided the formalities of the notarial recognizance or credit sale, either through cash transactions, through merchandise exchange or through more informal credit techniques which escape notice.

Historians have long recognized the importance of credit in medieval trade.[98] In Montpellier, as in Toulouse, Pisa and England, indeed throughout medieval Europe, credit furthered commercial expansion in an era of bullion shortages and problems of velocity of circulation of coins.[99] Sale credits in the form of recognizances filled this need admirably.[100] In market transactions as in business partnerships, the extension of credit made commercial activities possible for some who could not otherwise engage in trade.[101] Credit transactions eliminated the

[98] P. Wolff, *Commerces et marchands de Toulouse*, p. 366. See also the discussion by Michel Lacave, "Note sur une source de l'histoire monétaire méridionale, XVe-XVIe siècles," *Revue historique de droit français et étranger* 4th ser., 51 (1973), 418-424.

Mireille Castaing-Sicard, *Les contrats dans le très ancien droit toulousain (Xe-XIIIe siècles)* (Toulouse, 1959), has traced the use of credit sales back to the tenth century (962) in the region of Toulouse. On credit sales, see pp. 102-106.

A.-E. Sayous maintained that credit sales were characteristic of inland towns and of local commerce and were only common in these contexts. See "Dans l'Italie à l'intérieur des terres: Sienne de 1221 à 1229," *Annales d'histoire économique et sociale* 3 (1931), 202. The evidence of credit sales in Marseille, a maritime town, has been signaled by Pierre Racine, "À Marseille en 1248: l'activité des hommes d'affaires de Plaisance," *Annales du Midi* 78 (1966), 226. If the evidence from Montpellier is considered that of a maritime town, the contention of Sayous must be revised with regard to the international trade of the south of France, where credit sales were common.

[99] Michael M. Postan, "Credit in Medieval Trade;" P. Wolff, *Commerces et marchands de Toulouse*; and David Herlihy, *Medieval and Renaissance Pistoia. The Social History of an Italian Town* (New Haven, 1967).

[100] D. Herlihy, *Medieval and Renaissance Pistoia*, p. 169, cited the problems of important commercial companies in "obtaining cash payments." His study of Pistoia suggested that the number of local customers able to pay cash was limited by the absence of a mint and by the small size of the town.

[101] P. Wolff, *Commerces et marchands de Toulouse*, pp. 355-356, and *Les 'estimes' toulousaines*, p. 71, maintained that credits due from sales by merchants represented a large share of their operating capital. Further, Wolff, *Commerces et marchands*, pp. 366-373, found considerable variety among the percentages of credit involved in commercial associations of Toulousains from 3.2% to 78.5%. He argued that the credit sale was no more expensive than the cash sale because, given the lack of cash in the economy, the only way to do business and preserve a clientele was to sell on credit. The luxury

need for the transport of coins or bullion over long distances. Problems of primitive road infrastructure and vehicles were thereby circumvented as were the risks of robbery. Credits and debits might be cancelled, especially between merchants, without the exchange of money. A system of mutual trust underlay medieval trade and was essential to its operations.[102]

---

trade transactions of Montpellier do not permit exploration of the costs of credit. The trade in agricultural products suggests that credit transactions were somewhat more costly in Montpellier.

A contrary opinion to Wolff's is that of A. Udovitch, "Credit as a Means of Investment in Medieval Islamic Trade," *Journal of the American Oriental Society* 87 (1967), 260-264, who argued that credit transactions were more costly than cash sales.

[102] R. S. Lopez has made this point on a number of occasions. See, for example, "Italian Leadership in the Medieval Business World," *Journal of Economic History* 8 suppl. (1948), pp. 66-67.

3

Loans

Lending operations in the Middle Ages could fulfill one of several financial functions.[1] Loans for consumption or distress loans served as vehicles of credit in a cash shortfall, providing the means of obtaining necessities for subsistence. Commercial or business loans offered the convenience of credit to merchants and artisans in need of ways to cope with cash flow and to further the expansion of trade.[2] Risks of nonpayment underlay these operations, but precautions such as late payment penalties and collateral pledges protected lenders from losses.[3]

Loans were rarely made without an expected financial return.[4] The practice of lending money at interest was recorded in the south of France as early as the tenth century.[5] The *Cartulaire de Maguelone* and the *Cartulaire de l'abbaye de Gellone* contain loans on security in the form of a *carta pignoratis* or *mort-gage* dating from the end of the eleventh century.[6] In this contract a piece of real estate could be transferred by the borrower to the lender for the duration of the loan.[7] The revenues stemming from the property represented the interest on the loan for the lender.[8] In contrast to the *vif-gage*, the interest on the *mort-gage* in no way

[1] A.-E. Sayous, "Les opérations des banquiers italiens en Italie et aux foires de Champagne pendant le XIIIe siècle," *Revue historique* 170 (1932), 2-6, viewed lending as the primitive banking function. Raymond de Roover, *Money, Banking and Credit in Mediaeval Bruges*, p. 311, believed that neither deposits nor lending would give rise to medieval banking but rather foreign exchange. See also his "Early Banking before 1500 and the Development of Capitalism," *Revue internationale d'histoire de la banque* 4 (1971), 1-16 and "New Interpretations in the History of Banking," *Journal of World History* 2 (1954), 38-76.

[2] For the distinctions between distress loans and business loans, see for example, N. J. G. Pounds, *An Economic History of Medieval Europe*, pp. 405-409.

[3] See nn. 12, 13 and 14 below.

[4] See my article, "Les opérations de crédit dans la coutume et dans la vie des affaires à Montpellier au moyen âge: le problème de l'usure."

[5] On early forms of interest-bearing loans, see the studies by J. de Malafosse, "Contribution à l'étude du crédit dans le Midi aux Xe et XIe siècles: Les sûretés réelles," *Annales du Midi* 63 (1951), 105-148 and Mireille Castaing(-Sicard), "Le prêt à intéret à Toulouse aux XIIe et XIIIe siècles," *Bulletin philologique et historique*, années 1953 & 1954 (Paris, 1955), 273-278.

[6] J. de Malafosse, "Contribution à l'étude du crédit," pp. 127-131. These practices preceded the recovery of Roman law. See p. 109.

[7] J. de Malafosse has analyzed contracts with and without depossession. See, for example, p. 116.

[8] M. Castaing(-Sicard), "Le prêt à intéret," p. 273.

diminished the amount of money owed in reinbursement by the borrower.[9] Regional cartularies and the *Liber Instrumentorum Memorialium* of the Guilhem of Montpellier preserved examples of *pignorationes* of the twelfth century.[10]

The *consuetudines* of 1204 in Montpellier treated the practice of lending at interest, prohibiting it unless the transactions were sealed by oaths.[11] Interest was controlled by one article of these statutes which prohibited the accumulation of interest beyond the equivalent of the principal; in other words interest could not exceed the principal.[12] These same statutes of 1204 governed the pledge of personal effects and of real property as collateral in loans. The lender holding a pledge or *pignus* of personal effects was empowered to sell the article after one year if the borrower had been duly informed of the lender's intent and had refused to reimburse the loan.[13] The pledge of personal effects in a loan was representative of pawnbroking which was given legal recognition by these statutes. When the security pledge was real property, the lender could sell the *pignus* after three years had elapsed, provided that the borrower had been notified of the lender's intent and had failed to repay the loan.[14] *Fidejussores*, personal guarantors of borrowers, were also governed by the 1204 statutes.[15]

Among credit instruments the *mutuum* contract or simple loan has occupied a vastly influential, if controversial, place. It was first noted in the Montpellier documents in the last quarter of the twelfth century after the recovery of Roman law, which had been encouraged by the presence of Placentinus here.[16] The *mutuum* in Roman law meant a loan which was instituted when a sum of money, or an amount of fungibles, was given by a debtor to his creditor.[17] The borrower was to return to the lender at the term of the loan or in due time the same quantity and quality of fungibles or amount of money which had been lent. In the Roman and medieval periods, interest (*fenus* or *usurae*) generally accompanied such a transaction.

[9] On the *vif-gage*, see Étienne Fournial, *Les villes et l'économie d'échange en Forez*, pp. 695-696 and M. Castaing-Sicard, *Les contrats dans le très ancien droit toulousain*, pp. 317-320.

[10] See for example, *LIM*, act LIII: *carta pignoris*. *Le Cartulaire de Maguelone* contains thirteenth-century examples of the *mort-gage*. See for example, 2: 198: 1219.

[11] See my discussion in "Les opérations de crédit." See also Pierre Tisset, "Placentin et l'enseignement du droit à Montpellier. Droit romain et Coutume dans l'ancien pays de Septimanie," *Recueil*, fasc. II (Montpellier, 1951), 81-82.

[12] *Layettes*, 1: 264, article 116.

[13] *Layettes*, 1: 259, article 40.

[14] *Ibid.*

[15] See P. Tisset, "Placentin et son enseignement à Montpellier," p. 82.

[16] Edmondo Meynial, "De l'application du droit romain dans la région de Montpellier aux XIIe et XIIIe siècles," pp. 14-15.

On the recovery of Roman law in the region of Montpellier, see *ibid.*, P. Tisset, "Placentin et son enseignement à Montpellier," pp. 67-94, and A. Gouron, "Les étapes de la pénétration du droit romain au XIIe siècle dans l'ancienne Septimanie," pp. 103-120.

[17] Adolf Berger, *Encyclopedic Dictionary of Roman Law* (Philadelphia, 1953), p. 591. According to Berger, loans can be traced back to ancient civilizations such as the Babylonian. See also Roger Aubenas, *Cours d'histoire du droit privé des anciens pays de droit écrit (XIIIe-XIVe siècles)* V: *Contracts et obligations d'après les actes de la pratique* (Aix-en-Provence, 1956): and Robert S. Lopez and Irving W. Raymond, *Medieval Trade in the Mediterranean World* (New York, 1955), pp. 143-161.

The extant loan contracts in Montpellier took the form of a recognition of debt *ex causa mutui*, *ex causa veri et legitimi mutui* or, on occasion, *ex causa gratuiti mutui*.[18] The latter may have been, as its terminology implies, a charitable loan; the former undoubtedly involved the profit of interest (i.e., *lucrum*) although there was no mention of it in the act itself.[19] In these contracts, interest was probably included in the face value of the debt due.[20] The borrower might have received 100 *l.* and agreed to reimburse the lender for 120 *l.* Other arrangements providing the lender with interest were also possible. A pre-arranged agreement between lender and borrower might have resulted in a failure of prompt reimbursement permitting the invocation of late payment penalty charges.[21] In the *mutuum* loan, the borrower recognized owing a specific sum, or less frequently, certain agricultural goods, to be repaid to the lender.[22] The borrower stated in cash loans that he had received the loan money *in pecunia numerata*, renouncing the exception of Roman law, *exceptio non numerate pecunie*, which thereby eliminated the possibility of any future recriminations about the amount received.[23]

Mutuum loans were generally guaranteed by the borrower with the obligation of person and goods.[24] A *fidejussor* or *fidejussores* might be called upon to stand as surety for the borrower, to be responsible in the event of the latter's default on the loan, for its reimbursement.[25] Thus, on 4 March 1348, a moneyer of Pignan recognized owing 10 gold *denarii ex causa mutui* to a merchant of Montpellier.[26]

[18] For examples of these formulae, see A. D. Hérault, II E 95/375, P. de Pena, ff. 2v, 46r, 88v and 100v. Variant formulae were also utilized. Thus one finds *ex causa veri et legitimi mutui* with farther on in the act *amicabiliter et gratioze* in A. D. Hérault, II E 95/374, G. Nogareti, f. 30r. P. Bouges, "La pratique contractuelle," 1: 242, remarked that all of the loans in the notarial registers which he sampled were gratuitous. In an exhaustive study of those loans of 1293-1348 exceptions to this statement have been found. There are extant three hundred eighty-four *mutuum* loans of which thirty-six are old loans or mentions of loans.

The Montpellier terminology can be compared with that of Toulouse; see P. Wolff, *Commerces et marchands de Toulouse*, 361 ff. and with P.-L. Malausséna, *La vie en Provence orientale*, p. 218.

[19] This practice of "underground" interest was widespread. See the examples in Lopez and Raymond, *Medieval Trade*, pp. 160-161.

On gratuitous loans, *pro amore*, in Venice, F. C. Lane, "Investment and Usury," pp. 8-9, commented, "Some of these free loans probably hide the payment of usury; some were probably really accommodation loans such as businessmen have used during the centuries."

See also Robert S. Lopez, "The Dawn of Medieval Banking," *The Dawn of Modern Banking* (New Haven and London, 1979), p. 17.

[20] See P. Wolff, *Commerces et marchands*, p. 363.

[21] P.-L. Malausséna, *La vie en Provence orientale*, pp. 219-222 for various ploys of dissimulation.

[22] As an example of a loan in kind, see A. M. Montpellier, II 1, J. Grimaudi, f. 13v in which the Jew Vidas lent a mixture of wheat and barley to an inhabitant of the village of Prades-le-Lez.

[23] See P. Riesenberg, "Roman Law, Renunciations and Business," pp. 209-211; P. Bouges, "La pratique contractuelle," 1: 241 and A. Berger, *Encyclopedic Dictionary*, p. 459.

[24] P. Bouges, "La pratique contractuelle," 1: 244. For examples, see A. D. Hérault, II E 95/369, J. Holanie, ff. 71v and 77r.

[25] See, as examples, A. M. Montpellier, II 1, J. Grimaudi, f. 15v; A. D. Hérault, II E 95/370, J. Holanie, ff. 21r and 22v; II E 95/372, J. Holanie *et al.*, f. 148r; and II E 95/377, B. Egidii, ff. 305r and 318r.

[26] A. D. Hérault, II E 95/377, B. Egidii, f. 305r.

Two other moneyers obligated themselves with him for the debt. An alternative technique involved two borrowers who established a joint obligation which was followed by a mutual grant of indemnity from damages.[27]

The *mutuum* loan, accompanied by pledges of personal property furnished by the borrower to the lender, was noted in the extant Montpellier contracts. Among the personal pledges of *mutuum* loans were objects of considerable value: copies of the *Decretals*, a gold crown, cups, spices and a coat.[28] No one profession seems to have specialized in pawnbroking in Montpellier. Changers, moneyers, merchants, Jews, and members of the retail/wholesale trades accepted personal pledges as guarantees in loans. The amounts loaned in cases where pledges were given varied widely. A loan of 4 *l.* current money (1.32 *l.* in the money of 1330) was accompanied by a pledge to the lender of two cups.[29] In 1348 the loan of 100 gold florins by a Montpellier changer to a *miles* was guaranteed by the pledge of a gold crown with pearls and "various other stones." [30] Many other instances of pawnbroking in Montpellier may have taken place without the establishment of a formal notarial obligation of debt.

Pawnbroking practices frequently escaped the notice of historians because this type of lending was not frequently accompanied by a written act. Raymond de Roover cited Pistoia as the only town where fragments of medieval pawnbrokers' accounts have survived.[31] He found evidence of the practice in Lombard hands in Bruges, however.[32] R. W. Emery in his study of the Jews of Perpignan noted little evidence of securities offered as collateral in loans, but he suggested that the prevalence of pawnbroking was implicit in the absence of very small loans in the notarial registers.[33] The Jewish lender would not have demanded a formal obligation of debt since he had the object of property in hand.

[27] A. D. Hérault, II E 95/372, J. Holanie *et al.*, f. 92v and A. M. Montpellier, II 1, J. Grimaudi, f. 79v. Grants of protection to *fidejussores* against eventual losses sustained on account of the borrower's default were a frequent technique of credit arrangements in Toulouse and Provence as in Montpellier. See P.-L. Malausséna, *La vie en Provence orientale*, pp. 226-227 and P. Wolff, *Commerces et marchands de Toulouse*, p. 373.

[28] A. M. Montpellier, II 1, J. Grimaudi, f. 89r; A. D. Hérault, II E 95/375, P. de Pena, f. 99v; II E 95/372, J. Holanie *et al.*, f. 23v; II E 95/377, B. Egidii, ff. 257v and 281r.

[29] A. D. Hérault, II E 95/377, B. Egidii, f. 257v.

[30] A. D. Hérault, II E 95/377, B. Egidii, f. 281r.

[31] R. de Roover, *Money, Banking and Credit in Mediaeval Bruges*, pp. 120-124.

[32] *Ibid.*, p. 117. R. de Roover, *Money, Banking and Credit in Mediaeval Bruges*, p. 313, noted that regulations in Bruges prohibited money changers from the acceptance of a pledge of personal property. There existed no such prohibitions for the changers of Montpellier. See also de Roover, "The Three Golden Balls of the Pawnbrokers," *Bulletin of the Business History Society* 20 (1946), 117-124.

On this institution, in Roman law, see A. Berger, *Encyclopedic Dictionary*, *pignus*, p. 630: "*Pignus* differed from other types of security, *fiducia* and *hypotheca*, in that by *fiducia* ownership was transferred to the creditor, and by *hypotheca* the thing was not handed over at all, whereas through *pignus* only possession of the *res pignorata* was conveyed to the creditor." On these distinctions, see also Paul Ourliac and J. de Malafosse, *Histoire du droit privé*. I. *Les obligations* (Paris, 1957, 1969), pp. 331-376.

[33] R. W. Emery, *The Jews of Perpignan*, pp. 31-33.

Real property was offered on occasion as collateral in a *mutuum* loan. This loan resembled the earlier *pignoratio* or *mort-gage*. The lender benefitted from the revenues of the land, but these were not applied, as they were in the *vif-gage*, against the outstanding debt. Houses, vineyards, fields and even salt exploitations were among those pledges of real property recorded.[34] The pledge of houses in town accompanied larger loans than did that of agricultural lands, suggesting that there was a relationship between the amount of the loan and the value of the pledged property.[35] By foreclosing on such pledges, the ambitious artisan or merchant financier could hope to accumulate a landed fortune.[36]

The *vif-gage* can be distinguished from the *mort-gage* in that in the former context property holdings were transferred to a lender by the borrower for the period of time necessary to pay off the debt.[37] The lender's remuneration from the use and revenues of the property was cancelled against the value of the loan. Loan reimbursements were effectuated at times by borrowers with the assignment to the lender of the rents and fruits from lands, from houses and from ecclesiastical revenues for the period necessary to pay off the loan.[38] In one instance a seller of cooked meat (*cabasserius*) arranged for a loan of 18 *l. t.* on 15 May 1333, to finance the purchase of two vineyards.[39] He promised the total grape harvest in diminution of his debt. These procedures were not numerous compared to cash loans, and in this respect the region of Montpellier resembled that of Toulouse where M. Castaing-Sicard found little evidence of the use of the *vif-gage*.[40]

***

Three hundred and eighty-four acts regarding *mutuum* loans have been preserved in the notarial registers; these transactions represent approximately 8.3% of the extant notarial evidence of the period 1293-1348.[41] This bulk of evidence for loan credit compares favorably with the "hundreds" of loans which Philippe Wolff noted in his study of fourteenth- and fifteenth-century Toulouse.[42] The Montpellier contracts cannot rival in number the 1,643 cases of debts by Christians to Jews which R. W. Emery found in the thirteenth-century notarial registers of Perpignan.[43]

[34] A. M. Montpellier, II 1, J. Grimaudi, ff. 13r, 15v, 78r, 86r; A. D. Hérault, II E 95/369, J. Holanie, f. 82r; II E 95/372, J. Holanie *et al.*, f. 162r.

[35] *Ibid.*

[36] See Chapter 4, "Deposit Banking and the Recovery of Debts."

[37] See n. 9 above.

[38] A. M. Montpellier, II 1, J. Grimaudi, f. 66v; A. D. Hérault, II E 95/370, J. Holanie, f. 95r; II E 95/371, J. Holanie, 140v.

[39] A. D. Hérault, II E 95/369, J. Holanie, f. 36v. On the means of reimbursement of loans, see also P. Bouges, "La pratique contractuelle," 1: 241.

[40] M. Castaing-Sicard, *Les contrats dans le très ancien droit toulousain*, pp. 317-320.

Lending operations were in the hands of a cross-section of the urban population of Montpellier in Table 1. The professional money handlers, whom Raymond de Roover defined as the pawnbrokers, the money changers and the merchant bankers, were well represented.[44] Also active at the end of the thirteenth century were the Jews of Montpellier.

[41] Lenders – Loans

Notarial Register	Year	Total	Merchants	Changers/ Moneyers	Retail/ Wholesale	Nobles/ *Burgenses*	Professions/ Education	Jews	Royal Administration	Ecclesiastics	Women	Artisans/ Service	Food Trades	Agriculture	Foreigners	Unidentified Local	Unidentified Other
AM II 1	1293-1294	151	2	5	5	1	2	127		1		2	2		4		
AM II 2	1301-1302	8	2				1				1				3		1
AD II E 95/368	1327-1328	69	10	1	12		3			4	9	10	2	9	4	5	
AD II E 95/369	1333	36	2		2		2		2	1	10	2	1	3	5	4	2
AD II E 95/373	1333	1										1					
AD II E 95/370	1336	35	11	3	2		1		4	1	3	2	2	2	4		
AD II E 95/374	1337-1342	9	7		1					1							
AD II E 95/375	1339-1340	13	3		3		2				2				3		
AD II E 95/371	1342	15	3	1	1					3	1			1	3		2
AM II 3	1342-1343	2		1	1												
AD II E 95/372	1343-1344	19	5	1					3		1	3		1	5		
AD II E 95/376	1346	1	1														
AD II E 95/377	1347-1348	25	1	7	2					2	2	1		3	3	4	
TOTALS		384	47	19	29	1	11	127	9	13	29	21	7	19	34	13	5

Borrowers – Loans

Notarial Register	Year	Total	Merchants	Changers/ Moneyers	Retail/ Wholesale	Nobles/ *Burgenses*	Professions/ Education	Jews	Royal Administration	Ecclesiastics	Women	Artisans/ Service	Food Trades	Agriculture	Foreigners	Unidentified Local	Unidentified Other
AM II 1	1293-1294	151	3		7	3	1	7		2	10	9	2	9	87	2	9
AM II 2	1301-1302	8	1	1		1					2				2		1
AD II E 95/368	1327-1328	69	3		10		1			2	7	11	1	20	14		
AD II E 95/369	1333	36	1	2	3	1	1		1	1	1	6	5	4	8		2
AD II E 95/373	1333	1										1					
AD II E 95/370	1336	35	2	1	4		1				2	4	1	4	15		1
AD II E 95/374	1337-1342	9								1			1		7		
AD II E 95/375	1339-1340	13			2		1				2	4		1	2	1	
AD II E 95/371	1342	15	1		1						1	3	1		7		1
AM II 3	1342-1343	2				1								1			
AD II E 95/372	1343-1344	19	1						1	2	3	1	2	2	7		
AD II E 95/376	1346	1											1				
AD II E 95/377	1347-1348	25		1	1					1	2	5		3	12		
TOTALS		384	12	5	28	6	5	7	2	9	30	44	14	44	161	3	14

[42] P. Wolff, *Commerces et marchands de Toulouse*, p. 362.
[43] R. W. Emery, *The Jews of Perpignan*, p. 26.
[44] See Raymond de Roover, "The Organization of Trade," pp. 42-118.

TABLE 1: LENDERS IN LOANS *EX CAUSA MUTUI* OF THE MONTPELLIER NOTARIAL EVIDENCE (1293-1348) (384 acts)

	Total Loans	Lenders' % of Total Loans[1]	Lenders' % of Non-Jewish Loans
Merchants	47	12.2%	18.3%
Changers/ Moneyers	19	4.9%	7.4%
Retail/ Wholesale	29	7.6%	11.3%
Nobles/ *Burgenses*	1	0.3%	0.4%
Professions/ Education	11	2.9%	4.3%
Jews	127	33.0%	–
Royal Administration	9	2.3%	3.5%
Ecclesiastics	13	3.4%	5.1%
Women	29	7.6%	11.3%
Artisans/ Service	21	5.5%	8.2%
Food Trades	7	1.8%	2.7%
Agriculture	19	4.9%	7.4%
Foreigners	34	8.9%	13.2%
Unidentified			
Local	13	3.4%	5.1%
Other	5	1.3%	1.9%

[1] Figures are rounded to the nearest tenth of a percent. This table reflects extant Jewish loans prior to the 1306 expulsion.

The Jews were well established in Montpellier as early as 1121.[45] Through the early thirteenth century they enjoyed favorable business conditions. The *consuetudines* of 1204 and 1205 regulated Jewish and Christian money-lending,

[45] *LIM*, act XCIV, pp. 172-176. See R. W. Emery, *The Jews of Perpignan*, Appendix 3, pp. 131-133 on the Jews of Montpellier.

For background on Jewish communities in the south of France and in Montpellier in particular, see Salomon Kahn, *Étude sur les Israélites de Montpellier au moyen âge* (Nîmes, 1924) and "Documents inédits sur les Juifs de Montpellier," *Revue des études juives* 19 (1889), 259-281; 22 (1891), 264-279; 28 (1894), 118-141. See also Gustave Saige, *Les Juifs de Languedoc antérieurement au XIVe siècle* (Paris, 1881). Some of these older works are fraught with errors, as R. W. Emery, *The Jews of Perpignan*, pp. 2-3, has demonstrated.

acknowledging the role of Jewish business within the community.[46] In the course of the thirteenth century this position degenerated.[47] While Jacme I, king of Aragon and Majorca and lord of Montpellier, attempted to protect the Jews from unjust treatment, ecclesiastical and consular legislation assumed an increasingly severe stand on Jewish usury.[48] From 1306 on, Philip IV and his successors resorted to condemnations, confiscations and banishment in a series of fiscal expediencies.[49]

The loan transactions of the Jews were recorded in the notarial registers of Johannes Grimaudi, of 1293-1294 and 1301-1302.[50] No Jewish loans have survived in later registers. Representing thirty-three percent of the lenders in the total pool of Montpellier loans, their lending operations accounted for only 1,637 *l. t.* of 8,058 *l. t.* of loan capital, or twenty percent of the total.[51] Graphs 1 and 2 give the average levels of their transactions and the maximum new loans in years where evidence has been preserved. These levels were lower than those of the pool of Christian lenders. G. Nahon has suggested on the basis of two surviving loans from a Christian to a Jew that the Jews may have enjoyed some infusion of Christian capital in their lending operations.[52] They may also have financed their lending activities through business partnerships.[53] The Jews made loans in cash and in mixtures of cash and kind to villagers of the Montpellier countryside and served an urban clientele of rural nobles and town people including modest artisans, members of the retail/wholesale trades and merchants.[54] R. W. Emery has remarked on the similarities in the clienteles of the Jews in Perpignan and in

[46] See the *Consuetudines* of 1204, arts. 68 and 116. The validity of the Jewish oath was affirmed by an article of 1205.

[47] S. Kahn, "Documents inédits sur les Juifs de Montpellier," 19 *Revue des études juives* (1889), 259-261, suggested that the Cathar heresy and the Albigensian Crusade had adverse repercussions on the Jews.

[48] A church council of 1258 declared void any contract made by a Jew which had not been preceded by an oath on the Mosaic law. The council also maintained that it was sufficient for a Christian to swear that usury was present to be liberated from his debt. See S. Kahn, "Documents inédits sur les Juifs de Montpellier," 19 *Revue des études juives* (1889), 261-262. See also "Les opérations de crédit dans la coutume et dans la vie des affaires à Montpellier au moyen âge: le problème de l'usure," for a discussion of Jewish usury. Consular legislation prohibited the Jews from lending any sum to a Christian under twenty-five years of age without his parents' consent. See *Le Petit Thalamus*, pp. 139-140.

[49] On French anti-Jewish activities, see "Les opérations de crédit dans la coutume et dans la vie des affaires à Montpellier au moyen âge: le problème de l'usure."

[50] A. M. Montpellier, II 1 and 2, J. Grimaudi.

[51] See Chapter 1, Graphs 1, 2 and 3, for a comparison of the capital involved in commercial partnerships.

[52] Gérard Nahon, "Condition fiscale et économique des juifs," in *Cahiers de Fanjeaux*, 12: *Juifs et judaïsme de Languedoc* (Toulouse, 1977), pp. 66-67.

Jews borrowed four times from Christians, three times from other Jews in the remaining loans. See A. M. Montpellier, II 1, J. Grimaudi, ff. 21r, 35v, 47r and 48r for Christian loans to Jews. See ff. 52r, 76v and 94r for Jewish loans to Jews.

[53] See nn. 68 and 69 of Chapter 1.

[54] See R. W. Emery, *The Jews of Perpignan*, Appendix 3, p. 132, chart. Compare the Perpignan clientele, p. 39, chart. My figures differ somewhat as I based my calculations on both old and new loans while Emery used only new loans.

Montpellier and on comparable "type and economic significance" of the loans made by both Jewish communities.[55] The Jews provided an important source of short term credit in small loans.[56]

GRAPH 1: AVERAGE NEW LOANS

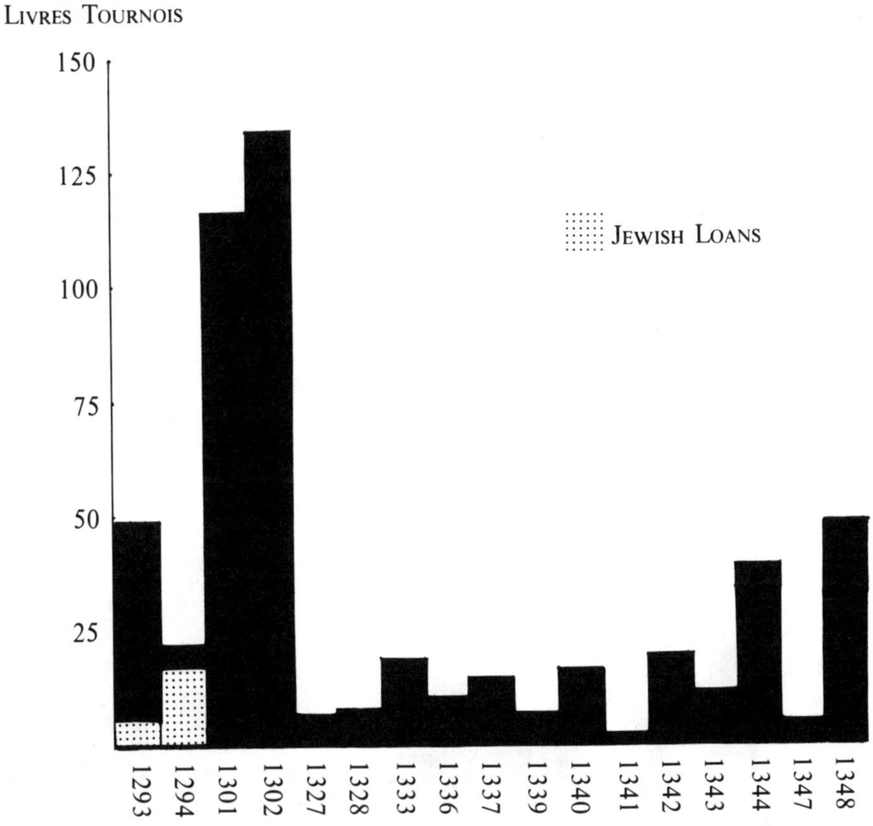

Another group of professional money lenders, the Lombards, performed services similar to those of the Jews. The term "Lombard" was a designation covering Italians from northern Italy. They often shared a leading role in the

[55] *Ibid.*, pp. 132-133.

[56] See also P. Bouges, "La pratique contractuelle," 2: 105, n. 259, on the Jews' activities. Further information on Jewish business is preserved in the notaries of Montpellier from 1361 on; see A. D. Hérault, II E 95/378-383, Pons Emeric, for Jewish acts. The Jews were invited to return to France by an ordinance of July 1315. See *Ordonnances*, 1: 595 and P. Wolff, *Commerces et marchands de Toulouse*, p. 398.

It is interesting to compare the regulation of Jewish lending in Venice; see Reinhold C. Mueller, "Les prêteurs juifs de Venise au moyen âge," *Annales: ESC* 30, no. 6 (1975), 1277-1300.

lending business with the Jews.[57] In fourteenth-century Montpellier, Lucchese exiles joined the Lombards in the lending of money *ex causa mutui*.[58] There were similarities between the positions of these Italian immigrants and the Jews. The Italians were often political exiles. Both groups were, in effect, without a homeland, remaining generally unassimilated in their medieval town of adoption during the first generations. The Italian exiles were of mercantile background. They brought with them at least part of their personal fortune which would facilitate their entry into the lending business. However, the Lombards, like the Jews, were subject to pursuit by royal authorities for usurious practice in the fourteenth century.[59]

GRAPH 2: MAXIMUM AMOUNTS OF NEW LOANS[1]

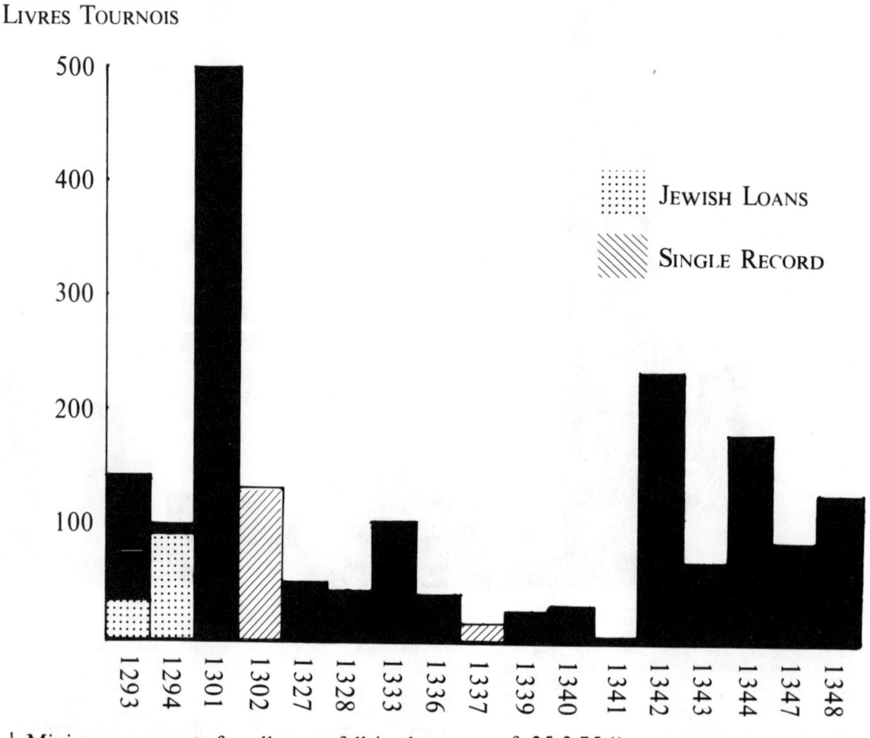

[1] Minimum amounts for all years fall in the range of .25-2.75 livres.

[57] On the Lombards, see Yves Renouard, *Les hommes d'affaires italiens du moyen âge* (Paris, 1949; rev. ed., 1968). For an attempt to renew study of the Lombards, see the article of Kurt Grunwald, "Lombards, Cahorsins and Jews," *The Journal of European Economic History* 4 (1975), 393-398.

[58] On the Lucchese in France, see Florence Edler de Roover, "Lucchese Silks," *Ciba Review* 80 (1950), 2902-2931 and "The Silk Trade of Lucca during the Thirteenth and Fourteenth Centuries," Diss. University of Chicago, 1930. See also my forthcoming article, "I lucchesi in Montpellier al tempo di Castruccio: il commercio e le finanze," *Castruccio Castracani e il suo tempo. Convegno internazionale* (Lucca).

[59] See J. B. Henneman, "Taxation of Italians;" Arthur Layton Funk, "Confiscation of Lombard Debts in France, 1347-1358," *Medievalia et Humanistica* 7 (1952), 51-55.

While Jewish activities were easily isolated for censure, the problem of usurious practice by non-Jews in Montpellier was a topic of some ambiguity as far as the local officials were concerned. Montpellier had its share of royal ordinances controlling the activities of the Lombards.[60] On occasion, however, French officials were overzealous in their suppression of usury, proceeding, according to consular complaints, not only against blatant usurers but against merchants engaged in legitimate business activities.[61] These same merchants were generally influential, wealthy inhabitants of the Majorcan sector of the town.

The lending activities of the Italians were of several sorts. Like the Jews, they extended credit to villagers of the surrounding region. They lent large sums on occasion to village corporations. For example, in 1345 the Lucchese Raymundus Arnulphini, inhabitant of Montpellier, loaned 600 *l. t.* to the inhabitants of Cournonterral for the purchase of a consulate from the king of France.[62] In another instance Ardusso Mutonis, immigrant from Chieri, bourgeois of Montpellier, lent money in 1339 to the consuls of Loupian.[63] The same type of activity was practiced by Italians who were in transit in Montpellier. The Falletti, well-known financiers of Alba, made loans of 800 *l. t.* and 300 *l. t.* to the consuls of Montpellier in 1339.[64] In 1342 Antonius Falettis (*sic*), son and heir of Symondin, acquitted the consuls. Reimbursements had been made in the form of allocations from the collections of *tailles*. The traditional role of financier remained an important part of the identity of merchants of northern Italy in southern France.

Italian immigrants such as Ardusso Mutonis and Boninus de Meldeo of Novara also lent funds to artisans and agricultural workers of Montpellier. These Italians had, in fact, a variety of business activities in Montpellier. Meldeo was involved in trade, land acquisitions and various financial transactions such as the pursuit of his outstanding credits and money exchange contracts.[65]

Ardusso Mutonis was active in Montpellier in the years 1336-1343. By 1339 he had acquired the title of *burgensis*.[66] Mutonis left record of a series of acquittals of debts and cessions of rights against debtors which amply testify to his role in the lending business.[67] Engaged in finance, Mutonis can also be traced in land

[60] See my article, "Les opérations de crédit," and my forthcoming study, "I lucchese in Montpellier."

[61] For example, A. M. Montpellier, *Grand Chartrier*, Louvet no. 1217: 1325.

[62] A. D. Hérault, "Répertoire des archives communales de Cournonterral," inventory in manuscript by Danièle Neirinck (Montpellier, 1969), AA 14.

[63] A. D. Hérault, II E 95/375, P. de Pena, f. 93r.

[64] A. M. Montpellier, II, 3, J. Laurentii, f. 69v. The Falletti also made loans to individuals. See, for example, A. D. Hérault, II E 95/375, P. de Pena, f. 61r and II E 95/369, J. Holanie, ff. 43r and 64r. See also Jean Combes, "Quelques remarques sur les bourgeois de Montpellier au moyen âge," *Recueil*, fasc. 7, *Mélanges Pierre Tisset* (Montpellier, 1970), 125.

[65] A. D. Hérault, II E 95/369, J. Holanie, ff. 29v, 32r, 82v and II E 95/370, J. Holanie, ff. 11v, 92v and 93v.

[66] A. D. Hérault, II E 95/375, P. de Pena, ff. 46r, 48v. See J. Combes, "Quelques remarques sur les bourgeois," p. 125.

[67] A. D. Hérault, II E 95/370, J. Holanie, ff. 16v and 70r; II E 95/375, P. de Pena, 21v and 46r; II E 95/372, J. Holanie *et al.*, 115v and 160v.

investments, especially vineyards. For both Meldeo and Mutonis the foreclosure of debts probably led to the acquisition of real property.

Yet another type of credit activity practiced by the Italians involved furnishing funds to their compatriots and to other foreigners. While these credit operations most often took the form of money exchange contracts, occasionally the loan *ex causa mutui* was utilized. Thus, in 1343 Ardusso Mutonis lent 87 *l. t.* current money to a merchant of Puigcerda.[68] In this context the Italians along with international merchants of Montpellier and elsewhere extended and acquired credit according to the needs of their commerce and finance.

Italians and Jews belonged to a class of professional financiers in which international merchants, changers and moneyers of Montpellier should also be included.[69] Their participation in lending was to be expected since they possessed considerable liquid financial resources and were involved in the contemporary credit network. Second to the Jews in frequency of loans, merchants of Montpellier made a total of forty-seven loans representing 12.3% of all loans extant and 18.3% of all non-Jewish loans.[70] Changers and moneyers were also frequent money lenders. Like the Italians, these professional lenders who specialized in the handling of money often made large loans surpassing 100 *l. t.*[71]

In general, loans made by merchants, changers and moneyers to foreign merchants and financiers were larger than those made to other Montpelliérains. The clientele of these Montpellier lenders included compatriots, inhabitants of the surrounding region and foreign merchants. In spite of these lenders' predilection for large loans, they might on occasion lend small amounts extending consumer credit. Thus, the changers Jacobus and Johannes de Sancto-Michaele lent 65 *s. t.* to a *domicellus* of the village of Poussan on 17 July 1336 and 28 *s. t.* to an inhabitant of another village, Clapiers, on 8 August 1336.[72]

The involvement of professional financiers as creditors in contracts *ex causa mutui* was a common medieval phenomenon, long recognized by economic historians.[73] The participation of virtually every social group in Montpellier in lending activities, however, deserves emphasis (Table 1).[74]

[68] A. D. Hérault, II E 95/372, J. Holanie *et al.*, f. 115v.

[69] R. de Roover, *Money, Banking and Credit in Mediaeval Bruges*, p. 4, discerned three categories of professional money handlers in Bruges: Italian merchant bankers, Lombards or Italian pawnbrokers and money changers. For Montpellier the categories of professional financiers were somewhat broader in that local inhabitants participated at all levels in financial activities.

[70] See Table 1, "Lenders in loans *ex causa mutui*."

[71] For example, in 1344 the merchant Bertholomei lent 225 *l. t.* to the widow of a *burgensis* of Aigues-Mortes. See A. D. Hérault, II E 95/372, J. Holanie *et al.*, f. 162r.

[72] A. D. Hérault, II E 95/370, J. Holanie, ff. 83v and 106v. Mireille Castaing-Sicard, *Les contrats dans le très ancien droit toulousain*, p. 240, argued that the Toulousain loans were "prêts à la consommation" not investment loans. P. Bouges, "La pratique contractuelle," 1: 235, made the same argument regarding the *mutuum* loans of Montpellier. However, the variety of the extant *mutuum* loans of Montpellier would seem to admit of the hypothesis that some of them – those in excess of 100 *l. t.* for example, or those extended by one merchant to another, or by an Italian to a foreign colleague – had investment or business overtones.

[73] See R. de Roover, *Money, Banking and Credit in Mediaeval Bruges*, p. 139.

[74] See the comments of T. Blomquist, "De Roover on Business, Banking and Economic Thought," p. 826.

TABLE 2: WOMEN LENDERS' AND BORROWERS' BACKGROUND IN LOANS *EX CAUSA MUTUI* OF THE MONTPELLIER NOTARIAL EVIDENCE (1293-1348) (29 acts)

	Lenders		Borrowers	
	No. of Acts	% Total Acts	No. of Acts	% Total Acts
Merchants	1	3.4%	1	3.3%
Changers/ Moneyers	2	6.9%	1	3.3%
Retail/ Wholesale	3	10.3%	1	3.3%
Nobles/ *Burgenses*	1	3.4%	–	–
Professions/ Education	–	–	–	–
Jews	–	–	–	–
Royal Administration	–	–	–	–
Ecclesiastics	1	3.4%	–	–
Artisans/ Service	4	13.8%	5	16.7%
Food Trades	2	6.9%	–	–
Agriculture	4	13.8%	6	20.0%
Foreigners	2	6.9%	15	50.0%
Unidentified				
Local	9	31.0%	1	3.3%
Other	–	–	–	–

Table 2 provides the distribution of women lenders by social and occupational background. Participation of all groups with the exception of the Jews, professions/education and royal administration can be noted. R. W. Emery in his study of Perpignan Jews noted women lenders.[75] It would seem that the Montpellier evidence of Jewish loan operations has a lacuna here, especially in light of the participation of Jewish women in other business activities.[76] In northern Europe Jewish women lent money as William C. Jordan demonstrated

[75] R. S. Emery, *The Jews of Perpignan*, p. 26..

[76] S. Kahn, "Documents inédits," *Revue des études juives* 28 (1894), mentions several Jewish women. See, for example, p. 129, document IV, taken from A. M. Montpellier, II, 2, f. 75r, and document VII, f. 120v.

in his discovery of a "two-tiered credit system" in Picardy with Jewish women lenders granting small loans of a "domestic" nature to other women.[77]

Table 3 gives the marital status of women lenders in Montpellier. The participation of single and widowed women was of equal frequency. Married women were noted somewhat less frequently as lenders of money. If married in the south of France, a woman surrendered her dowry to her husband but retained control of her personal possessions or *paraphernalia*. Upon the death of her husband, a widow regained control of part of her dowry and the usufruct of her marital gift.[78] It would seem that widows and single women had somewhat greater resources to devote to lending operations than did married women.

TABLE 3: MARITAL STATUS OF WOMEN LENDERS AND BORROWERS IN THE MONTPELLIER NOTARIAL EVIDENCE (1293-1348)

		Single	Widowed	Married
Lenders	(29)	11	11	7
Borrowers	(30)	6	17	7

Women participated fully in medieval credit operations, and in this context, they frequently lent money. Recorded loans by women rarely surpassed 25 *l. t.* Generally they were more modest. Thus, in 1333 the widow of a *burgensis* lent 59 *s. t.* to another *burgensis* and his wife.[79] Typical of the woman lender of non-noble origin was the widow Maria Bertholomiene whose sons exercised the occupation of shoemaker and fisherman. In addition to financing their trades, Maria lent small sums to agricultural workers.[80]

The presence of members of the clergy among the lenders of money (5.1 % of non-Jewish loans) shows the degree to which this credit practice was accepted in the Montpellier community. Some but not all of the loans by clergy employed the formula *ex causa gratuiti mutui* which may have referred to interest-free loans.[81] There is no proof of the existence of such free *mutuum* loans, however, in the Montpellier evidence. Included in the group of clergy were wealthy churchmen, canons of Maguelone, who were also priors of village churches in the surrounding region, and priests. The clerical benefice whether belonging to the

[77] William C. Jordan, "Jews on Top: Women and the Availability of Consumption Loans in Northern France in the Mid-Thirteenth Century," *Journal of Jewish Studies* 29 (1978), 53 and 56.

[78] See Jean Hilaire, *Le régime des biens entre époux dans la région de Montpellier du début du XIIIe siècle à la fin du XVIe siècle* (Montpellier, 1957), on the property rights of women. See also P. Tisset, "Placentin et l'enseignement à Montpellier," p. 87.

[79] A. D. Hérault, II E 95/369, J. Holanie, f. 10v.

[80] A. D. Hérault, II E 95/369, J. Holanie, ff. 97r, 99v and 103r.

[81] See T. P. McLaughlin, "The Teaching of the Canonists," 2: 1-3, on the punishments of clerics guilty of usury. For example, A. D. Hérault, II E 95/377, B. Egidii, 103r. It is, however, by no means certain that this formula guaranteed an interest-free loan.

middle or upper class clergy suffered in the fourteenth century from the problems associated with fixed revenues in an era of inflation and currency debasements.[82] Clergy may have chosen to supplement fixed income and low-yielding investments with loans. The standards of consumption set by the papal court at Avignon may have accentuated the cash needs of the clergy.

Jurists, notaries and royal officials occasionally extended loan credit. They occupied influential positions in society, performing tasks which were lucrative and unspeculative in nature. These professionals did not need commercial credit as did the merchant and the retailer for the acquisition of merchandise and the conduct of affairs. On the contrary, they may often have had surplus funds to invest. In 1333, the royal servant, Bernardus Fornerii, made four loans of 8 *s. t.* to 60 *s. t.* to the wives of a grain merchant and a wood merchant, to a notary and to an innkeeper.[83]

Artisans and agricultural workers generally lent modest sums. However, these groups were not without their occasional capitalist. The cultivator Symon Lambruscala disposed of considerable resources. On 20 September 1333, he lent 90 *l. t.* to a butcher.[84] The butcher repaid his loan four days later and at the same time borrowed 104 *l. t.* from the same Lambruscala.[85] Unfortunately, the source of Lambruscala's fortune remains undetermined. More typical of loans made by agricultural workers was that of 18 June 1347, involving 20 *s. t.* current money lent by the cultivator Rose to another cultivator, Boneti.[86]

The one social group rarely recorded as lenders in the extant loan contracts was the urban and regional nobility, comprised of *domicelli*, *milites*, *burgenses*, and *domini*.[87] Although often related to mercantile and financial families, members of the nobility were rarely recorded in business activities. Their fortune consisted essentially of lands, revenues from long-term leases and rights of eminent domain both urban and rural. Their lack of participation in credit operations would seem to reflect a reluctance to engage in commercial and financial ventures after ennoblement.[88]

*
**

[82] On the papal court at Avignon, see, for example, Bernard Guillemain, *La cour pontificale d'Avignon (1309-1376): étude d'une société* (Paris, 1962); and Yves Renouard, *Les relations des papes d'Avignon et des compagnies commerciales et bancaires de 1316 à 1378* (Paris, 1941).

[83] A. D. Hérault, II E 95/369, J. Holanie, ff. 57v, 64v, 72r and 74v. See Joseph R. Strayer, *The Reign of Philip the Fair* (Princeton, 1980), pp. 55-68, for a discussion of royal officials' salaries.

[84] A. D. Hérault, II E 95/369, J. Holanie, f. 71v.

[85] A. D. Hérault, II E 95/369, J. Holanie, f. 77r.

[86] A. D. Hérault, II E 95/377, B. Egidii, f. 84r.

[87] The *burgenses* were titled bourgeois inhabitants of Montpellier; the *domicelli* were holders of noble title in the town and in the countryside; the *milites* represented the traditional urban nobility of the twelfth-century Guilhem family's entourage. *Dominus* was a title applied to nobles in the town and region. Even the twelfth-century lord of Montpellier was so designated.

See J. Combes, "Quelques remarques sur les bourgeois;" see also the discussion in Reyerson, "Commerce and Society in Montpellier," 1: 12-17.

[88] On the urban nobility in the south of France, see P. Dognon, "De quelques mots employés au moyen âge dans le Midi pour désigner des classes d'hommes: *platerii*, *platearii*," *Annales du Midi* 11

TABLE 4: BORROWERS IN LOANS *EX CAUSA MUTUI* OF THE MONTPELLIER NOTARIAL EVIDENCE (1293-1348) (384 acts)

	Total Loans	Borrowers' % of Loans[1]	Borrowers in Non-Jewish Loans	Borrowers' % of Non-Jewish Loans[1]
Merchants	12	3.1%	10	3.9%
Changers/ Moneyers	5	1.3%	5	1.9%
Retail/ Wholesale	28	7.3%	26	10.1%
Nobles/ *Burgenses*	6	1.6%	3	1.2%
Professions/ Education	5	1.3%	4	1.6%
Jews	7	1.8%	4	1.6%
Royal Administration	2	.5%	2	.8%
Ecclesiastics	9	2.3%	8	3.1%
Women	30	7.8%	20	7.8%
Artisans/ Service	44	11.5%	38	14.8%
Food Trades	14	3.6%	13	5.1%
Agriculture	44	11.5%	35	13.6%
Foreigners	161	41.9%	79	30.7%
Unidentified				
Local	3	.8%	3	1.2%
Other	14	3.6%	7	2.7%

[1] Figures are rounded to the nearest tenth of a percent. Jewish borrowers were those recorded in the extant evidence before the 1306 expulsion.

Just as urban lenders were represented among all social groups, borrowers were also drawn from a cross-section of the population as Table 4 shows. Among borrowers *ex causa mutui*, foreigners were by far the most numerous. Almost thirty-five percent, excluding women and ecclesiastics, came from the region around Montpellier. About seven percent of male foreign borrowers hailed from a

(1899), 348-358; Robert Michel, "Les chevaliers du château des Arênes de Nîmes aux XIIe et XIIIe siècles," *Revue historique* 102 (1909), 45-61; and H. Richardot, "Le fief roturier à Toulouse aux XIIe et XIIIe siècles," *Revue historique du droit français et étranger*, 4th ser., 14 (1935), 307-359, 495-569.

distance of over fifty kilometers. Approximately five percent from within a fifty-kilometer radius were members of the nobility. About fifty-three percent of female borrowers were foreigners, the vast majority of whom were from the immediate region. Five borrowers of the clergy were foreigners. Montpellier was an important urban center, acting as a magnet for regional residents in search of credit.[89]

Among urban borrowers, artisans and inhabitants associated with agriculture were frequently in need of loans. They borrowed sums ranging, in general, from 50 *s. t.* to 20 *l. t.*[90] Members of the food trades were less assiduous borrowers. Although recorded only seven times, butchers received sizeable loans.[91] Representatives of the urban nobility, of royal officialdom, of the legal classes and of the clergy occasionally sought funds through loans.[92]

Women were recorded borrowing money with approximately the same frequency as they lent it. The reasonably broad distribution of women borrowers is given in Table 2. Half of the women borrowing money were from outside Montpellier, as noted above. The loans recorded for women borrowers were small.[93] Table 3 gives the marital status of women borrowers. Widows made the greatest use of the *mutuum* loan to obtain necessary consumer credit, recording over twice as many loans as single and married women. In some instances, the financial status of the widow in Montpellier seems to have required loan credit. The women borrowing money in this fashion, it must be pointed out, were judged sufficiently good credit risks to obtain a loan.

The commercial and financial classes, large retailers, merchants, changers and moneyers, utilized loan credits regularly just as they had frequent recourse to recognitions of debt, to money exchange contracts and to commercial partnerships. Changers borrowed in large amounts while retailers and merchants were recorded in all manner of loans, large and small.[94]

*
**

[89] On the attraction of Montpellier, see my article, "Patterns of Population Attraction and Mobility: The Case of Montpellier, 1293-1348," *Viator* 10 (1979), 257-281.

[90] For example, on 6 April 1336, a cauldron maker borrowed 30 *s. t.* from a royal servant. See A. D. Hérault, II E 95/370, J. Holanie, f. 36v.

[91] Butchers were often capitalists of some importance. See the interesting study of the butchers of Toulouse by Philippe Wolff, "Les bouchers de Toulouse aux xiie-xve siècles," *Annales du Midi* 65 (1953), 375-393.

[92] For example, on 27 September 1343, a royal servant borrowed 100 *s.* of current money from another royal servant. See A. D. Hérault, II E 95/372, J. Holanie *et al.*, f. 88v.

[93] For example, on 28 August 1336, the widow of a cultivator borrowed 22 *s. t.* from another woman. See A. D. Hérault, II E 95/370, J. Holanie, f. 126r.

[94] For example, on 1 May and 20 May 1333, a local changer obtained loans of 100 *l. t.* each from a royal notary. See A. D. Hérault, II E 95/369, J. Holanie, ff. 25r and 40r. A much smaller sum, 100 *s. t.* was borrowed in 1336 by a local merchant from another merchant. See A. D. Hérault, II E 95/370, J. Holanie, f. 16r.

TABLE 5: DATES OF CONTRACTION OF LOANS IN THE MONTPELLIER NOTARIAL EVIDENCE (1293-1348)

The 347 loans of this table were new loans or acts regarding loan obligations in which the date of contraction was mentioned. The remainder of the 384 loans or mentions of old loans did not refer to this date.

Notarial Register	Year	Jan	Feb	Mar	Apr	May	Jun	Jul	Aug	Sept	Oct	Nov	Dec
AM II 1	1293-1294	15	18	9						13	24	26	15
AM II 2	1301-1302	1			1	1	1				1		
AD II E 95/368	1327-1328	3	1	12				3	7	11	10	8	14
AD II E 95/369	1333			4	2	7			5	9	3	4	2
AD II E 95/373	1333											1	
AD II E 95/370	1336			1	9	5	2	6	11	1			
AD II E 95/374	1337-1342		1	1			2	1					4
AD II E 95/375	1339-1340		1		1		1	2	1		1	4	1
AD II E 95/371	1342			1	3	1	3	2		1	3		
AM II 3	1342-1343												
AD II E 95/372	1343-1344	7				4				3	2	3	
AD II E 95/376	1346	1											
AD II E 95/377	1347-1348	1	4	2	3	4	4	1	1		2	2	1
TOTALS		28	25	30	19	22	13	15	25	38	45	49	37

The demand for loan credit in Montpellier was not uniform throughout the calender year. Table 5 giving dates of establishment of loan contracts indicates that urban inhabitants and foreigners of the surrounding region borrowed funds or grain mixtures in the fall and winter months. The pattern which emerges from the loans resembles that which Richard W. Emery discerned in examining loans made by Jews in thirteenth-century Perpignan.[95] Emery argued that such a

[95] R. W. Emery, *The Jews of Perpignan*, p. 26.

distribution in the months following the harvest was not indicative of borrowing in distress. It may well be that those agricultural workers in difficult financial straits resorted in the lean months before the harvest to the sale of futures in grapes and grain, examined earlier. June and July were the months of lightest borrowing in Montpellier as they were in Perpignan.[96]

TABLE 6: "ON DEMAND" TERMS IN LOANS OF THE MONTPELLIER NOTARIAL EVIDENCE (1293-1348)

Notarial Register	Year	Numbers	Percentage of Total
AM II 1	1293-1294	4	2.7%
AM II 2	1301-1302	2	25%
AD II E 95/368	1327-1328	40	58%
AD II E 95/369	1333	16	44%
AD II E 95/373	1333	0	
AD II E 95/370	1336	20	57.1%
AD II E 95/374	1337-1342	4	44%
AD II E 95/375	1339-1340	1	7.7%
AD II E 95/371	1342	5	33.3%
AM II 3	1342-1343	0	
AD II E 95/372	1343-1344	11	57.9%
AD II E 95/376	1346	0	
AD II E 95/377	1347-1348	4	16%
TOTALS		107	27.9%

The term of credit in the loans of Montpellier was most frequently "on demand," that is, at the request of the creditor as it was in recognitions of debt for the purchase of movables and real property. The potential demand for immediate reimbursement thus existed here as in the recognition of debt. If this provision

[96] *Ibid.*, p. 64.

were invoked and the borrower were unable to pay, the fine of double indemnity in the case of default could result.[97]

The term of repayment, "on demand," was present in approximately forty-four percent of the loans contracted in the fourteenth century as Table 6 shows. With the inclusion of thirteenth-century Jewish loans this percentage drops to 27.9%. None of the loans extended by Jewish creditors in 1293-1294 was established on an "on demand" basis.[98] The Jews of Perpignan do not seem to have utilized such terms, and it may be that such a practice would have rendered Jewish lenders more vulnerable than necessary to accusations of extortion.

TABLE 7: DATES OF TERM IN LOANS OF THE MONTPELLIER NOTARIAL EVIDENCE (1293-1348)

Notarial Register	Year	Jan	Feb	Mar	Apr	May	Jun	Jul	Aug	Sept	Oct	Nov	Dec
AM II 1	1293-1294	2	4	4	8		5	1	43	17		16	8
AM II 2	1301-1302			1					1	1			
AD II E 95/368	1327-1328	1	5	1	5		3		2	3	3	1	5
AD II E 95/369	1333		4		2	1	2			3		1	
AD II E 95/373	1333												1
AD II E 95/370	1336			1		2	2		3	1		2	2
AD II E 95/374	1337-1342								1				
AD II E 95/375	1339-1340		1		1		1					3	2
AD II E 95/371	1342			1	1	1	2		1		1		
AM II 3	1342-1342												
AD II E 95/372	1343-1344		1		1	1	1			2			1
AD II E 95/376	1346												
AD II E 95/377	1347-1348				2	1	1		4	5			2
TOTALS		3	15	8	20	6	17	1	55	32	4	23	21

[97] Some skepticism must be raised here with regard to the likelihood of the invocation of this kind of "on demand" payment. Only in the earliest Genoese loans did such formulae appear, and, according to R. S. Lopez, who shared this comment with me, loans at the discretion of the lender are reflective of a primitive economy.

[98] See R. W. Emery, *The Jews of Perpignan*, Appendix 3, p. 133, for a table on the dates of term of Jewish loans to villagers in the region of Montpellier.

Table 7 details the distribution of terms of payment other than "on demand" when they were recorded in the loans. The most frequent months of term were August and September. Jewish dates of term, in particular, were concentrated in these months. The major dates of term in the loans of Montpellier, as in the recognitions of debt, were associated with religious events: Lent, Easter, the feast of Saint John the Baptist, the Ascension of the Virgin, the feast of Saint Michael, All Saints' Day and Christmas. Other saints' days such as those of Saint James (25 July), Saints Peter and Paul (29 June), Saint Gilles (1 September) and Saint Andrew (30 November) were occasionally mentioned. Emery suggested that the absence of major religious holidays in July and October was one reason few terms in the Jewish loans of Perpignan were scheduled in those months.[99] The same infrequency of repayment in these months can be noted in Montpellier.

Terms of three to six months were common in the fourteenth century whereas the Jewish loans of 1293-1294 carried a longer term, in many instances, nine months to a year. The majority of the Jewish clientele was composed of villagers of the region around Montpellier for whom loans contracted in the fall and winter months could be most easily reimbursed at the next harvest period in August and September.[100] P.-L. Malausséna noted a diverse clientele for the Jews of Grasse, including villagers and village communities.[101] The majority of the Jewish clients in new loans in Perpignan in the thirteenth century were inhabitants from the surrounding villages.[102]

In addition, Jewish lenders also made loans in kind. About one-fourth of their total loans were made in kind or in a combination of cash and agricultural goods.[103] Grains or mixtures of grains such as that of barley and wheat formed the substance of these loans.[104] In the years 1327-1348 when no further Jewish acts were preserved, non-Jewish lenders recorded from one to three loans in kind per year (about eight percent) in the extant acts.[105] In the years 1347-1348 when a majority of villagers and agricultural workers again predominated as borrowers, terms of three to six months were scheduled to coincide with feasts in August and September.[106] The rhythm of the agricultural year governed these transactions in kind made to a rural clientele. For merchants and artisans the calendar was more flexible.

The *mutuum* loan was generally contracted in cash and reimbursed in cash. However, on occasion, other means of repayment were devised. Loans might be

[99] *Ibid.*, p. 66, n. 1.

[100] *Ibid.*, pp. 65-66 and Appendix 3, p. 133.

[101] P.-L. Malausséna, *La vie en Provence orientale*, pp. 261-262.

[102] R. W. Emery, *The Jews of Perpignan*, p. 39, chart. On the Jews of Toulouse as lenders, see P. Wolff, *Commerces et marchands de Toulouse*, pp. 397-399.

[103] All the remaining Jewish loans are preserved in A. M. Montpellier, II 1, J. Grimaudi. A total of 127 loans had Jewish creditors; 32 of these were loans in kind or in a combination of cash and kind.

[104] For example, A. M. Montpellier, II 1, J. Grimaudi, f. 28v.

[105] In the year 1333 one finds two such loans in kind: A. D. Hérault, II E 95/369, J. Holanie, ff. 43v and 66r.

[106] For example, A. D. Hérault, II E 95/377, B. Egidii, f. 83v: 16 June to 1 September.

repaid in work. Thus, on 21 September 1327, a cultivator and his wife agreed to reimburse the wife of a draper for a loan of 100 *s. t.* in work on colored articles of mercery, probably by the piece, performed by the cultivator's wife.[107] In a variation of the above, on 16 July 1342, a knifemaker was engaged as a journeyman by another knifemaker for one year.[108] In addition to a 2 *s. t.* per day salary, he received a 30 *s. t.* loan which he was to reimburse at 12 *d.* per week in those weeks when there were no religious feasts. Here the obligation was at a level consistent with the salary from which it was probably deducted. Four months later the loan was cancelled as repaid in full.

The *mutuum* loan was an instrument of short-term credit, destined for consumption rather than investment in most cases.[109] When the term of payment was "on demand," cancellation of the debt came often within a month of its establishment. It could come as much as nine months to a year later.[110] These delays in payment lend support to the hypothesis that in some loans arrangements were made to permit late reimbursement by the borrower with the collection of penalties by the lender as the interest on the loan. When a specific feast was cited as the due date, cancellation generally came within a month after that date.[111] When a delay occurred, it was usually an artisan, an agricultural worker or a villager who was behind in payments. In all, the rhythm of cancellations varied according to the vicissitudes of individual fortune and resulted in occasional, if not frequent, collection of fines.

The sums lent by *mutuum* contract were generally quoted in money of account, *livres tournois*. In periods of monetary crisis such as that preceding the currency reform of 8 April 1330, when the *pied de monnaie* was reduced from 24 to 12 officially, loans recorded in real money were common.[112] Such a practice assured the creditor that reimbursement would not be effected in a devalued currency. In the years 1339-1343, again an era of monetary instability, many quotations were given simply in "current money" with the specification of repayment in gold *denarii*, termed *angelus vetus* and *angelus novus*, both valued at 75 *s. t.* in the documents of Montpellier.[113] Local loans rapidly reflected currency revaluations. Thus on 3 February 1340, just after the devaluation of 29 January 1340, the wife of a merchant promised to repay a loan in 60 *l. fortis monete*.[114] For those loans which were quoted in money of account without the specification of the currency of repayment, the potential for loss was considerable in the years 1337-1342

[107] A. D. Hérault, II E 95/368, J. Holanie, f. 47v.

[108] A. D. Hérault, II E 95/371, J. Holanie, f. 80r. For the reimbursement in skirts, see II E 95/368, J. Holanie, f. 44r, promised by a skirtmaker (*juperius*).

[109] See P. Bouges, "La pratique contractuelle," 1: 235 on the consumption loan.

[110] As an example of a delay, see A. D. Hérault, II E 95/372, J. Holanie *et al.*, f. 115v. The loan was established on 8 November 1343, and cancelled on 12 June 1344.

[111] See A. D. Hérault, II E 95/370, J. Holanie, f. 113r. The date of term in this loan of 1336 was All Saints' Day (1 November), and the cancellation came on 13 November 1336.

[112] E. Fournial, *Histoire monétaire*, p. 94. See also Appendix 2, "Monetary Problems," below.

[113] See, for example, A. D. Hérault, II E 95/371, J. Holanie, ff. 16r and 63v.

[114] A. D. Hérault, II E 95/375, P. de Pena, f. 137r.

when mutations of the currency were frequent.[115] Loans reveal considerable sensitivity to the fluctuations of the currency on the part of all social groups.

***

The sums loaned *ex causa mutui* varied considerably over the period under study. Graphs 1 and 2 provide the average and maximum amounts lent in years when documentation remains.[116] The years from 1293-1302 witnessed the lending of sums greater than those of the first half of the fourteenth century. The availability of lending capital seems to have decreased over time. By the same token, the policing of lending activities by the French crown increased.[117]

The loan evidence from the Montpellier contracts does not permit the calculation of interest levels. The 1204 statute allowing the accretion of interest to a level of the principal suggests a rather tolerant attitude on the part of the urban community in the early thirteenth century.[118] In Montpellier there was no counterpart of Foulques of Marseille, Bishop of Toulouse (1206-1231), who vigorously pursued an anti-usury policy.[119] The "campaign against usury," according to John Baldwin, should be situated in the years 1195-1215 with further pursuit under Foulques.[120] In fact, canon law legislation and decretals of the late twelfth century denote a mounting tide of condemnation of usury which culminated in the pronouncements of the Council of Lyon (Lyon II, 1274) and the Council of Vienne (1311).[121] At Vienne, "those who authorized or protected usurers," in the words of Jacques Le Goff, were subject to excommunication.[122]

The French king took action against usury in the thirteenth century. The attitude of Saint Louis hardened with regard to interest of any kind during his reign; he forbade Christian usury in 1230 and prohibited the taking of interest even by Jewish lenders in 1254.[123] The king of Aragon-Majorca, Jacme I, lord of Montpellier from 1213-1276, was more tolerant with regard to the Jews, permitting them to exact twenty percent interest in contracts of less than one year

[115] An example of possible devaluation occurs in A. M. Montpellier, II 3, J. Laurentii, f. 95v. On 14 January 1343, acquittal for a loan of 27 *l. t.* was made by the son of Salvator Guillelmi, draper of Montpellier, to a *legum doctor* of Montpellier. The 27 *l. t.* lent at an undetermined date were worth 63 *l.* 15 *s. t.* in 1343, when the *pied de monnaie* was at 60. See Appendix 2, "Monetary Problems."

[116] See Appendix 2 for a discussion of these premises upon which these tables were constructed. The problem of currency conversions remains one of the most acute in medieval economic history. The data for 1302 and 1337 represent single loans.

[117] See the discussion in Reyerson, "Les opérations de crédit dans la coutume et dans la vie des affaires à Montpellier au moyen âge: le problème de l'usure."

[118] See my discussion in "Les opérations de crédit."

[119] On Foulques see the brief comments of Jacques Le Goff, "The Usurer and Purgatory," in *The Dawn of Modern Banking* (New Haven, 1979), p. 30.

[120] *Ibid.*, and John W. Baldwin, *Masters, Princes, and Merchants: The Social Views of Peter the Chanter and His Circle*, 2 vols. (Princeton, 1970), 1: 296-311 and 2: 204-211.

[121] Le Goff, "The Usurer and Purgatory," pp. 27-29.

[122] *Ibid.*, p. 30.

[123] *Ordonnances des rois de France de la troisième race*, ed. Eusèbe de Laurière (Paris, 1723), 1: 53-54, December 1230 and 1: 75, December 1254. On royal legislation against the Jews, see Gérard Nahon, "Le crédit et les Juifs dans la France du XIIIe siècle," *Annales: ESC* 24 (1969), 1121-1148.

in duration and 16 2/3% for all other contracts.[124] In 1262 Jacme I permitted the Jews of Montpellier to add principal and interest into one sum which could be claimed if the borrower failed to repay the debt.[125] The French attitude towards interest changed under the rule of Philip IV and his successors. Although the French kings confiscated Jewish and Lombard property for usurious practices from time to time throughout the first half of the fourteenth century, they tolerated in other moments, from 1311 on, interest rates of between fifteen and twenty percent.[126] No individual cases of exorbitant interest claims have survived in the notarial registers, but the town consuls of Montpellier requested French intervention against notorious usurious practice on several occasions with regard to the Jews and the Lombards.[127]

In conclusion, the main traits of the lending business can be highlighted. Within the broad base of urban participation in loan credit the Jews stand out as professionals providing short-term consumer or distress credit to the rural population of the region surrounding Montpellier. The Lombards joined them in extending credit to regional villagers and to village corporations. The penetration of urban credit into the rural, agricultural world is well illustrated in the Montpellier lending operations.[128] This credit in the hands of the professionals, Jews and Lombards, was vulnerable to the usurpations and confiscations of the French monarchy, which alternated with official tolerance of interest rates of between fifteen and twenty percent.[129] The fourteenth and fifteenth centuries are generally accepted as an era when interest was lower than it had been in the twelfth and thirteenth centuries.[130] Consumer loans were in demand in the fourteenth century while profitable investment opportunities were growing scarce.[131]

[124] R. W. Emery, *The Jews of Perpignan*, p. 84.

[125] *Ibid.*

[126] John Bell Henneman, "Taxation of Italians by the French Crown (1311-1363)," *Mediaeval Studies* 31 (1969), 17. In 1332 Philip VI authorized an interest rate of 21.6% or 1 *d./l./*week. See Raymond Cazelles, "Quelques reflections à propos des mutations de la monnaie royale française (1295-1360)," *Le moyen âge* 72 (1966), 92. An interest rate of twenty percent seems to have been the rule in Genoa and in San Gimignano and in twelfth-century Venice. See the comments of Thomas Blomquist, "De Roover on Business, Banking and Economic Thought," *Journal of Economic History* 35 (1975), 826. See also F. C. Lane, "Investment and Usury," p. 7. P. Wolff, *Commerces et marchands de Toulouse*, p. 398, suggested a 43 1/3% interest rate for the Jews. For further discussion of interest rates, see Reyerson, "Les opérations de crédit," p. 197, n. 38.

[127] On the possibility of compound interest, see the discussion in Reyerson, "Les opérations de crédit," and the hypothetical case of escalating interest cited by the consuls in an undated document in *Le Grand Chartrier*, Louvet no. 1931. M. Castaing-Sicard, *Les contrats dans le très ancien droit toulousain*, p. 251, found few examples of compound interest in Toulouse.

[128] See Jacques Heers, *L'Occident aux XIVe et XVe siècles. Aspects économiques et sociaux* (Paris, 1970), 382-383, and Georges Duby, *L'Économie rurale et la vie des campagnes dans l'Occident médiéval* (Paris, 1962), 2: 631-634, for the European perspective on this phenomenon.

[129] See n. 126 above.

[130] See Benjamin Z. Kedar, *Merchants in Crisis*, pp. 62-65.

[131] Bernard Schnapper, "La répression de l'usure et l'évolution économique (XIIIe-XVIe siècles)," *Tijdschrift voor Rechtsgeschiedenis* 37, fasc. 1 (1969), 47-75, has put forward some interesting theories about the relation of economic conditions and interest.

The conveniences of loan credit to the consumer and to the business community had gradually overridden any constraint on lending practice because of usury prohibitions present at the beginning of the thirteenth century in Montpellier. Loans of the years 1293-1348 in Montpellier were similar to lending practices across all of southern France.[132] While few inhabitants outside professional money lenders probably derived their incomes from such activities, loans provided a means of augmenting other revenues. Sale credit and loan credit were the foundations of daily economic operations in Montpellier.

[132] The secondary works cited in the footnotes of this chapter bear out the similarities between Montpellier and other towns of southern France in regard to lending practices.

4

Deposit Banking and the Recovery of Debts

The evolution of medieval banking was closely connected with the credit techniques of the economy as a whole.[1] Three banking functions stand out in the Middle Ages: money lending, foreign exchange and deposit banking.[2] It was in these operations that the professionals of medieval finance, the credit specialists, were particularly active. Montpellier enjoyed the presence of mechant-bankers, money changers, pawnbrokers, Jews and Lombards, as did most medieval towns.

Methods for the recovery of debts and the repayment of financial obligations are tied to the system of banking, credit and investment. The degree of negotiability of obligations and the transferability of assets and credits affected the means through which debts were repaid. The velocity of circulation within the economy and the volume of economic transactions were related, in turn, to these techniques.[3] Although the concept of endorsement developed only in the Early Modern era, the negotiability of credit instruments and a process of discounting debts have been noted in the surviving notarial evidence of

[1] The collected papers of a recent symposium on the history of banking provide new insights into the late medieval period. See *The Dawn of Modern Banking* (New Haven and London, 1979).

[2] The emergence of the earliest medieval banking practices can be traced to twelfth-century Italy. R. S. Lopez has suggested that the eleventh-century appearance in western Europe of terms such as *trapezita* (of Byzantine origin) meaning banker-changer, represented a prelude to banking activities *per se*. Lopez emphasized that the functions of moneyer and changer were often mixed in this early period; yet, the seeming lack of specialization was not necessarily a sign of backwardness. The needs of the existing economy were probably best served in this way. The distinguishing traits of the *bancherius* were already clear. Such individuals operated banks, tables of money-changing and foreign exchange.

See Lopez, *La prima crisi della banca di Genova, 1250-1259* (Genoa, 1956); "Continuità e adattamento nel medio evo: un milliennio di storia delle associazioni di monetieri nell 'Europa meridionale," in *Studi in onore di Gino Luzzatto* (Milan, 1950), 2: 74-137; and "An Aristocracy of Money in the Early Middle Ages," *Speculum* 28 (1953), 1-42.

The early admixture of banking functions helps to explain the disagreement among financial historians regarding the origins of banking in the Middle Ages. Abbott P. Usher, "The Origins of Banking: The Primitive Bank of Deposit, 1200-1600," *Economic History Review* 4 (1934), 399-428, emphasized the deposit function.

[3] For a recent discussion of velocity of circulation and the operation of credit in the economy, see Harry A. Miskimin, "The Impact of Credit on Sixteenth Century English Industry," in *The Dawn of Modern Banking* (New Haven, London, 1979), pp. 275-289.

Montpellier.[4] Medieval methods of liquidating debts were not as efficient as the modern system of checking accounts and credit cards, but the evolution of clearing house techniques, based on the deposit banking of changers at the Champagne fairs, in Bruges and in Tuscany permitted the cancelling of debts between clients of the same banker or between clients of changers who carried mutual accounts.[5]

Deposit banking had developed several facets by the early fourteenth century.[6] Of the many functions which banks perform today, the deposit function is perhaps the most obvious banking operation. The banks receive money from a depositor allowing that individual to draw checks on those funds, if they were placed in a checking account, to receive modest returns on the money if it was deposited in a savings account, and in some instances, to do both in the newest form of bank accounts. Term deposits and "on demand" deposits can both be found in modern savings arrangements as they were in the most evolved form of medieval deposit banking. The historical precedent of Roman law underlying such operations was the *depositum irregolare*, or irregular deposit, which permitted the deposit of money or fungibles that were to be returned to the depositor in quantity but not necessarily as the same physical objects.[7] If the

[4] On the sale of obligations, see P. Wolff, *Commerces et marchands de Toulouse*, pp. 377-379. On the concepts of negotiability, endorsement and discounting, see Abbott P. Usher, "The Origins of Banking: The Primitive Bank of Deposit, 1200-1600," pp. 399-428. Usher assigned the growth of negotiability to the sixteenth century, that of endorsement to the seventeenth century. Herman Van der Wee, "Anvers et les innovations de la technique financière aux XVIe et XVIIe siècles," *Annales: ESC* 22 (1967), 1067-1089, has found earlier instances of negotiability by endorsement.

[5] Abbott P. Usher, *The Early History of Deposit Banking in Mediterranean Europe* (Cambridge, Mass., 1943) 1: 3-25. He has succinctly enumerated the handicaps and facilities of medieval banking in his study of early deposit banking: "Banks could not buy and sell short time paper in the open market. They could accumulate credits and sell exchange. They could lend deposit credit against a bill or a note. But they could not convert particular bills or notes into cash before maturity. The paper work of a bank could not assume its modern form until the jurists had developed the concept of negotiability. The essential purposes of all these dealings in credit could be achieved, but by modes that would seem strange and unfamiliar to the modern banker." (p. 8).

Raymond de Roover viewed transfer banking, the essence of the medieval clearinghouse at fairs, as developing from the deposit capacity of money changers. On transfer banking, see R. de Roover, *Money, Banking and Credit in Mediaeval Bruges*, pp. 249 ff. On banking at the Champagne fairs, see A.-E. Sayous, "Les opérations des banquiers italiens en Italie et aux foires de Champagne pendant le XIIIe siècle," *Revue historique* 170 (1932), 2-6; and R.-H. Bautier, "Les foires de Champagne. Recherches sur une évolution historique," *Recueils de la société Jean Bodin*, 5: *La Foire* (Brussels, 1953), pp. 97-148.

[6] A. P. Usher argued that the deposit function was primordial in the development of banking. He elaborated his ideas regarding medieval and early modern banking in *The Early History of Deposit Banking in Mediterranean Europe*, 1, and in "Deposit Banking in Barcelona, 1300-1700," *Journal of Economic and Business History* 4 (1931), 121-155, and "The Origins of Banking: The Primitive Bank of Deposit, 1200-1600," *Economic History Review* 4 (1934), 420, for example.

A.-E. Sayous acknowledged the existence of the deposit function as typical of banking but offered the hypothesis that before bankers achieved the public confidence necessary to attract deposits, their primitive function was that of lending money. With the passage of time, according to Sayous, those loan bankers became credit bankers and changers. See "Les opérations des banquiers italiens," pp. 2-6.

[7] A. Berger, *Encyclopedic Dictionary*, p. 432.

proviso of use of this money or these fungibles was part of the contract, it became legally a loan made by the depositor to the bank. The distinction between a *mutuum* loan and the irregular deposit lay in the legal interpretation of the *mutuum* function as that of consumption, the deposit function as that of use.[8]

Security deposits also existed in the Middle Ages as they do today in the safety deposit vault functions of banks. The security deposit was legally in Roman law a *depositum regolare* or regular deposit, which entailed no use of the objects or money deposited on the part of the bank and required the return "on demand" of the exact same objects with all "proceeds and accessories." [9] Philippe Wolff noted an evolution in the connotation of the regular deposit: from that of simple security placed in safekeeping with changers, "deposits had become transferable rights over a certain sum of money." [10] Changers invested part of the funds conveyed to them in this fashion. Wolff dated this evolution to the twelfth century in Genoa, to the thirteenth century in the Low Countries.[11] The deposit banks of medieval changers and merchant-bankers were the fruits of this evolution.

In all only twenty-four contracts of deposit have survived in the Montpellier evidence. This survival rate is less impressive than that which Philippe Wolff found in the Toulousain documents.[12] In both Toulouse and Montpellier, investigation of deposit banking is hindered by the lack of survival of deposit account books, especially those of changers.[13] In the Montpellier evidence as in that of Toulouse, not only changers accepted deposits but others did so – merchants, jurists, women, foreign merchants, friars, and institutions such as local *caritas* associations.[14]

The deposit function is the most difficult banking practice to trace in Montpellier before 1350.[15] The contract of *depositum* here as elsewhere in the Mediterranean world was present in several forms. The most primitive was a simple act of custody of an object or a sum of money. More sophisticated forms involved the use of deposited assets by the recipient and the payment of interest to the depositor.[16] Merchants and changers of Montpellier were the most frequent

[8] See the comments by P.-L. Malausséna, *La vie en Provence orientale*, pp. 217-218. See also, P. Ourliac et J. de Malafosse, 1, *Les obligations*, pp. 254-258.

[9] A. Berger, *Encyclopedic Dictionary*, p. 432.

[10] P. Wolff, *Commerces et marchands de Toulouse*, p. 381: "les dépôts étaient devenus des droits transférables sur une certaine somme d'argent."

[11] *Ibid.*

[12] P. Wolff, *Commerces et marchands de Toulouse*, p. 381.

[13] *Ibid.*, pp. 383-384. It is to be regretted that no account book on the order of the remarkable journal of Lippo di Fede del Sega has survived. On the latter see Charles de la Roncière, *Un changeur florentin du Trecento: Lippo di Fede del Sega (1285 env.-1363 env.)* (Paris, 1973).

[14] See the examples below.

[15] R. S. Lopez and I. W. Raymond, *Medieval Trade*, p. 212, offer an explanation for the limited remaining evidence of deposits: "By the beginning of the thirteenth century, if not earlier, bank ledgers were accepted as binding evidence in court. This explains why the number of deposit contracts which has come down to us is comparatively small; an entry in a ledger was enough."

[16] On distinctions in deposits, see A. P. Usher, *The Early History of Deposit Banking*, 1: 16ff. On deposit contracts, see R. S. Lopez and I. W. Raymond, *Medieval Trade*, pp. 212-215. The deposit had Roman roots in the *depositum irregolare*. See also A. Berger, *Encyclopedic Dictionary*, p. 432.

recipients of deposits; occasionally retailers and foreigners were the beneficiaries of deposit contracts. The rate of interest was never specified. However, it perhaps fell in the range of the five to ten percent current in fourteenth-century deposit banking and commercial investments.[17] The expansion of credit in the fourteenth century led to a gradual lowering of the interest rate.[18] A variety of formulae were employed in the local deposit contracts. The recipient recognized in a notarial document to the depositor that he or she (the banker) was holding cash or precious items *causa depositi*, *causa custodie*, *causa depositi seu comande* or *causa comande cum custodia*.[19] The duration of a contract might vary from an "on demand" return upon request to several years.

Among acts of *custodia* the safekeeping function of the deposit was pre-eminent. In one case a chest was confided to a Franciscan friar for safekeeping; here it would seem that the concepts of interest and profit were absent.[20] Some ambiguity regarding purpose and notarial terminology persists even in *depositum* contracts. Merchants might employ such contracts as a means of security. For example, Petrus Guersii, the merchant whose *comanda* engagements for Cyprus have been examined in some detail, placed 108 white *besants* of Cyprus *causa depositi* with another merchant of Montpellier on 18 May 1333.[21] The latter was to restore this currency immediately upon request. In September of the same year Guersii recorded his *comanda* contracts for his forthcoming trip.[22] He may have retrieved his *besants* in preparation for this voyage.[23]

In other deposit contracts interest was in all likelihood anticipated. For example, in 1333 the consuls of the changers' *caritas* deposited thirty-one silver *marcs* of Montpellier *causa comande cum custodia* for one year with another changer.[24] Since money changers periodically supplied silver to local mints, in addition to engaging in commercial investments, there was a strong probability that the recipient changer put these funds to profitable use during the year. The

[17] According to Yves Renouard, *Les hommes d'affaires italiens du moyen âge*, p. 243, interest for principal depositors varied from six to ten percent. R. S. Lopez, "Hard Times and Investment in Culture," *The Renaissance. A Symposium* (New York, 1953), pp. 19-32, noted that five to eight percent was a common rate.

[18] Marie-Odile Piquet-Marchal, "Doctrines monétaires et conjoncture aux XIVe et XVe siècles," *Revue internationale de l'histoire de la banque* 4 (1971), 373-374.

[19] See the comparable findings of P. Wolff, regarding formulae in Toulouse, *Commerces et marchands de Toulouse*, p. 38, n. 1-3. For his analysis of deposits, see pp. 381-384.

[20] A. D. Hérault, II E 95/369, J. Holanie, f. 20v.

[21] A. D. Hérault, II E 95/369, J. Holanie, f. 38r.

[22] See Chapter 1, "Investment in Business Partnerships."

[23] For additional examples of this type of *depositum* contract, see A. D. Hérault, II E 95/369, J. Holanie, f. 63v, for the deposit of a quantity of salt for two years. In II E 95/372, J. Holanie *et al.*, f. 36r, for the deposit of Florentine florins which technically did not qualify as legal tender in Montpellier.

[24] A. D. Hérault, II E 95/369, J. Holanie, f. 8v. The *marc* of Montpellier weighed 239.126 grams, that of Troyes 244.753 grams. In another act of greater ambiguity of function consuls of the *caritas* of mercers acknowledged holding *causa custodie seu garde* on 19 June 1343, nine ounces and eighteen *denarii* of gold (*marc* of Troyes) which they promised to return on Ascension Day in May. They were joined by a *fidejussor*. The intent of this deposit may have been simple safekeeping, but the possibility of use of the funds for investment and profit cannot be excluded. (A. D. Hérault, II E 95/372, J. Holanie *et al.*, f. 42v).

mid 1330s was an era of silver shortages which made such stores particularly valuable.[25]

The profit motive underlying some deposit receipts was clearly evident on 7 November 1293, when Jacobus and Petrus de Crusolis, merchants of Montpellier, recognized the acceptance at their changers' table in Toulouse of 6700 *l. t.* from the bishop of Toulouse.[26] The Crusolis were to hold this money for a term of two years using it for their profit and their risk. No doubt the bishop expected a return from the money thus placed at the disposal of businessmen. On another occasion the Crusolis acquitted a representative of the abbot of the monastery of Montmajor for the payment of a debt contracted ten years before. It was not uncommon for merchants to have such dealings with members of the higher clergy. In late thirteenth-century Perpignan, R. W. Emery noted that the merchant Arnaldus de Codaleto held funds of the bishop of Elne on deposit and had deposit dealings with members of the cathedral chapter.[27] Codaleto also accepted deposits from other persons as a means of increasing his operating capital.[28]

Depositors with the Crusolis may, in fact, have realized a very limited return since the latter were having trouble with their creditors as early as December 1294. At that time the Crusolis obtained from the king of France a safe conduct valid until early January 1295, to permit negotiations over their debts.[29] By April 1295, they were attempting to collect credits owed them in connection with trade at the Champagne fairs.[30] In the same month they were themselves pursued for debts by the guards of the fairs on behalf of another merchant.[31] Deposit banking was only one of a variety of commercial and financial activities of the Crusolis. If other deposits which they received reached the level of that of the bishop, they may have financed some of their trade in Champagne and in Montpellier through such sources of capital.

Another case of deposit banking involved the Salas family of changers. In 1293 Bernardus Salas recognized before the notary Grimaudi that he owed his sister, the widow of a furrier, 200 *l. melg.* (182 *l. t.*) held on deposit and guaranteed by the obligation of all his goods with the exception of a silver goblet and a silk blanket which he had from his sister.[32] In December 1329 and January 1330, a

[25] J. B. Henneman, *Royal Taxation in Fourteenth-Century France*, pp. 336-339, cited the closing of the mints from March 1335 to February 1337. R.-H. Bautier, "L'Or et l'argent en Occident de la fin du XIIIe siècle au début du XIVe siècle," *Académie des Inscriptions et Belles Lettres, Comptes rendus* (1951), 169-170, isolated three periods of silver shortages for the royal mints of the first half of the fourteenth century: 1308-1314, October 1329-September 1330, March 1334-February 1336.

[26] A. M. Montpellier, II 1, J. Grimaudi, f. 27v.

[27] R. W. Emery, *The Jews of Perpignan*, pp. 122-123.

[28] *Ibid.*, p. 119.

[29] Eugène Martin-Chabot, *Les archives de la Cour des Comptes, Aides et Finances de Montpellier. Avec un essai de restitution des premiers registres de la sénéchaussée*, Bibliothèque de la Faculté des Lettres de l'Université de Paris, 22 (Paris, 1907), no. 215, f. 60, pp. 38-39.

[30] *Ibid.*, no. 213, ff. 56v-58r, p. 38.

[31] *Ibid.*, no. 214, f. 58r, p. 38.

[32] A. M. Montpellier, II 1, J. Grimaudi, f. 37v.

Bernardus Salas, the same changer or perhaps a descendant, received a total of 134 *marcs* at the weight of St. Louis (presumably *marcs* of Troyes) in deposit from a jurist of Montpellier. Salas was to reimburse the jurist in money *de Valoys* with each *valoys* quoted at two *deniers* and one *obole*. On 5 June 1332, this obligation was transformed into a *comanda* and deposit, *causa depositi seu comande*.[33] It was specifically stated that a return of half of the profits was expected with the reimbursement of the principal. The productive function of these deposits was thus assured. Also suggested in these acts was the money changer's role in converting sums from one coinage to another.

Late thirteenth-century Perpignan witnessed the same sort of terminology in contracts termed *in deposito sive comanda nomine societatis*. In this fashion, as R. W. Emery has shown, the merchant Arnaldus de Codaleto deposited large sums with merchants for investment in trade on land or on sea on several occasions. R. W. Emery also noted that Jews of Perpignan made deposits with Christians and Christians with Jews. In the former instance, he suggested that Christians might be acting as a "dummy creditor" to facilitate interest-loans between Jews, a practice which Jewish law prohibited.[34] Such a practice is not documented in Montpellier.

Deposits were accepted by changers who traditionally had their tables located around the church of Nôtre-Dame-des-Tables.[35] For example, on 11 March 1294, Nicholas de Sancto Egidio rented a *mensam nummulariam*, table and shop *in trapezetis* next to another changer's table.[36] An indirect reference to deposits at the changers' tables is preserved in an act of procuration of 16 December 1302.[37] A draper named a procurator to recover all credits due to him and his late father; the sum thus assembled was to be deposited at the *tabula nummularia* of the Alamandini brothers, associated changers and apothecaries, who shipped spices to Paris and participated in a circuit of foreign exchange from Genoa to the Champagne fairs.[38]

Among the specialists of medieval finance, money changers were the most closely associated with deposit banking. The changers' profession had been of importance in the south of France since at least the twelfth century. A remarkable list of twelfth-century changers (about one hundred and thirty) occurs at the end

[33] A. D. Hérault, II E 95/370, J. Holanie, ff. 87v-88r.

[34] R. W. Emery, *The Jews of Perpignan*, Appendix 4: Documents, nos. 142 and 143, pp. 192-193, for examples, and text pp. 117-118, on Codaleto. Regarding Jews' deposits with Christians, see pp. 35 and 69-71.

[35] Louise Guiraud, "Recherches topographiques sur Montpellier au moyen âge," *Mem. soc. arch. Mplr.*, 2nd ser., 1 (1899), pp. 115-116.

[36] A. M. Montpellier, II 1, J. Grimaudi, f. 88v.

[37] A. M. Montpellier, II 2, J. Grimaudi, f. 60v.

[38] On the terminology of the changer's table, see R. S. Lopez, *La prima crisi*, p. 26.

A. M. Montpellier, II 1, J. Grimaudi, ff. 4v, 15r and 15v. See also Renée Doehaerd, *Les relations commerciales entre Gênes, la Belgique et l'Outremont d'après les archives notariales génoises aux XIIIe et XIVe siècles*, 3 (Brussels, Rome, 1941), acts 1658, 1669 and 1670.

of the statutes granted by the count of Toulouse to the money changers of Saint-Gilles.[39] These statutes addressed the fashion in which the changers of Saint-Gilles were to deal with pilgrims on the road to Santiago de Compostella. The proximity of Saint-Gilles to Montpellier and the presence in Montpellier of a pilgrimage church dedicated to Nôtre-Dame around which the changers of Montpellier had their tables render plausible some early influence from the financial center of Saint-Gilles on that of Montpellier. Genoese interest in both towns may have facilitated the cross-fertilization of financial development.[40] The presence of the mint of Melgueil in the proximity of Montpellier further contributed to its emergence as a center of finance.[41]

The profession of changer was among the most prestigious in Montpellier in the period 1293-1348. The first two consuls in the hierarchy of twelve town consuls were in most years changers.[42] The profession of changer counted a considerable number of adherents who may, as in the case of the Alamandini, have exercised several other business functions. This business versatility was not uncommon among medieval financiers. The changers of Lyon, studied by Michèle Bonnet for the period 1350-1450, showed a tendency to exercise more than one profession.[43] In Montpellier, professional designations were still flexible at the mid-fourteenth century.[44]

The average number of changers noted in the notarial registers was nineteen, but this figure rose as high as forty-two in 1342.[45] In a study of changers of the kingdom of France under Louis XI, Robert Favreau listed Montpellier among towns of the late fifteenth century with fewer than ten changers.[46] The numbers of adherents to the financial profession had thus declined with the decrease in

[39] See A. Teulet, *Layettes*, 1: 119-October 1178: Statutum quo vicarius Tolosani comitis declarat quomodo cambiatores S. Egidii cum romeis agere debeant." See the publication of excerpts drawn from the original document of the Archives Nationales J. 304, Toulouse, II, no. 16 in A. Gouron, *La réglementation des métiers en Languedoc au moyen âge* (Geneva, Paris, 1958), pp. 48-49, nn.

[40] See Chapter 1, "Investment in Business Partnerships."

[41] See Appendix 2, "Monetary Problems," for a brief history of the mint.

[42] *Le Petit Thalamus*, pp. 98-100, for the hierarchy established in 1252. A. Gouron, *La réglementation des métiers en Languedoc au moyen âge*, discussed the municipal election procedures, pp. 56ff. It is interesting to note that in the description of a parade formation in Montpellier in the mid-fourteenth century, the silversmiths, scarlet drapers, changers and pepperers led the procession of town trades. See Gouron, p. 268. The first two consuls were chosen by lot from nine money changers and one pepperer.

[43] Michèle Bonnet, "Les changeurs lyonnais au moyen âge (1350-1450)," *Revue historique* 249 (1973), 235-352.

[44] A. Gouron, *La réglementation des métiers*, p. 283.

[45] See Reyerson, "Commerce and Society in Montpellier," 2, Appendix 3, "Demographic Tables," pp. 135-143 for a breakdown by notarial register of changers, and the other urban professions and trades. The largest number of merchants recorded in any one register was one hundred fifty-two, but the profession of merchant was much less specialized than that of changer. Pepperers were recorded in numbers comparable to changers and there were, in relative terms, fewer silk merchants, grain merchants, spice merchants, apothecaries and *canabasserii* noted. Only mercers and drapers among prestigious trades were present in numbers greater than those of the changers.

[46] Robert Favreaux, "Les changeurs du royaume de France sous le règne de Louis XI," *Bibliothèque de l'École des Chartes* 122 (1964), pp. 216-251.

Montpellier's population in the late Middle Ages. It is noteworthy, however, that by the date of the reign of Louis XI (1461-1483), there were only five towns in France which had over thirty changers. In the course of the fourteenth and fifteenth centuries the king of France had come to assert greater control over the changers' profession through licensing of their activities.

In 1342 the changers' profession of Montpellier drew up its statutes of organization.[47] The only regulation regarding incoming members was the obligation of any individual installing a new changer's table to pay 20 *s.* to the changers' *caritas*. The changers in their statutes defended themselves against all accusations of monopoly and illicit activities and against any usurpations of rights belonging to the king of Majorca, the bishop of Maguelone and the king of France. Such a defensive posture may have resulted from the involvement of Montpellier changers in the illicit export of silver bullion to Genoa and to Barcelona in the early years of the fourteenth century.[48] The statutes enregistered contain conventional clauses consistent with the incorporation of such a trade. Each changer owed 5 *s.* a year to the *caritas*. Attendance at funerals of colleagues and their spouses was required. Changers were obliged to submit to consular inspections. Apprentice changers owed contributions to the *caritas* as well. A competent changer was to be elected to arbitrate disputes; a graduated percentage of the sums involved in the disputes was to be contributed to the *caritas*. Visits to sick colleagues were encouraged, and the visitors were to exhort the sick member to make a legacy to the chandelier which the changers maintained in the church of Nôtre-Dame-des-Tables. Any changer failing to observe the regulations of the statutes was to be deprived of all his prerogatives and labelled a rebel in the consular registers. The changers pledged to follow the letter of the statutes, and the consuls of the town duly approved the statutes.

Apprenticeship in the changers' profession was the most active branch of career training recorded in the extant evidence.[49] Changers' apprentices were recruited from throughout the Midi. Moreover, the extended families of most local changers included members who were international merchants, apothecaries, pepperers, *canabasserii*, silk merchants, grain merchants, and mercers, the most prominent local business professions.

Changers of Montpellier were often engaged in international trade. On 13 April 1336, Hugo de Vilari and Jacobus Valaranga, changers, sent 1141 *l. t.* invested in saffron and woolen cloth of France to the Byzantine Empire in a *comanda* investment confided to a merchant of Figeac.[50] Vilari sent another 50 *l. t.* invested

[47] A. M. Montpellier, II 3, J. Laurentii, ff. 52r-55v.

[48] Marc Bompaire, "L'Atelier monétaire royal de Montpellier," has a long appendix on the prosecution of such abuses by the changers and other prominent inhabitants of Montpellier in 1322. See v. 2, Notes, Pièce justificative no. 1, pp. 1-10. R. H. Bautier referred to these problems in "L'Or et l'argent en Occident de la fin du XIIIe siècle au début du XIVe siècle," *Académie des Inscriptions et Belles Lettres, Comptes-Rendus* (1951), 169-174.

[49] See the discussion in my article, "Patterns of Population Attraction and Mobility," pp. 272-273.

[50] A. D. Hérault, II E 95/370, J. Holanie, f. 12r. Another changer, Symon de Sancto Egidio, also invested in trade with the Byzantine Empire. See A. D. Hérault, II E 95/371, J. Holanie, f. 12v and 13r.

in local woolen cloths to Salerno with Pons Alamandini, merchant, his *comanda* partner.[51] The Levant trade might be a joint venture among changers. In 1342 Bremundus Fabri, changer, acquitted Jacobus de Valaranga, Johannes de Calvinhaco and Johannes de Crusolis, changers and consuls of the changers' *caritas*, for a sum, 28.6 *l. t.* which they had invested *causa comande* in a voyage to Cyprus, for the probable purpose of expanding the endowment of the charitable organization.[52] Changers might engage in business ventures with individuals outside their trade. In 1342 the changer Petrus de Bello Podio established a *societas* with an innkeeper of Montpellier, the former investing 100 l., the latter 50 *l. t.*[53] The partnership provided for the support of two apprentices in the house of the changer. Profits were to be divided in a two-thirds/one-third split between the changer and the innkeeper respectively.

The lending operations of changers such as those of the de Sancto Michaele brothers have been examined in the Chapter "Loans." Table 1 of "Loans" shows their participation among non-Jewish lenders at 7.4%. They made large loans probably destined to finance business ventures and small consumer loans. They also borrowed money, perhaps acquiring additional lending capital in this fashion.

While the involvement of Montpellier changers in exchange contracts passed in Montpellier cannot be demonstrated from the surviving evidence, the Alamandini, alternatively termed changers and apothecaries, and the Bordelis, changers, were borrowing by exchange in Genoa for repayment at the Champagne fairs in the early fourteenth century.[54] In Montpellier professional designations remained flexible until the mid-fourteenth century.[55] The Crusolis, witnessed above, could be designated as merchants while maintaining changers' tables. There is no indication in Montpellier that deposit banking was a separate province of the changers or that changers did not participate in foreign exchange operations, a natural complement to their interest in international trade.

The changers of Montpellier were entrusted with the policing of monetary circulation. They complained on occasion about the receipt of forbidden coins by local businessmen.[56] They oversaw the rates of exchange of moneys.[57] They responded to royal orders to transport money and objects of precious metal to the

[51] A. D. Hérault, II E 95/371, J. Holanie, f. 85r.

[52] A. M. Montpellier, II 3, J. Laurentii, f. 71r.

[53] A. D. Hérault, II E 95/371, J. Holanie, f. 123r.

[54] See Ch. 5, "Foreign Exchange," n. 89. Raymond de Roover's more limited assessment of changers' activities is thus not borne out in the case of Montpellier.

In one local operation regarding exchange the participation of a foreign changer can be shown. See A. D. Hérault, II E 95/370, J. Holanie, ff. 85v-89v. On 8 October 1333, merchants of Minorca received an acquittal in Montpellier from the *mancipus* and *negociorum gestor* of a changer of Lerida for 500 gold *réaux* owed by exchange in Minorca.

[55] See A. Gouron, *La réglementation des métiers en Languedoc au moyen âge* (Geneva, Paris, 1958), pp. 179 and 282-283.

[56] See for example, A. M. Montpellier, *Grand Chartrier*, Louvet no. 3010.

[57] *Ibid.*

mints.[58] Sometimes they too fell victim to abuse regarding traffic in foreign money.[59]

The Montpellier changers were jealous of their prerogatives. In October 1342, changers appeared before the notary Holanie to empower procurators to negotiate an exemption for the changers from the levy of a royal hearth tax on notaries, royal servants, brokers and changers in the *sénéchaussée* of Beaucaire and Nîmes. This order was being implemented by Jean de Marigny, bishop of Beauvais and royal lieutenant in Languedoc. Changers were assimilated here with fiscally privileged groups.[60]

Changers of Montpellier may have overseen and indeed participated in the holding of deposits connected with litigation as the changers did in Toulouse.[61] Upon the occasion of an annulment of a real estate sale, a changer, Johannes de Fantaneis, witnessed the two acts described below. The first document involved the agreement of Maria, wife of Boninus de Meldeo, merchant and immigrant from Novara, to an annulment of a sale of real estate made to her by a *domicellus* of the diocese of Maguelone. On 4 October 1333, Maria renounced the *Senatus-consultum Velleianum* and accepted the annulment contingent upon the restoration of the purchase price of 20 *l. t.*[62] On the same day in a subsequent act the *domicellus* confirmed having given 20 *l. t.* in deposit to a scribe of the court who transferred it to a *legum doctor* again in deposit (*causa depositi*) to be paid to Maria de Meldeo on the *domicellus'* behalf.[63]

That changers be involved in litigation concerning indebtedness would not be surprising, given the variety of their activities and the complexities of matters of debt. The extensive indebtedness revealed in the credit operations examined heretofore deserves further consideration. The notarial registers of Montpellier are full of allusions to the difficulties of recovery of debts from recalcitrant debtors. This evidence preserves records of partial payments of debts and of prolongations of debt terms.[64] There was practical justification for the clauses of protection accorded creditors in debt contracts.

According to the Montpellier statutes of 1204, the creditor might proceed against the person of the debtor and against his or her goods, once a request for reimbursement of debts had been formulated before the *bayle's* court.[65] The

[58] A. M. Montpellier, *Grand Chartrier*, Louvet nos. 3326 and 439. On the delivery of precious metals to mints by the changers, see the comments of Marc Bompaire, "L'Atelier monétaire royal de Montpellier," pp. 167-179.

[59] A. M. Montpellier, *Grand Chartrier*, Louvet no. 415, for example.

[60] See A. D. Hérault, II E 95/371, J. Holanie, ff. 126v-127v. See also J. B. Henneman, *Royal Taxation in Fourteenth Century France*, pp. 162 and 311-312.

[61] P. Wolff, *Commerces et marchands de Toulouse*, p. 382.

[62] A. D. Hérault, II E 95/369, J. Holanie, f. 82v.

[63] A. D. Hérault, II E 95/369, J. Holanie, f. 83r.

[64] On old debts and new debts of the Jews of Montpellier, see R. W. Emery, *The Jews of Perpignan*, Appendix 3, p. 131. On debt prolongation in Provence, see P.-L. Malausséna, *La vie en Provence orientale*, pp. 225-229.

[65] P. Tisset, "Placentin et son enseignement à Montpellier," p. 83.

creditor could seize the debtor bodily in the case of non-payment of obligations or in the event that the debtor attempted to flee.[66] The creditor was authorized to imprison the debtor in chains with a bread and water diet until satisfaction had been obtained.[67] The use of personal effects and of property as collateral surrendered by the debtor to the creditor was governed by the statutes of 1204.[68] Provided that the debtor had been duly notified and had refused to reimburse his or her debt, the sale of collateral of personal effects was authorized after one year, of real property after three years.

The harsh measures of personal imprisonment of debtor by creditor gave way over time to more refined legal procedures directed against the goods of the debtor.[69] The debtor might obligate himself or herself in person and in goods using the general legal obligation of *omnium bonorum* which furnished the creditor with a means of recourse for the recovery of debts.[70] According to the statutes of 1205, the debtor's goods were seized until he furnished satisfaction and a *fidejussor* to stand surety for him.[71] Failing the personal surety and sufficient possessions, the debtor was at the mercy of the court. Such strictures upon the debtor were not extended to his family or to the *fidejussor*.[72] Further refinement of actions against the debtor was provided in consular statutes of 1212, 1221 and 1223.[73] By the end of the thirteenth century, the *bayle*'s court had the power to order an execution of sale (a forced public sale) of the debtor's property.[74] The obligation of *omnium bonorum* provided the creditor with guarantees of recovery of his assets and permitted the debtor to avoid imprisonment for debts.[75]

A practical illustration of this legal procedure regarding debts was preserved in the notarial register of Johannes Grimaudi of 1301-1302. Grimaudi acted, on occasion, as the notary of the court of the *bayle* in Montpellier. On 30 March 1302, Petrus Corrigerii, pepperer, acting for himself and for other creditors, the changer Guillelmus Ceruti, the merchant B. de Maburia and R. de Montaniaco who represented the heirs of Johannes de Asperis, requested before the court of the *bayle* a sentence of execution for debt against the property of one Johannes Ceruti, merchant, "secundum formam statutorum novorum Montispessulani." [76]

[66] *Ibid.* See *Layettes*, 1, article 32, p. 258. See also article 16, p. 257.

[67] See P. Tisset, "Placentin et son enseignement à Montpellier," p. 83. See also *Layettes*, 1, article 35, p. 259.

[68] See my discussion in "Les opérations de crédit."

[69] See P. Tisset, "Placentin et son enseignement à Montpellier," p. 83.

[70] See P. Bouges, "La pratique contractuelle," 1: 62-66 for comments on the obligation *omnium bonorum*.

[71] P. Tisset, "Placentin et son enseignement à Montpellier," p. 83.

[72] *Ibid.*

[73] On the statutes of Montpellier, see André Gouron, "La *potestas statuendi* dans le droit coutumier montpelliérain du treizième siècle," *Diritto comune e diritti locali nella storia dell'Europa. Atti del Convegno di Varenna* (12-15 June 1979) (Milan, 1980), pp. 95-118.

[74] See below for an example.

[75] For the evolution of this institution in medieval jurisprudence, see Michel Lacave, "Recherches sur la *cessio bonorum* dans le droit méridional à la fin du moyen âge," *Recueil*, fasc. 9, *Mélanges Roger Aubenas* (Montpellier, 1974), pp. 443-460.

[76] A. M. Montpellier, II 2, J. Grimaudi, ff. 98v, 127r.

The statutes in question were those of 1223. In the case of a *cessio bonorum* for which the pepperer Corrigerii had instituted legal procedures, the statutes provided for a six-week delay to enable the debtor to sell goods. If the debtor failed to do so, the court undertook to arrange a sale within two weeks under the supervision of a court-appointed procurator.[77] In the Ceruti case the creditors, cited above, produced two obligations owed by Ceruti: 155 *l.* 12 s. 8 *d. melg.* due Guillelmus Ceruti and 221 *l.* 22 *d. melg.* due Maburia and Asperis. The *bayle* accorded two weeks to the procurator of Johannes Ceruti for his defense. Since the extension of six weeks accorded to Ceruti by his creditors for the sale of goods had almost elapsed, the court assigned him a curator in the person of a lawyer of the court to this end. The provisions of the judical procedure of 1223 were clearly in operation here.[78]

These legal procedures outlined in debt litigation in Montpellier had their counterparts elsewhere in the south of France. Similar practices of the debtor offering as collateral goods which might be sold at the elapse of a specific term of debt were noted by Philippe Wolff in Toulouse.[79] The *capitouls* of Toulouse, members of the local town government, authorized action first against the personal effects and then against the real property of a debtor.[80] Compromise with at least a partial reimbursement usually resolved cases of imprisonment for debt.[81] Wolff found evidence of frequent excommunication for debts before ecclesiastical tribunals, a practice which has not been noted in the extant notarial registers of Montpellier.[82]

In his examination of the notarial registers of Grasse, P.-L. Malausséna discerned procedures of cession of goods, seizure of the person of the debtor and imprisonment.[83] He also noted the practice of excommunication for debts in eastern Provence. He suggested that the application of this measure of excommunication was most often employed in the case of an ecclesiastical debtor.[84]

In addition to collateral of personal effects or property, a *fidejussor* or personal surety might be associated with the debtor as a guarantor of good faith and as

[77] M. Lacave, "Recherches sur la *cessio bonorum*," p. 447, saw the evolution of this procedure as a means for the debtor to avoid prison.

[78] See *Layettes*, 2: 7, for the passage of the statutes of 1223 implied: *De solutione debitorum*: "Et si debitor cessaverit solvere infra dictos xv. dies, curia capiat tantum de bonis illius mobilibus vel se moventibus, vel nominibus liquidis et bonis, juxta electionem creditoris (cod. justa electione creditoris), que valeant decimam partem plus debito. Que si non suficiant, ultimo loco de [non] mobilibus supleantur secundum arbitrium curie. Que bona tradantur vel quasi tradantur jure pignoris creditori; et admoneatur debitor a curia ut, infra vi. septimanas proximas conputandas post dictorum xv. dierum lapsum, res illas vendat. Quod si non fecerit, curia faciat res illas vendi infra alios xv. dies proximos per procuratorem ad hoc a curia constitutum; ..."

[79] P. Wolff, *Commerces et marchands de Toulouse*, p. 372 ff.

[80] *Ibid.*, p. 374.

[81] *Ibid.*, p. 375.

[82] *Ibid.*

[83] P.-L. Malausséna, *La vie en Provence orientale*, p. 228.

[84] *Ibid.*, p. 229.

security for a debt.[85] The *fidejussor* obligated person and possessions and promised solidarity with the debtor for the responsibility of the whole debt.[86] Occasionally, a separate act established the obligations of the *fidejussor*.[87] The institution of *fidejussor* was widely used, not only in recognitions of debt but in commercial and property transactions such as loans, exchange transactions, rentals and pledges of apprenticeship.[88]

The statutes of 1204 in Montpellier and those of other *consuetudines* of the south of France such as Perpignan and Carcassonne required the *fidejussor* to pay, in accordance with his engagement as surety without the protection of Roman law remedies.[89] The institution of *fidejussor* was invoked in Montpellier to assure the debtor's attendance in court when necessary.[90] The obligations of the *fidejussor* in Montpellier did not pass to heirs.[91]

The principal debtor could record his desire to protect the *fidejussor* from any damages which might be incurred as a result of his joint obligation.[92] Thus, in November 1342, two silversmiths, father and son, acknowledged that a third party had become their *fidejussor* in regard to a debt owed another silversmith according to an arbitrated decision; they stated that they would reimburse any damages which the *fidejussor* suffered.[93] The promise of indemnification of a *fidejussor* on the part of the principal debtor was a commonly noted practice in Toulouse and in Grasse.[94] The *fidejussor* in the south of France might be a business colleague, a relative, perhaps a wife or a husband.[95]

It happened in business practice that the *fidejussor* played an active role in the financial affairs of his principal. In 1336 the *canabasserius* Petrus de Vineriis arranged the refinancing of his debts over a period of eight years following an amiable composition with his creditors, arbitrated by an apothecary, another *canabasserius* and a merchant.[96] For reasons which were not related in the act, Vineriis entrusted the administration of repayment to his *fidejussor*, Symon de Sancto Egidio, *canabasserius*, whose activities have left an impressive record in

[85] For example, A. D. Hérault, II E 95/372, J. Holanie, ff. 19v and 47r. See also P. Bouges, "La pratique contractuelle," 1: 66.

[86] For background on the institution of *fidejussor*, see Mireille Castaing-Sicard, *Les contrats dans le très ancien droit toulousain*, pp. 379-403.

[87] For example, A. D. Hérault, II E 95/371, J. Holanie, f. 103r and II E 95/369, J. Holanie, ff. 19r and 30v.

[88] A. D. Hérault, II E 95/369, J. Holanie, ff. 15r, 85r-85v; II E 95/370, J. Holanie, f. 21r and II E 95/372, J. Holanie, f. 19r for examples.

[89] *Layettes*, 1, articles 13, 72 and 73. See also P. Tisset, "Placentin et l'enseignement à Montpellier," p. 82.

[90] P. Tisset, "Placentin et l'enseignement à Montpellier," p. 82.

[91] *Ibid.*

[92] A. D. Hérault, II E 95/369, J. Holanie, f. 47r.

[93] A. D. Hérault, II E 95/371, J. Holanie, f. 148v.

[94] P.-L. Malausséna, *La vie en Provence orientale*, pp. 225-227, and P. Wolff, *Commerces et marchands de Toulouse*, pp. 372-373.

[95] P.-L. Malausséna, *La vie en Provence orientale*, p. 227.

[96] A. D. Hérault, II E 95/370, J. Holanie, f. 49ff.

Montpellier. Vineriis provided Sancto Egidio with linen, woolen cloths, almonds and salted meat worth a total of 580 *l. t.* It was Symon's responsibility to obtain as much profit from this merchandise capital as possible in order to make annual payments to eighteen creditors including pepperers, mercers, drapers, changers, *canabasserii*, *jurisperiti* and merchants of Montpellier, as well as men of Mâcon, Le Puy and Lyon. Vineriis cancelled his old obligations before the notary according to the terms of arbitration and established in almost every instance new recognitions of debt. He also obtained two loans worth 35 *l. t.* and 12 *l.* 14 *s.* 8 *d. t.* from a *jurisperitus*, a merchant and a changer.[97] In 1342, although Petrus de Vineriis was since deceased, Symon de Sancto Egidio was still administering the repayment of his debts.[98] The record of Vineriis' indebtedness reveals the potential responsibility of the *fidejussor* who was probably tied in this case by professional solidarity and personal friendship to the debtor.

There were several means available to facilitate the recovery of debts. The creditor might resort to the appointment of a third party as procurator or legal representative to act on his behalf to recover debts.[99] The delegation of authority through procuration was recorded in three hundred sixty-eight surviving acts.[100] The majority of these appointments did not include the specific pretext for the nomination. However, the mandate of the procuration might be directed to the recovery of all credits or of specific outstanding credits. For example, on 3 November 1343, the pepperer Egidius Dalmassii designated two other pepperers to pursue the reimbursement of credits owed to him.[101] On 20 January 1344, Johannes Naturalis, another pepperer, acting for himself and another associate, named a cloth finisher of Toulouse to be his procurator to receive 24.4 *l. t.* owed in gold *denarii* from three Toulousains.[102]

The repayment of debts resulted in some cases in the acquittal of the debtor by the creditor.[103] The settlement of outstanding debts in this fashion might be made *ex causa finalis computi*.[104] A formal acquittal before the notary was at times accompanied by a return to the debtor of the instruments or contracts of debt.[105] Renegotiation of the terms of debt might be necessary to adjust for coinage alterations which could wreak havoc with long-term obligations.[106]

[97] A. D. Hérault, II E 95/370, J. Holanie, ff. 50v and 60v.

[98] A. D. Hérault, II E 95/371, J. Holanie, f. 36v.

[99] On the appointment of third parties to pursue debts in Toulouse, see P. Wolff, *Commerces et marchands de Toulouse*, pp. 378-379. A percentage of the overall credits might be assigned for this service.

[100] See Reyerson, "Commerce and Society in Montpellier," 2, Appendix 1, p. 119.

[101] A. D. Hérault, II E 95/372, J. Holanie *et al.*, f. 112r.

[102] A. D. Hérault, II E 95/372, J. Holanie *et al.*, f. 154r.

[103] A. D. Hérault, II E 95/375, P. de Pena, f. 49r.

[104] A. D. Hérault, II E 95/377, B. Egidii, f. 93v.

[105] Mention of the return of the instruments of debt can be found in II E 95/372, J. Holanie *et al.*, f. 43v and II E 95/375, P. de Pena, f. 76v.

[106] For example, A. D. Hérault, II E 95/371, J. Holanie, f. 8r, specified currency to be used in payment of a debt for grain.

A dispute over debts might lead to a friendly settlement *ex causa amicabilis compositionis*.[107] Debtors and creditors might submit to arbitration before the notary.[108] Failure to respect an arbitrated decision could result in the imposition of a fine on the defaulting party.[109] As the Vineriis case showed, the arbiters were not necessarily legal specialists; Vineriis' debts had been arbitrated by an apothecary, a *canabasserius* and a merchant.[110]

An "amiable composition" might take place before the *bayle*. An accord of 13 November 1301 of this sort involved the agreement of two merchants of Barcelona and a pepperer of Montpellier to terms of payment of 2,383 *l.* current money owed by the pepperer.[111] Within a week 900 *l.* were to be paid in merchandise; then 300 *l.* in cash within two weeks and another 200 *l.* at the feast of St. Hilary in January. The remainder of the debt was due in thirds at the fairs of Lagny, Bar and at the May Fair of Provins.

If measures of compromise proved unsuccessful as a means of arranging a debt settlement, litigation remained as a recourse for the recovery of debts. The tribunals before which debt litigation has been recorded were first and foremost the court of the *bayle* of the king of Majorca in Montpellier. The French *Cour du Petit Scel* and the *Cour des Conventions Royaux* of Nîmes were also debt forums.[112] There is evidence in 1310 in Montpellier of debt litigation before the *officialité* of Maguelone.[113] In Toulouse and Grasse where the procedure of excommunication for debts was invoked on occasion, litigation might pass before ecclesiastical tribunals.[114]

Generally, in regimes of consular government in southern France, the local lord retained extensive powers of justice.[115] In theory, the seigneur of Montpellier – in this case the king of Majorca – controlled the court of the seigneurial quarter, termed the court of the *bayle*.[116] According to the *Consuetudines* of 1204, the court of the *bayle* was endowed with civil, commercial and criminal jurisdiction.[117] In practice the consuls controlled this court since they were granted the right to participate in the choice of the *bayle*.

Although records of commercial litigation are scarce, Johannes Grimaudi preserved a series of judicial decisions of the *bayle*'s court condemning debtors to

[107] As examples, A. D. Hérault, II E 95/370, J. Holanie, ff. 5v, 20v; II E 95/371, J. Holanie, ff. 8r, 93v and 108v.

[108] Changers agreed to arbitration in A. D. Hérault, II E 95/377, B. Egidii, f. 241r.

[109] See n. 135 below.

[110] See n. 96 above.

[111] A. M. Montpellier, II 1, J. Grimaudi, f. 48r.

[112] On the installation of French administration in the south of France, see Robert Michel, *L'Administration royale dans la sénéchaussée de Beaucaire au temps de Saint Louis* (Paris, 1910).

[113] *Cartulaire de Maguelone*, 4, p. 119, act MCCLIX.

[114] See nn. 81 and 84 above.

[115] On consular jurisdiction, see Jean-Marie Carbasse, "Consulats méridionaux et justice criminelle au Moyen Âge," Thèse, Faculté de Droit et des Sciences Économiques de Montpellier – Université de Montpellier – I, 1974.

[116] Details on the court system in the seigneurial quarter of Montpellier can be found in *LIM*, acts CCXXXIX-CCXLIV, pp. 400-407. See also the works of Archibald R. Lewis, Introduction, n. 16 above.

[117] *Layettes*, 1: 225-266.

pay their debts.[118] In most cases no pretext for the debt was cited, although orders of repayment of a loan and of payment of rent due for a house were mentioned.[119] Jews as well as Christians could be condemned to pay debts in the *bayle*'s court.

Jews could be both plaintiffs and defendants in cases which appeared before the *bayle*. On 29 November 1301, the *vice-bayle* of the court sentenced a merchant to pay a debt of 25 *l. t.* to the Jew Vitalis de Mauguio.[120] The merchant owed 8 *l. t.* at the feast of John the Baptist, 9 *l. t.* at Lent and the remainder of the debt at Michaelmas. The condemnation of a Jew to pay a Christian has also been noted. On 14 June 1302, the *bayle* sentenced Crescas den Mascip to pay one B. Garrigas 100 *l. t.* of 300 *l. t.* which Crescas owed to Blanca and Johanna, daughters of the deceased mercer Philippus de Orlhaco, in connection with the purchase of a house.[121] The Orlhaco sisters had borrowed in turn from Garrigas to finance an overseas investment. Finally, debts between Jews were also submitted to the court of the *bayle* for judgment. On 16 August 1301, the *bayle* sentenced the Jew Cresten Cohen to pay 33 *l.* 5 *s. melg.* to Samuel, son of Vinas de Naserena; 14 *l.* 10 *s. melg.* were due at All Saints, the rest on 15 August of the following year.[122] The Jewish litigants submitted here to terms of payment on Christian holidays as did their Christian counterparts.

On occasion the judge indicated the fashion in which a debt was to be liquidated. For example, the *vice-bayle* pronounced a sentence on 5 October 1301 against a goldsmith and his wife who owed 16 *l. t.* to another goldsmith for the purchase of tools of the trade.[123] They were ordered to pay their debt once they had sold the three barrels of wine which they had in their cellar. An inspection of their assets revealed that 4 *s. t.* was still outstanding after the proceeds of the sale had been surrendered.

The tribunal of the *Petit-Scel* had a reputation in commercial litigation throughout the south of France. References to its jurisdiction appeared in the evidence of Toulouse and in that of the Forez.[124] This jurisdiction was frequently invoked in the formal clauses of assurance in debt contracts drawn up in Montpellier, as earlier shown. Its institution in Montpellier was the result of Philip IV's purchase of Montpelliéret in 1293.[125] At numerous sites in Languedoc, the king of France had installed courts, entitled *sceaux aux contrats*, that imitated

[118] A. M. Montpellier, II 2, J. Grimaudi. Some judgments are also mentioned in II 3, J. Laurentii.

[119] A. M. Montpellier, II 2, J. Grimaudi, f. 71v.

[120] A. M. Montpellier, II 2, J. Grimaudi, f. 53v. For another case, see II 2, J. Grimaudi, f. 43v. On the recovery of Jewish debts in Perpignan, see R. W. Emery, *The Jews of Perpignan*, p. 80ff.

[121] A. M. Montpellier, II 2, J. Grimaudi, f. 133r.

[122] A. M. Montpellier, II 2, J. Grimaudi, f. 25v.

[123] A. M. Montpellier, II 2, J. Grimaudi, f. 38v. On the legal personnel of Languedoc, see Joseph R. Strayer, *Les gens de justice du Languedoc sous Philippe le Bel* (Toulouse, 1970).

[124] P. Wolff, *Commerces et marchands de Toulouse*, p. 372 and E. Fournial, *Les villes et l'économie d'échange en Forez*, p. 707.

[125] See André Gouron, "L'Origine du Tribunal du Petit-Scel de Montpellier," *Fédération historique* (Montpellier, 1955), pp. 57-70.

northern ecclesiastical courts which had gained the competence of ratifying contracts through the apposition of a seal.[126]

In the south of France the notarial act continued to stand alone without need for further authentication. However, submission to a voluntary jurisdiction such as the *Petit-Scel* added assurance for the enforcement of obligations carrying its seal and the rapid execution of justice in case of abuse. Before the installation of the *Petit-Scel* there were no courts of voluntary jurisdiction in the *sénéchaussée* of Beaucaire-Nîmes.[127] The first reference to the *Petit-Scel*'s operation came in a letter of Philip IV of 1296 in which he prohibited the pursuit of debtors living in the lands of the bishopric of Maguelone without the notification of the bishop but subjected debtors to the jurisdiction of his seal.[128] In 1302, the submission of a merchant of Montpellier to the king's seal in Montpellier regarding a debt contracted before a local notary is indisputable proof of the court's operation.[129] The submission resulted in the judicial sale of the property of the debtor, Philippus Fortanerii.

In spite of its reputation there remain few records of litigation before the *Petit-Scel*, and the profits of its operation were apparently never very impressive.[130] The procedure of the court, formulated in written form in 1344, was nonetheless of influence as a model for other courts.[131]

The third tribunal mentioned in debt litigation in the notarial registers was the *Cour des Conventions Royaux* in Nîmes.[132] In 1339 Petrus de Bordelis, member of a prominent Montpellier merchant family with business in Italy and at the Champagne fairs, was pursued in justice by over thirty creditors for debts contracted in Champagne. These creditors, most of whom were Italians and especially Lucchese merchants of Montpellier and Nîmes, took their case to the *Cour des Conventions*.[133] Bordelis had taken refuge in the Franciscan monastery in Montpellier for fear of bodily seizure by his creditors.[134]

[126] A. Gouron and Jean Hilaire, "Les 'sceaux' rigoureux du Midi de la France," *Recueil*, fasc. 4 (Montpellier, 1958), 41-77.

[127] *Ibid.*

[128] *Ibid.*, p. 50.

[129] A. M. Montpellier, II 2, J. Grimaudi, f. 72v. In fact, it was necessary for the creditor to seek action from the court of the *bayle* although he held his obligation under the seal of the court of the king of France in Montpelliéret, i.e. the *Petit-Scel*.

[130] A. Gouron and J. Hilaire, "Les 'sceaux' rigoureux," pp. 51-52.

[131] *Ibid.* Some conflicts of jurisdiction between the courts of the French and Majorcan kings in Montpellier arose in the fourteenth century. The Fortanerii case of 1302 demonstrated a creditor's need to have recourse to the court of the *bayle* of the king of Majorca for legal action against the property of a debtor of the Majorcan quarter of the town. In 1321 the king of Majorca and the king of France came to an agreement over the division of profits of the *Petit-Scel*. (See A. D. Hérault, Série A, 4, f. 57r.) To alleviate political conflicts, in 1345 Philip VI released the towns of the kingdom of Majorca from their submission of obligations to the *Petit-Scel*. (See *H.L.*, 10, *preuves*, no. 387).

[132] A. Gouron and J. Hilaire, "Les 'sceaux' rigoureux," p. 60, on this court, which served Italian merchants in particular.

[133] A. D. Hérault, II E 95/375, P. de Pena, f. 124ff. On the Bordelis family activities, see R. Doehaerd, *Les relations commerciales entre Gênes, la Belgique et l'Outremont*, 3, act 1658. See also my forthcoming article, "I lucchesi in Montpellier."

[134] On the issue of refuge from debts in a church, see *Layettes*, 1: 519-520 for the statutes of 1221: "Si pro injuria vel delicto aliquis ad ecclesiam vel domum religionis confugerit, vel a Montepessulano

An agreement, negotiated by the *legum doctor*, Johannes Ysbarre of Lucca, inhabitant of Nîmes and *tutor* of the children of the late Pucchinus Ysbarre, one of Bordelis' creditors, arranged for the safety and freedom of Bordelis for fifteen years in return for his surrender of all business records and credit commitments to facilitate the reimbursement process. The creditors gave assurance of their good faith by agreeing to a 1000 *l. t.* fine if they broke the agreement. They also consented to accept Bordelis' word at face value on the penalty of 306 gold *agneaux* for refusal. For his part, Bordelis promised to reveal all of his debits, credits, possessions, rights and all "salvatasias et res absconsas" which he had *in comanda* or on deposit. In addition, he was to submit all his commercial records, account books and written forms contained in a sealed sack.[135] He guaranteed his good faith by agreeing to a 1000 *l. t.* fine for non-performance.

Beyond local and regional courts, the submission of merchants of Montpellier to other commercial courts has been mentioned earlier. The Crusolis, merchants and changers of Montpellier, were held for debts negotiated under the seal of the warden of the fairs of Champagne.[136] The authority under which debt obligations were established generally determined the court of litigation in the case of disputes over repayment or failure of reimbursement.

Various means of repayment of debts were available to inhabitants of Montpellier and the immediate region. Concessions of the fruits of real property for the time necessary to reimburse an obligation occurred on 6 June 1343, when an inhabitant of Saint-Laurent d'Hierle went before the notary Holanie to cede his share of the fruits and revenues of several mills to his father-in-law, in order to reimburse the latter for expenses incurred in the repair of these mills.[137]

Debts might be repaid through work, perhaps through the performance of the skilled labor of a trade.[138] The transfer of partnership rights could be used as a means of repayment.[139] Sales of real estate rights might be used in repayment of commercial debts.[140] The transfer of credit obligations by a debtor to a creditor was a form of negotiability of credit instruments.

The complexity of the international merchant's credit operations, revealed in the Bordelis and Crusolis proceedings, probably favored the growth of trans-

---

se absentaverit, et inventus alicubi et a curia citatus sive amonitus non venerit infra decem dies, vel non inventus, precone publice clamante ut ad curiam veniat, infra triginta dies curie se non presentaverit, ex publica preconizatione, habito ipso pro legitime citato, pro convicto vel conffesso criminis vel injurie habeatur; et si sententia pecunialiter ferri postuletur a dampnum vel injuriam passo, contra talem absentem, tanquam vere confessum et contumacem, proferatur, super injuria facta, vel delicto et quantitate condempnationis, primo facto sacramento a conquerente, et a judice taxatione premissa; et a tali sententia nemini sit licitum appellare, immo per res et facultates condempnati exsequtioni sententia celeriter demandetur." If a debtor fled into a church and remained for thirty days, he might be declared publicly guilty.

135 A. D. Hérault, II E 95/375, P. de Pena, f. 126r.

136 See above, nn. 29, 30, 31.

137 A. D. Hérault, II E 95/372, J. Holanie *et al.*, f. 34v.

138 A. D. Hérault, II E 95/368, J. Holanie, f. 47v and II E 95/371, J. Holanie, f. 80r.

139 A. D. Hérault, II E 95/369, J. Holanie, f. 43r.

140 A. D. Hérault, II E 95/369, J. Holanie, f. 40r.

ferability of a creditor's rights. These could be transmitted from one person to another in Montpellier as in Toulouse.[141] Seventy acts of cession of rights against debtors have been preserved. A creditor might, in ceding his credit obligations, use them to reimburse an outstanding debt. Cessions of debts to third parties by creditors could also result in the reimbursement of the original creditor for the amount owed. For example, on 5 April 1343, an inhabitant of Montpellier ceded to a mercer all rights and actions against the son of a late shoemaker by reason of 66 *s.* 8 *d.* current money owed in a larger debt of 10 *l. t.* established by an instrument of 26 August 1342.[142] The creditor acknowledged receiving payment of the 66 *s.* 8 *d.* The credit instrument here had become a negotiable instrument.

In cessions of credits the original creditor might seek to obtain his money immediately without awaiting the term of the debt. The liquidation of credits could serve any number of business or personal needs. The new creditor might have greater facility for the collection of the debt.[143] When foreign merchants were involved as debtors, a Montpellier creditor might cede or sell a credit to a foreign colleague of the same locality as that of the debtors.[144]

In cessions of rights against debtors to third parties, the original creditor might make an acquittal on his behalf in favor of the debtor renouncing any further claim to the obligation.[145] The original creditor might further promise the purchaser of the credit to protect the latter from damages in the event that the recovery of the credit obligation proved impossible.[146] Cessions of credits were common practice among foreign merchants and professional financiers.[147] They provided a convenient means of clearing obligations. In spite of the lack of endorsement in the Middle Ages, the cession of credits in towns such as Montpellier and Toulouse offered medieval businessmen flexible means of cancelling obligations.

In ceding a credit to a third party, the creditor might have been willing to take a loss on the original debt and in this sense to discount the credit in favor of the new purchaser. An example will serve to illustrate this process. In 1339, the procurator of a merchant ceded to a foreigner a credit of 8 *l. t.* for grain drawn up on 12 March 1338 (n.s.) when a stronger currency (4/3 times stronger) was in

[141] P. Wolff, *Commerces et marchands de Toulouse*, pp. 377-379.

[142] A. D. Hérault, II E 95/372, J. Holanie *et al.*, f. 9r.

[143] P. Wolff, *Commerces et marchands de Toulouse*, pp. 377-380, discussed various pretexts for the cession of credits in Toulouse. He saw the cession of credit as a means of displacing or obtaining other credit.

[144] A. D. Hérault, II E 95/375, P. de Pena, f. 36v, for an illustration.

[145] See, for example, A. D. Hérault, II E 95/375, P. de Pena, ff. 48v-49r. Ardusso Mutonis, immigrant from Chieri and *burgensis* of Montpellier, ceded all his rights against a cultivator of Montpellier by reason of 100 *s. t.* remaining from two debts of 1332 and 1333 to a moneyer. Mutonis made an acquittal in favor of the cultivator, stating that he was satisfied in the present cession with regard to the cultivator's debts.

[146] See, for example, A. D. Hérault, II E 95/370, J. Holanie, f. 105v and II E 95/369, J. Holanie, f. 16r.

[147] For example, A. D. Hérault, II E 95/372, J. Holanie *et al.*, ff. 51r and 115v regarding the merchant Thomas Hugonis of Huesca, inhabitant of Montpellier and Ardusso Mutonis.

circulation.[148] Acknowledging the receipt of 8 *l. t.* the procurator stated that he would be content with 20 *s.* of the remaining 40 *s.* Here a discount of an original debt seems to have been linked to an alteration of coinage values. In his study of Toulouse Philippe Wolff suggested that the original creditor in cessions of credits might have been willing to take a sacrifice and even derive no benefit at all to avoid the difficulties of debt collection.[149] With regard to an old credit, some financial concession on the part of the creditor may have been necessary. The numerous appointments of procurators suggest that debt recovery was a complex process and a long one, as the Vineriis case revealed. The transferability of credit obligations facilitated the negotiability of assets, contributing to the volume of economic transactions and alleviating problems of coinage circulation.[150]

The extension of credit tested the limits of the medieval banking system. Many precautions were taken to protect the creditor and to provide him with the means of recovering his funds. Compromise, arbitration and litigation were methods of facilitating debt repayment. Procuration was a further device. The deposit contract might also be used in debt recovery operations.

The absence of surviving changers' account books in Montpellier makes it impossible for the historian to learn as much about their deposit banking activities as that known about changers in the Low Countries and in Italy.[151] Concrete proof is lacking for mutual accounts among changers of Montpellier, a facet of operations which would have facilitated transfer banking functions. There remain no records of Montpellier changers employing *scritti di banchi* on behalf of their clients.[152] Yet, given the place of Montpellier as a center of European foreign

[148] A. D. Hérault, II E 95/375, P. de Pena, f. 36v. See also Appendix 2, "Monetary Problems."

[149] P. Wolff, *Commerces et marchands de Toulouse*, p. 378.

[150] The most plentiful evidence on the recovery of debts comes from A. M. Montpellier, II 2, J. Grimaudi, 1301-1302. Elsewhere in the notaries, there were scattered references to debt litigation. See, for example, A. D. Hérault, II E 95/377, B. Egidii, f. 293v regarding litigation over the repayment of a loan.

It is not within the scope of this chapter to explore all the legal ramifications of debt. Compare the disclaimer of P. Wolff, *Commerces et marchands de Toulouse*, p. 372, n. 70. A useful brief treatment of unpaid debts is that of R. S. Lopez and I. R. Raymond, *Medieval Trade in the Mediterranean World*, pp. 278-282; on loan sharks see pp. 273-276; on business failures, pp. 277-302.

[151] The banks of the money changers of Bruges revealed a technical development which overshadowed that recorded in Montpellier. Raymond de Roover found that bank transfers outnumbered cash transactions in the changers' accounts. He identified four main transactions at the Bruges changers' banks: the depositing of money, the withdrawal of funds, the transfer of credit from one account to another at one changer's bank; the same sort of transfer between changers. De Roover noted that all the money changers of Bruges carried accounts with colleagues in the town. Although medieval banks did not issue money, de Roover argued with regard to Bruges that "exchange banks of changers created purchasing power or money as effectively as if they had been granted the privilege of issuing notes." See R. de Roover, *Money, Banking and Credit in Mediaeval Bruges*, pp. 267-272, 321.

A further comparative context for changers is Tuscany. See Thomas Blomquist, "The Castracani Family of Thirteenth-Century Lucca," *Speculum* 46 (1971), 459-476; Charles M. de la Roncière, *Un changeur florentin du Trecento: Lippo di Fede del Sega (1285 environ-1363 environ)* (Paris, 1973).

[152] On *scritti di banchi*, Florence Edler (de Roover), *Glossary of Medieval Terms of Business: Italian Series* (Cambridge, Mass., 1934), pp. 264-265. On bank money, see Reinhold C. Mueller, "The Role of Bank Money in Venice, 1300-1500," *Studi Veneziani* new series, 3 (1979), 47-96.

exchange and the importance of the commercial and deposit banking activities of the local changers, there is no reason to doubt that the changers of Montpellier performed transfer banking functions and extended overdraft credit to their clients.[153] The broad range of financial and commercial activities of the Montpellier changers lends even greater plausibility to their clearinghouse role. However, the early importance of the changers in the south of France and in Montpellier through the mid-fourteenth century did not lead in the Languedocian town to developments in deposit banking comparable to those in Genoa and in Barcelona in the late Middle Ages.[154]

[153] The caveats raised by Philippe Wolff with regard to banking in Toulouse bear repeating in the context of Montpellier. Wolff suggested that if payment by deposit and by transfer of deposits had been a common practice in Toulouse, more trace of such operations would have survived. See P. Wolff, *Commerces et marchands de Toulouse*, pp. 381-384. He asserted, p. 384, "Or c'est seulement dans la mesure où les mêmes dépôts servaient, à concurrence de leur montant et au-delà, à des paiements par virements, tout en étant ailleurs partiellement investis, qu'ils créaient vraiment une monnaie fiduciaire." Wolff concluded that the structure of credit in Toulouse did not depend heavily upon the deposit banking foundation.

[154] A. P. Usher, "Deposit Banking in Barcelona, 1300-1700," *Journal of Economic and Business History* 4 (1931), 125-127; and M. Riu, "Banking and Society in Late Medieval and Early Modern Aragon," in *The Dawn of Modern Banking*, pp. 149-156 on the public bank of Barcelona. See Jacques Heers, *Gênes au XVe siècle. Activité économique et problèmes sociaux* (Paris, 1961), pp. 97ff on the Casa di San Giorgio.

5

Foreign Exchange

Foreign exchange represented another important aspect of medieval banking and finance. Exchange transactions had originally been confined to manual manipulations of local and foreign coinage at the tables of changers.[1] Addressing himself to a changer's table, a medieval merchant could obtain in exchange for foreign coins the funds in local coinage necessary to carry out his commercial purchases and cover his expenses. According to the type of coinage under consideration, the sphere of circulation might vary considerably, just as weights and measures had greater or lesser geographic sway.

To meet the needs of commercial expansion there developed as early as the twelfth century the practice of drafting a contract of exchange which permitted a borrower to obtain credit from a local creditor in the form of local coinage which the borrower promised to repay in another coinage at another geographic location.[2] As the use of exchange contracts proliferated, networks of correspondents evolved. Creditors could direct repayment to colleagues in other towns, and debtors might delegate the performance of reimbursement to their representatives. The mature exchange operation of the Montpellier notarial evidence involved two principals, a debtor and a creditor, in one location, and their respective correspondents in another area.

The notarial contract of exchange, the *instrumentum ex causa cambii*, as it was generally termed, involved the advance of a sum of money in one coinage with the expectation that reimbursement would take place in another coinage at another location and at a later time with some addition to the initial sum to cover

[1] R. S. Lopez has dealt with the early history of banking in a number of works; see, for example, *La prima crisi della banca di Genova, 1250-1259* (Genoa, 1956); "Continuità e adattamento nel medio evo: un millennio di storia delle associazioni di monetieri nell'Europa meridionale," *Studi in onore di Gino Luzzatto* (Milan, 1950), 2: 74-117; R. S. Lopez, "An Aristocracy of Money in the Early Middle Ages," *Speculum* 28 (1953), 1-42.

[2] The classic study of exchange remains that of Raymond de Roover, *L'Évolution de la lettre de change* (Paris, 1953). One can compare A.-E. Sayous, "L'Origine de la lettre de change. Les procédés de crédit et de paiment dans les pays chrétiens de la Méditerranée occidentale," *Revue d'histoire du droit français et étranger* 4th ser., 12 (1933), 66-112. See, finally, the brief but useful summary with examples in R. S. Lopez and I. W. Raymond, *Medieval Trade*, pp. 162-173.

the costs of the extension of credit.[3] The notarial contract of exchange placed emphasis on the credit function of the operation.[4] The contract took the form of a recognition of debt with the formula *confiteor me debere vobis* introducing the transaction; the reason for indebtedness, *ex causa cambii, ratione cambii* or *pro cambio*, then followed.[5] In the exchange contracts of Montpellier the amount advanced in local currency was rarely included. Only the type of currency was mentioned. In contrast, the sum to be reimbursed in foreign currency was specifically quoted.[6] The interest or fee for the exchange was included in the face value of the sum owed. The level of profit was subject to the actual exchange rate between the two currencies at the time of repayment.[7]

The guarantees for the exchange contract were similar to those of the recognition of debt and the loan. *Fidejussores* were at times associated as sureties.[8] A standard formula generally obligated the debtor in the transaction in his person and possessions. The debtor also made an assertion of his good faith.

The classic exchange contract, defined by the scholastics as a *permutatio*, carried risks sufficient, because of coinage fluctuations, to exonerate the profits of the operation from the categorization of usury.[9] No medieval merchant or

[3] The exchange rate envisioned by the principals at the outset was undoubtedly favorable to the creditor. However, at the time of repayment, the rate of exchange might have been altered by changing monetary circumstances.

[4] See Appendix 1, "Documents," for a sample exchange contract.

[5] P. Bouges, "La pratique contractuelle," 1: 193-235, discussed at length the contract of exchange.

[6] Some contracts, in contrast, carried only a sum quoted in local currency, *livres tournois*. See the discussion of "dry" exchange below. It has not proved possible to develop a comparative table for the contracts of exchange, as was done in the case of loans, *comanda* and *societas* contracts. The major obstacle encountered was the multiplicity of currencies quoted, money of account such as *livres melgoriens* and *livres tournois*, florins, pounds of Genoa and Portugal, and real money, such as varieties of Spanish money, of Majorca, Valencia and Barcelona, French *réaux*, *agneaux*, and *écus* and, of course, *deniers tournois*, with the addition of money termed simply current.

[7] For example, A. D. Hérault, II E 95/369, J. Holanie, f. 55r.

[8] See the sample exchange contract in Appendix 1, "Documents."

[9] Raymond de Roover, "*La pensée économique des scolastiques: doctrines et méthodes* (Montreal and Paris, 1971), pp. 27 and 84. De Roover attributed the redefinition of the exchange operation as a *permutatio* to Alexander of Alexandria († 1314). Redefinition, according to de Roover, removed the obstacles to the development of banking by defining the *cambium* as a *permutatio*, thereby eliminating its usurious stigma. Usury was technically "certain" gain and given the fluctuation of exchange rates, exchange transactions were speculative, resulting at times in losses as well as in high profits. See Raymond de Roover, "The Scholastics, Usury and Foreign Exchange," *Economic History Review* 41 (1967), 257-271.

For de Roover the operations of foreign exchange in the Middle Ages gave rise to the origin of modern banking. De Roover believed that the medieval doctrine of usury made it necessary for individuals engaged in business to avoid loan practices, for fear of condemnation, and to find other means of covering their shortfalls of capital and of regulating the debts and credits involved in international trade. See also Raymond de Roover, "New Interpretations of the History of Banking," reprinted in *Business, Banking, and Economic Thought in Late Medieval and Early Modern Europe: Selected Studies of Raymond de Roover*, ed. Julius Kirshner (Chicago and London, 1974), pp. 200-238.

My own examination of usury in Montpellier ("Les opérations de crédit") has led me to believe that the prohibition of usury was no real barrier in lending practices. See Chapter 3, "Loans," for further development of this position. I would argue that de Roover overstated the case for foreign exchange on these grounds. There is no denying, however, that foreign exchange was an important medieval banking function.

changer could satisfactorily predict what the rates of exchange between coinages would be at a particular place at a specific time. The demands of international trade led Montpelliérains to avail themselves of the notarial contract of exchange which provided conveniences beyond those of commercial loan credit on the local market.

Exchange practices showed little evolution in the period under study. The *instrumentum ex causa cambii* persisted in the second half of the fourteenth century, and it was only in the 1350s in Montpellier that the bill of exchange made its appearance.[10] The bill of exchange was an informal holograph letter in contrast to the formal notarial instrument. In Montpellier as in Marseille and Toulouse, such bills appeared later than in Italy and Flanders.[11] The use of the bill of exchange in Barcelona also dated from the end of the fourteenth century, providing a chronological parallel of financial development with Montpellier preceding the emergence of public banking functions in the Catalonian capital in 1401.[12] There is evidence in Montpellier that foreigners used the bill of exchange on the Montpellier market earlier than did Montpelliérains. Thus, as early as 1358, changers of Avignon drafted a bill of exchange in Montpellier scheduling repayment in Bruges.[13] The limited survival of evidence in Montpellier makes an exact chronological dating of the evolution of the bill of exchange impossible.

There are divergences of opinion among scholars regarding the origin of the bill of exchange. Raymond de Roover argued that the letter of notification, which frequently accompanied the notarial instrument of exchange, was the immediate precursor of the bill itself.[14] A.-E. Sayous believed that the letter of notification was, in fact, rarely sent, and that it had no direct link with the notarial

[10] P. Bouges, "La pratique contractuelle," 1: 196ff. Bouges noted that, according to his sampling, the last contract of exchange, *instrumentum ex causa cambii*, was recorded in 1383; he found the first mention of a letter of exchange in 1398. Since there was obviously financial activity in the interim, it seems probable that an exhaustive search in the late fourteenth century, when notarial registers are relatively numerous, would produce letters of the 1380s at least.

[11] For the judgment of the 1955 Congress on Historical Sciences see M. Mollat et al., "L'Économie européenne aux deux derniers siècles du moyen âge." *Relazioni del x Congresso internazionale di Scienze Storiche, Storia del Medioevo*, 3 (Florence, 1955), regarding Marseille and Montpellier, p. 767: "Le change n'évolua pas vers la banque, et la lettre de change, qui n'apparut pas avant 1360, resta d'un usage limité aux seuls gros négociants en rapport avec la place d'Avignon, d'où la banque italienne s'intéressait aux affaires marseillaises, comme elle le fit de Lyon à la fin du xvème siècle." J. Combes, p. 768, n. 2 of the same commentary, stated that the same could be said of Montpellier.

[12] On Barcelona, see André-E. Sayous, "Les méthodes commerciales de Barcelone au xive siècle, surtout d'après de protocoles inédits de ses archives notariales," *Estudis universitaris catalans*, 18 (1933), 209-235; Sayous (p. 222) dated the *lettre d'avis* to 1376, the bill of exchange to 1388. On the deposit bank of Barcelona, see Abbott P. Usher, "Deposit Banking in Barcelona, 1300-1700," *Journal of Economic and Business History* 4 (1931), 121-155 and *The Early History of Deposit Banking in Mediterranean Europe*, 1 (Cambridge, Mass., 1943).

[13] A. M. Montpellier, *Grand Chartrier*, Louvet no. 3898: 1358.

[14] See the discussion in P. Wolff, *Commerces et marchands de Toulouse*, p. 385. See also R. de Roover, *L'Évolution de la lettre de change*, pp. 17-19, and "Le contrat de change depuis la fin du treizième siècle jusqu'au début du dix-septième siècle," *Revue belge de philologie et d'histoire* 24 (1946-1947), 111-128.

instrument.[15] He preferred to see the latter contract as the forerunner of the bill. Although there are no letters of notification extant prior to 1350, the Montpellier evidence contains a new element which contributes to this scholarly debate.

If the considerations of origin are broadened to admit additional hypotheses, a case can be made from the Montpellier evidence for the influence of the letter of payment, *littera pagamenti*, to be distinguished from the letter of notification.[16] P. Bouges has argued that this letter was the ancestor of the bill of exchange in Montpellier.[17] The letter of payment, which appeared in the early fourteenth century, was presented by the creditor or his correspondent to the debtor's correspondent for reimbursement, a practice characteristic of the bill of exchange. In contrast to the latter, the letter of payment in Montpellier was always associated with a notarial instrument.[18] In this respect it can be compared to the notarized letter of payment of Genoa extant from the mid-thirteenth century.[19] Here again, as in the case of business partnerships, Genoese influence was strong.[20]

Foreigners using the letter of payment in exchange transactions in Montpellier can be traced as early as 1316.[21] Local participation can be dated from 1343. In this year a Montpelliérain refused to honor a letter in favor of a Genoese merchant because the former had not received sufficient funds from his correspondent in Genoa.[22] The Genoese merchant, judging himself to be injured by this refusal, named a procurator to pursue his rights. In addition, he registered a formal protest before the notary. This procedure of protest had become common with regard to nonpayment of bills of exchange by the end of the fourteenth century.[23] This local case of 1343 indicates clearly that the system of the letter of payment was fully developed by that date.

It may be that the bill of exchange evolved in secondary, though important, financial centers such as Montpellier, from an instrument such as the letter of payment while elsewhere, in the primary centers, the evolution followed a different path.[24] The theories of de Roover and Sayous may both be valid depending on the region studied. The liberation of the bill of exchange from the

[15] A.-E. Sayous, "L'Origine de la lettre de change," p. 103, in particular.

[16] P. Bouges, "La pratique contractuelle," 1: 205, found no letters of notification (*lettres d'avis*) during the fourteenth century in Montpellier. For the *littera pagamenti*, see 1: 206.

[17] *Ibid.*, 1: 207.

[18] *Ibid.*, 1: 206.

[19] R. S. Lopez, *La prima crisi della banca di Genova*, p. 75, quotes a notarized letter of payment from Genoa of 1253.

[20] On Genoese influence on business practice, see Ch. 1, "Investment in Business Partnerships," pp. 11-12, 14, and 28 above.

[21] On 16 April and 13 May 1316, P. Truyars of Narbonne provided funds on four occasions to merchants of Barcelona from whom he was to receive sums of 100 *l. t.* upon the presentation of a *littera pagamenti* by his correspondent, also a Narbonnais, in Montpellier. The latter might in turn designate other individuals as recipients. See ACA, manual of P. de Torre: 1316.

[22] A. D. Hérault, II E 95/372, J. Holanie et al., f. 50r.

[23] P. Bouges, "La pratique contractuelle," 1: 196.

[24] R. de Roover, *L'Évolution de la lettre de change*, pp. 38-40, for examples.

notarial context, with or without a series of intermediate stages, was a logical response to the credit needs of late medieval commerce. The sedentarization of merchants and the multiplication of branch offices and correspondents of commercial companies and of individual merchants fostered this evolution.[25]

Several technical questions regarding exchange operations in fourteenth-century Montpellier, worthy of consideration, remain nonetheless unanswered. It has been impossible to determine the ways in which exchange rates involving foreign coinages were quoted on the Montpellier market. As Raymond de Roover has pointed out, when two financial markets of the Middle Ages were linked in exchange dealings, the exchange rate between those markets was based, generally, on the coinage of one of the two.[26] De Roover distinguished two methods of the quotation of exchange: "certain" and "uncertain."

In the language of the financial market, a "certain" quotation meant that the rate of exchange was quoted in foreign money on the basis of a fixed unity of local money. An "uncertain" quotation indicated that the rate of exchange in local money varied in relation to an unchanging quantity of foreign money.[27] The means of quotation determined the ways in which a particular financial market reacted to fluctuations in the value of currencies, and hence had an effect on the levels of profit of exchange transactions.

Another aspect of late medieval exchange operations involved the concept of *usance*, the fixed term of repayment with regard to specific financial markets.[28] Strictly speaking, *usance* did not appear in Montpellier before the fifteenth century.[29] In the period under study the duration of exchange transactions was extremely variable. Between Montpellier and Perpignan the delay was generally fifteen days, between Montpellier and Barcelona it might be as short as eight days, for Coimbra in Portugal as long as two months, for Lerida, two weeks, for Majorca from three to five weeks.[30] The only contract foreseeing repayment in

[25] On general economic changes, see R. de Roover, "The Commercial Revolution of the Thirteenth Century," *Bulletin of the Business Historical Society* 16 (1942), 34-39, and works of N. S. B. Gras, "The Growth of Rigidity in Business during the Middle Ages," *American Economic Review* 30 (1940), supplement, pp. 281-289; "Economic Rationalism in the Late Middle Ages," *Speculum* 8 (1933), 304-312; and *Business and Capitalism: An Introduction to Business History* (New York, 1939). See also his discussion of the bill of exchange, "Bill of Exchange," *Encyclopedia of the Social Sciences* 2 (1932), 539-540.

[26] R. de Roover, *Money, Banking and Foreign Exchange in Mediaeval Bruges*, p. 61. De Roover determined that "the exchange between Flanders and England was based on the *écu* both in Bruges and in London. In the same way the exchange was based on the Florentine florin and quoted in Flemish groats in both Florence and Bruges. Similarly the exchange ran upon the ducat in both Venice and Bruges and upon the *écu* in both Bruges and Barcelona. The only exception to this general rule was that of two places which used the same currency, such as Paris and Montpellier."

[27] R. de Roover, "Le marché monétaire au Moyen Âge et au début des temps modernes. Problèmes et méthodes," *Revue historique* 246 (1970), 17-18. De Roover noted for the fifteenth century, "Ainsi, avec Montpellier, Paris changeait franc pour franc, *meglio*, *pari* ou *peggio*, suivant les conditions du marché."

[28] *Ibid.*, pp. 19-20, on *usance* (*uso* or *usanza*).

[29] P. Bouges, "La pratique contractuelle," 1: 202.

[30] See the table in Reyerson, "Commerce and Society in Montpellier," 2, Appendix 6, pp. 269-278. As an example regarding Majorca, see A. D. Hérault, II E 95/369, J. Holanie, f. 61v, for a term of three weeks.

Bruges allowed a mere two weeks while terms of up to two months were recorded between Montpellier and Paris.[31] Twenty-five days were allowed for reimbursement in exchanges between Montpellier and Cuneo in northern Italy.[32] In view of the fluctuations of exchange rates, the actual delays of payment could be significant in the determination of profits and losses.

In Montpellier exchange contracts drawn on the Champagne fair towns, only the specific fair during which reimbursement was scheduled was mentioned in the contracts. Each Champagne fair lasted for approximately fifty days, leaving considerable margin in the term of repayment. Travel time between Montpellier and the fairs was about twenty days for merchant caravans, according to the extant transport contracts.[33] However, if the traditional dates of opening and closing for specific fairs are compared with the projected dates of repayment in the exchange contracts, there was not sufficient delay in every case for the trip to Champagne.[34] R. D. Face noted a similar problem of dates in a study of transactions between Genoa and Champagne in an earlier era.[35]

Several hypotheses can be presented to explain this seeming paradox of repayment time. The existence of permanent correspondents in Champagne may explain these credit connections between Montpellier and the fair towns.[36] Face proposed an extensive use of agents and partners for the late twelfth century. In the fourteenth century the use of correspondents has even greater plausibility.[37] An alternative explanation lies in less encumbered and therein faster travel. Finally, it is possible that settlements scheduled theoretically for Champagne were actually repaid in Montpellier, utilizing the approximate fair limits as terms of

[31] A. D. Hérault, II E 95/372, J. Holanie et al., f. 144r: Bruges; II E 95/375, P. de Pena, f. 4r: Paris; II E 95/370, J. Holanie, f. 73v: Paris.

[32] A. D. Hérault, II E 95/370, J. Holanie, f. 93v. It is difficult to account for the variations in these repayment delays. One might wonder whether the Bruges-Montpellier exchange was based upon maritime travel. By the same token, overland communication through mountain passes could prove difficult in winter, if routes were snowbound.

[33] See Reyerson, "Commerce and Society in Montpellier," 2, Appendix 5, pp. 261-267, for a table of transport contracts.

[34] This is not always the case for repayments in Champagne, but the example of A. D. Hérault, II E 95/375, P. de Pena, f. 118r of 10 February 1340, scheduled repayment at the fair of Lagny which closed on 22 February. A description of the dates of the cycle of six fairs can be found in Paul Huvelin, *Essai historique sur le droit des foires et des marchés* (Paris, 1897), pp. 598-599.

[35] R. D. Face, "Techniques of Business in the Trade between the Fairs of Champagne and the South of Europe in the Twelfth and Thirteenth Centuries," *Economic History Review*, ser. 2, 10 (1958), 427-438.

[36] Montpelliérains were present in Champagne as early as 1222 when the count of Champagne took several merchants under his protection stating that if ever they were prohibited access to the fairs, they could remain in his lands. In 1229 Thibaut le Chansonnier accorded privileges to Montpelliérains living in his lands. Hence, Montpelliérains could have served as correspondents from 1229 at least. On Montpelliérains at the Champagne fairs, see F. Bourquelot, *Étude sur les foires de Champagne* (Paris, 1865), 1: 155 and R.-H. Bautier, "Les foires de Champagne," p. 121. See also J. Combes, "Montpellier et les foires de Champagne," *Actes du 96e congrès national des sciences savantes (Toulouse, 1971), Philologique et historique* (Paris, 1978), 1: 381-428.

[37] R. D. Face, "Techniques of Business," pp. 433-438. This explanation has been questioned by Rosalind K. Berlow, "The Development of Business Techniques Used at the Fairs of Champagne from the End of the Twelfth to the Middle of the Thirteenth Century," *Studies in Medieval and Renaissance History*, 8 (1971), 3-32.

payment.[38] This final explanation takes into account the decline in the financial operations in Champagne which R.-H. Bautier dated from the years 1315-1320 and would have diffused criticism of the contracts as "dry" exchange.[39] One could always argue that if one fair could not be reached on time, reimbursement could be made at the next scheduled fair.

In Montpellier the level of profits, or for that matter, losses, experienced by the creditors in local exchange contracts cannot be satisfactorily calculated from the limited data of the notarial registers.[40] De Roover has suggested that in a case of *cambium con la ricorsa*, otherwise termed *cambium* and *recambium*, a nine percent profit might be expected. Such a contract, which has also been called "dry" exchange, permitted the elimination of risks through the specification of the rate of exchange.[41] This type of repayment on the same financial market in local currency, generally included in such acts, made them little different from loans.[42] The resemblance to a loan and the absence of risks led to the condemnation of this sort of contract by the critics of medieval usury.[43]

Specific evidence exists of *cambium* and *recambium* in Montpellier. In fact, a number of local exchange transactions left open the place of repayment; several specified that repayment was expected in Montpellier, with no pretense of the selection of another marketplace.[44] In the latter, the sum to be repaid might be quoted in local money, that is, in *tournois* currency or real coins with the amount of foreign currency left unidentified.[45]

The importance of foreign exchange operations in Montpellier and the significance of the town as a financial center can be best demonstrated through an

[38] See below the discussion of "dry" exchange in Montpellier. This hypothesis was suggested to me by Guy Romestan of the Faculté des Lettres et des Sciences Humaines de Montpellier, Université Paul Valéry.

[39] R.-H. Bautier, "Les foires de Champagne," pp. 133ff.

[40] On the question of exchange profits, R. de Roover discerned five forces regulating the rates of exchange: the interest rate; the changes in monetary standards locally or abroad; disturbances in the balance of payments between two financial centers; speculation in or manipulation of the market; the intervention of public authorities. See *Money, Banking and Credit in Mediaeval Bruges*, pp. 62-63.

[41] R. de Roover, "What is Dry Exchange? A Contribution to the Study of English Mercantilism," *The Journal of Political Economy* 52 (1944), 250-266.

The difficulties of determining what the exchange rates between coinages were at any given date are still too great to permit an attempt at calculations of gain. By the same token, no attempt has been made to develop tables of average values of transactions, as was attempted for loans and some articles of commerce. It is possible that, in the future, the research of Peter Spufford and Wendy Wilkinson on the exchange rates of medieval Europe will provide the key to such calculations. To date, however, the information in their Interim Listing (mss.) is not of sufficient assistance with regard to the Montpellier data.

[42] R. S. Lopez and I. W. Raymond, *Medieval Trade*, p. 163.

[43] R. de Roover, *La pensée économique*, p. 84.

[44] See, for example, A. D. Hérault, II E 95/370, f. 74r and II E 95/375, P. de Pena, f. 123v where the repayments were specifically scheduled for Montpellier.

[45] For other examples, of quotations of *tournois* equivalents in real money in exchange contracts, see A. D. Hérault, II E 95/374, G. Nogareti, ff. 11v and 39v.

On the usurious nature of "dry" exchange (*cambium* and *recambium*), see Terence P. McLaughlin, "The Teaching of the Canonists on Usury (XII, XIII and XIV Centuries)," *Mediaeval Studies* 1 (1939), 95-124.

examination of the origin and expansion of exchange transactions. The emergence of a financial market in Montpellier may well date from the eleventh century.[46] The stimulus of this market through Genoese business activities contributed much to its development. As early as the 1160s the Genoese were naming Montpellier as a place of repayment in primitive exchange contracts.[47] In this regard, they shifted their preference from the venerable financial market of Saint-Gilles to Montpellier. Saint-Gilles could lay claim to an impressive number of changers operating in the 1170s.[48] However, the influence of the count of Toulouse in Saint-Gilles may have inhibited Genoese activities.[49] In contrast, the seigneurs of Montpellier, Guilhem VI and Guilhem VII, had granted vast economic privileges to the Genoese in the mid-twelfth century.[50] Montpellier had the advantage of a stable local currency, the coinage of Melgueil.[51]

The earliest exchange activities of Montpelliérains themselves reflect Genoese influence. In the 1180s merchants of Montpellier, trading out of Genoa, were participating in exchange transactions linking Genoa and Sicily.[52] From these imitative beginnings, Montpelliérains expanded their financial operations in coordination with the enlargement of their commercial horizons.

Diplomatic contacts between Montpellier and Marseille in 1225 and 1229 laid the groundwork for a network of financial connections emanating from the Provençal town.[53] By 1233 Montpellier was serving as a place of reimbursement for exchange contracts drawn up in Marseille.[54] In 1248 merchants of Marseille used Montpellier as a center of repayment in transactions involving creditors from Barcelona and Piacenza.[55] In the same year merchants of Montpellier, using Marseille as a base of operations to trade with Saint-Jean-d'Acre, were employing exchange techniques.[56] Montpelliérains were directly involved in nine extant

[46] The first mention of the mint of Melgueil dates from the tenth century. See Mireille Castaing-Sicard, *Monnaies féodales et circulation monétaire en Languedoc (x^e-xiiie siècles)*, p. 29.

[47] *Giovanni Scriba*, 2, acts CMXLV, MLX, MLXXX, MXCVII, for acts of the early 1160s. In one contract of 1163 (act MLX) two Genoese merchants arranged to liquidate in Montpellier all financial obligations involved in a trip to Syria.

[48] A remarkable list of twelfth-century changers (about 130) occurs at the end of statutes granted by the count of Toulouse to the money changers of Saint-Gilles. See A. Teulet, *Layettes du Trésor des Chartes*, 1: 119, October 1178. A. Gouron, *La réglementation des métiers en Languedoc au moyen âge*, pp. 48-49, n. 73, has published excerpts from the original document of the Archives Nationales, Série J. 304, Toulouse, II, no. 16.

[49] A. Dupont, *Les relations commerciales entre les cités maritimes de Languedoc et les cités méditerranéennes d'Espagne et d'Italie*, for a discussion of these questions. See also Alexandre Germain, *Histoire du commerce de Montpellier*, 1: 99-107.

[50] A. Germain, *Histoire du commerce de Montpellier*, 1: 93-96.

[51] M. Castaing-Sicard, *Les monnaies féodales et la circulation monétaire en Languedoc (x^e-xiiie siècles)*, pp. 32-33.

[52] *Oberto Scriba de Mercato (1186)*, ed. Mario Chiaudano (Turin, 1940), 1, act 328.

[53] A. Germain, *Histoire de la commune de Montpellier*, 2: 446-455, acts XXVI-XXIX and 2: 457-461, act XXXI.

[54] L. Blancard, *Documents inédits sur le commerce de Marseille au moyen âge*, 1, acts of the Manduel brothers, no. 38.

[55] *Ibid.*, 2, acts of Amalric, nos. 833 and 843.

[56] *Ibid.*, 2, acts of Amalric, nos. 91, 145, 185, 409, 469, 511, 522, 691 and 910.

contracts: five times as creditors, four times as borrowers. Those who obtained credit through exchange were merchants traveling to Acre with northern French and Flemish cloths to sell.[57] In addition to serving as a base for commercial and financial connections with the Levant, Marseille was an international center of contact for Montpelliérains. They arranged exchange operations between Marseille and the Champagne fairs with merchants of Piacenza and Siena who were justly renowned for their banking activities.[58]

By the 1260s Montpellier had become an important regional place of financial exchange for Italian merchants in their trade with the Champagne fairs.[59] As the financial operations of the fairs evolved in the direction of a clearinghouse of accounts for European merchants, Montpellier came to occupy an important place as an intermediate link in the international financial network.[60] This role was particularly well developed with regard to merchants of southern Europe. The papacy availed itself of the money market of Montpellier from the late thirteenth century when transferring funds back and forth between Spain, Portugal and the papal court. When the papacy took up residence in Avignon, the possibilities of use of this financial circuit increased.[61]

The first large body of evidence for the role of Montpellier in this network comes from documents of the University of Bologna.[62] Acts of the university cartulary recorded the use of Montpellier as a financial center for transfers of money to Bologna for the account of students and as a place of repayment for funds borrowed in Bologna through loans and exchange operations. This network of financial operations was exploited fruitfully by banking companies of Pistoia and Florence.[63]

[57] The acts of Amalric are rich in allusions to this cloth trade between Marseille and Acre.

[58] *Ibid.*, 2, acts of Amalric, nos. 691 and 910. On the banking activities of the merchants of Piacenza in Champagne, see Pierre Racine, "I banchieri piacentini ed i campi sulle Fiere di Champagne alla fine del Duecento," *Studi storici in onore di Emilio Nasalli Rocca* (Piacenza, 1971).

[59] R. Doehaerd, *Les relations commerciales entre Gênes, la Belgique et l'Outremont*, 3, act no. 1224: on 19 April 1263, the Genoese Gilius Lavagius named a procurator and a *nuncius* to act for him with respect to contracts of exchange in Provence, in Montpellier, in France (*Francia*) and at the Champagne fairs.

[60] The emergence of this role is symbolized in the nomination of a Montpelliérain as "capitaneum consulem de Francia et mercatorum in Francia," with full authority, by Jacme I of Aragon and Majorca (act XV below). By 1290 the Montpellier captain had jurisdiction over merchants of Toulouse, Narbonne, Figeac, Aurillac, Saint-Flour, Combes, Saint-Thibéry, Saint-Guilhem-le-Désert, Béziers, Sommières and ten other towns. See A. Germain, *Histoire du commerce de Montpellier*, 1: 201-202, acts XIV, XV and XVI; pp. 307-325, act LXII. See also R.-H. Bautier, "Les foires de Champagne," pp. 133ff.

[61] See the comments of Jean Favier, *Philippe le Bel* (Paris, 1978), p. 276, regarding the operations of Boniface VIII. On the economic affairs of the papacy in Avignon, see Yves Renouard, *Les relations des papes d'Avignon et des compagnies commerciales et bancaires de 1316 à 1378* (Paris, 1941).

[62] *Cartularium Studii Bononiensis. Documenti per la storia della università di Bologna dalle origine fino al secolo XV*, 13 vols. (Imola, 1907, Bologna, 1913-1936).

[63] Sven Stelling-Michaud, "Le transport international des manuscrits juridiques bolonais entre 1265-1320," *Mélanges d'histoire économique et sociale en l'honneur du professeur Antony Babel* (Geneva, 1963), 1: 98ff. See also David Herlihy, *Medieval and Renaissance Pistoia. The Social History of an Italian Town* (New Haven and London, 1967), p. 165. The Ammannati of Pistoia had branches or correspondents at Bologna from 1261 and at Montpellier in 1277.

The sums involved in these transactions were never very large; they ran from 7 *l. t.* to 277 *l. t.* in the exchange contracts (29 *l.* Bolognese to 833 *l.* Bolognese) and from 8 *l.* Bolognese to 206 *l.* Bolognese in the loans.[64] Contracts transferring funds from Bologna to Montpellier were somewhat more numerous than transfers in the opposite direction. The typical process can be illustrated as follows: on 4 July 1268, Jacobus Boymondi of Sisteron, a student in Bologna, came before a notary to make a formal acquittal of the receipt of 353 *l.* Bolognese paid to him by a merchant of a company of Florence for the price of exchange of 120 *l. t.* received by a company associate in Montpellier from the brother of Jacobus.[65] The costs of this exchange which resulted in the transfer of funds to the student in Bologna were effectively hidden in the rate of exchange.

Among those students who transferred funds to Bologna in this fashion were Spaniards and Portuguese from Lerida, Barcelona, Saragossa, Ampurias, Urgel, Cuença, Gerona, Castile and Braga.[66] Roussillonnais students from Elne and Perpignan occasionally had recourse to the financial facilities of Montpellier to send funds to Bologna. Languedocians from Nîmes, Uzès, Alès, Carcassonne, Béziers, Aumelas, Toulouse, Montagnac and Narbonne participated in such operations. The Montpelliérains also utilized this type of exchange practice. Finally, students from Poitiers, Grenoble, Provence, Limoges, Bordeaux and other areas of northern France directed money transfers through Montpellier to Bologna.[67]

A similar pattern of geographic representation with emphasis upon southern French, Spanish and Portugese participation can be found among students borrowing money through loans and money exchange contracts with repayments scheduled in Montpellier, usually after a delay of several months.[68] S. Stelling-Michaud has found that this network of foreign exchange was closely related to a traffic in manuscripts of scholarly legal works which might serve as the collateral in these credit undertakings.[69]

For the years 1265-1269 Stelling-Michaud noted that eighty-two loans and contracts of exchange were established in Bologna and scheduled for reimbursement in Montpellier.[70] During the same period twenty-nine repayments from Bologna were destined for Paris and nine for the Champagne fair towns of Bar-sur-Aube and Provins. He also noted for the same years seventy-two acquittals

[64] For example, *Cartularium Studii Bononiensis*, 5, acts no. 125 and 222; 7, acts no. 52, 153 and 554.

[65] *Ibid.*, 7, no. 234.

[66] *Ibid.*, 8, no. 94; 11, no. 472; 7, no. 434; 7, no. 554; 5, no. 363; 10, no. 531; 11, no. 103; 7, no. 253; 5, no. 191; 11, no. 31; 11, no. 48.

[67] *Ibid.*, 5, nos. 79, 81, 371, 380, 475 and 479; 7, nos. 30, 31, 234, 277, 291, 311, 366, 429 and 435; 8, nos. 142 and 570; 10, nos. 93, 123, 267, 330, 424, 511, 512 and 517; 11, nos. 303 and 432.

[68] *Ibid.*, 5, nos. 66, 91, 129, 294 and 475; 7, nos. 105, 107, 122, 153, 195, 219, 280, 440 and 446; 8, nos. 22, 23, 196, 495 and 499; 10, nos. 106, 369, 373 and 381; 11, nos. 34, 160, 292 and 516.

[69] See n. 67 above.

[70] S. Stelling-Michaud, "Le transport international des manuscrits juridiques bolonais," pp. 100-101. The commercial foundations of these financial transactions lay in a lucrative trade in scholarly manuscripts.

preserved in Bologna for funds received in transfers from Montpellier to Bologna. These brief but intense financial connections between Montpellier and Bologna have left no further trace during the thirteenth century.[71] The university attendance of students from Montpellier, southern France, Spain and Portugal seems to have diminished in Bologna in the early fourteenth century, perhaps as a reflection of the revival of the law school of Montpellier in 1268.[72] Financial activities in Bologna were further dampened by a decline in the value of Bolognese coinage and by the bankruptcy of certain financial companies which had participated in the early exchange operations.[73]

Chronologically, the next available information on exchange operations involving Montpellier comes from the extant notarial registers. In 1293-1348 local merchants and changers had at their disposal a well-defined credit instrument to supplement shortages of cash capital and meet the needs of trade: the *instrumentum ex causa cambii* or notarial contract of exchange.[74] Fifty-seven contracts of exchange and twelve acquittals for engagements contracted outside Montpellier have been preserved.[75] Table 1 details their chronological distribution. Montpelliérains were present as creditors in thirty-six percent of the new acts and as debtors in 23.6%. They were present as debtors and creditors at the same level of twenty-three percent in the acquittals. The international nature of these exchange transactions is reinforced by the participation of a majority of foreigners in the monetary market of Montpellier.[76]

TABLE 1: CHRONOLOGICAL DISTRIBUTION OF EXCHANGE CONTRACTS OF THE MONTPELLIER NOTARIAL EVIDENCE (1293-1348)

	1293	1294	1327	1328	1329	1330	1333	1336	1337	1339	1340	1342	1343	1344	1347
Exchanges	4	3	8		1	1	8	5	1	12	4	4	4	1	1
Acquittals, Etc.		1	3	1			3	1			1		2		

[71] *Ibid.*, p. 101.

[72] On the revival of the law school, see A. Gouron, "Enseignement du droit, légistes et canonistes dans le Midi de la France," *Recueil* 5 (1966), 1-33 and "Les juristes de l'école de Montpellier," *Ius Romanum Medii Aevi*, pars 4, 3, a (Milan, 1971).

[73] S. Stelling-Michaud, "Le transport international," pp. 101ff.

[74] See n. 2 above.

[75] A table summarizing the extant exchange contracts can be found in Reyerson, "Commerce and Society in Montpellier," 2, Appendix 6, pp. 269-278.

[76] R. de Roover provided a definition of a "place bancaire ou cambiste" in "Le marché monétaire au Moyen Âge et au début des temps modernes. Problèmes et méthodes," *Revue historique* 244 (1970), 13: "un centre commercial où il y avait un marché monétaire organisé, et qui cotait régulièrement les cours du change sur plusieurs autres places." Montpellier was counted in his list of places of exchange. Harry A. Miskimin, *Money, Prices and Foreign Exchange* (New Haven, 1963), p. 18, stated, "Important banking centers, whose business is international in character, develop in France, at Paris and Montpellier, and in England at London."

The foreign participants in exchange operations in Montpellier and the money markets which they used in the organization of repayments from Montpellier reveal the place of Montpellier in the world of European finance of the Middle Ages. In 1293-1294 merchants of Figeac and Saint-Antonin, commercial towns of the Lot region of central France, received *melgorien* coinage in exchange from merchants of Montpellier who were to be reimbursed in *tournois* coinage at the fairs of Lagny.[77]

Parisians were employing the monetary market of Montpellier from the late thirteenth century with repayments scheduled for the Champagne fairs.[78] They continued to use these financial connections in the fourteenth century. For example, in 1339 Parisians borrowed funds through exchange from Montpelliérains, merchants of Aurillac and Anduze.[79] These Parisians had need of credit in Montpellier to purchase luxury products of the Mediterranean world: saffron, pepper, ginger, sugar and alum, destined for northern markets.[80]

The credit needs of northern merchants could be effectively served by funds acquired through exchange in Montpellier while corresponding requirements of Montpelliérains in the north were filled through reimbursements in Champagne and in Paris. Merchants of Montpellier shipped spices and leather to northern markets, a traffic which augmented their available capital for the purchase of cloths.[81] Woolen cloths of northern manufacture were the main exports of Montpelliérains in the lucrative Levant trade.[82]

A complementary current of exchange probably flowed from Champagne to Montpellier.[83] Northern merchants may have facilitated their cash flow in the south by advancing funds through exchange to southerners who reimbursed in Montpellier. Such a process would have permitted the repatriation of excess northern profits while at the same time offering to northerners and southerners alike the possibility of the financial profit of *cambium con la ricorsa*.[84]

A noteworthy feature of the exchange network between Montpellier and Champagne was its persistence as late as the 1340s.[85] In spite of the durability of

[77] A. M. Montpellier, II 1, J. Grimaudi, f. 52r. See also f. 18r.

[78] A. M. Montpellier, II 1, J. Grimaudi, ff. 15r, 17r, 34v and 51v for delayed payments.

[79] A. D. Hérault, II E 95/371, J. Holanie, f. 62v and II E 95/375, P. de Pena ff. 99r and 118r.

[80] The commercial interests of the Parisians in Montpellier are dealt with in Reyerson, "Commerce and Society in Montpellier," 1: 130-136.

[81] *Ibid.*, 2, Appendix 5, pp. 261-267, on the transport contracts.

[82] *Ibid.*, 2, Appendix 5, pp. 236-248, for the maritime *comanda* and *societas* contracts. Merchants of Aurillac and Anduze, it is interesting to note, could benefit from both ends of this commercial and financial circuit. On Aurillac, see M. Boudet, "Les marchands d'Aurillac et de Saint-Flour aux foires de Champagne et à Montpellier (XIIIᵉ-XIVᵉ siècles)," *Revue de la Haute-Auvergne* 15 (1913), 326-341. One exchange acquittal for 150 *écus* of 21 June 1343 in Montpellier between a borrower of Montpellier and a creditor of Perpignan was the fruit of an obligation contracted originally in Saint-Flour. See A. D. Hérault, II E 95/372, J. Holanie et al., f. 42r.

[83] The scarcity of records in Champagne renders proof of this hypothesis all but impossible. On the fragmentary records, see R.-H. Bautier, "Les registres des foires de Champagne. À propos d'un feuillet récemment découvert," *Bulletin philologique et historique* (1942-1943), 157-185.

[84] See n. 41 above.

[85] A. D. Hérault, II E 95/369, J. Holanie, f. 99v, II E 95/375, P. de Pena, ff. 39v, 69r, 99r; II E 95/374, G. Nogareti, f. 31rR; II E 95/371, J. Holanie, f. 62v. Merchants of Montpellier such as the

these contracts for over a century, Parisian markets of the fourteenth century drew an increasingly large share of southern commercial and financial business.[86] Shipments of commodities were multiplied; to the traffic in spices, almonds, dyes, paper, sugar and leather which can be traced in the late thirteenth century was added a major trade in saffron in the 1330s.[87] From the late 1330s Paris appeared as a center of repayment for financial exchanges established in Montpellier.[88] In 1342 an alternative of the Warm Fair of Troyes or Paris was provided as a repayment site.[89] In December 1343 Paris was mentioned as an alternative place of reimbursement for Bruges in the event of hostilities in the latter center.[90] The Parisan money market was expanding with the growth of the royal capital in the fourteenth century. The decadence of the Champagne fairs was a reality by 1350 while an active commercial and financial future awaited northern centers such as Bruges and Paris in the late fourteenth century.[91]

The expansion of the financial network of northern Europe was echoed by the intensification of southern exchange activity. The major thrust of financial connections between Montpellier and Spanish towns was in the years 1316-1335.[92] The continuing Majorcan domination of the seigneurial sector of Montpellier provided a favorable political context for these business contacts. Spanish foreign exchange connections with Montpellier have left traces in local sources but can be analyzed in greater detail thanks to the research of Guy Romestan in Spanish and Roussillonnais archives.[93] Tables 2 and 3 summarize Romestan's Spanish and Roussillonnais data, which is drawn from records in Valencia, Barcelona and Perpignan.[94] Participants in exchange linking Montpel-

---

Alamandini and the Bordelis were still borrowing by exchange in Genoa for repayment in Champagne in 1310 but it may be true that after 1315-1320, as R.-H. Bautier, "Les foires de Champagne," pp. 133ff suggested, there was a decline in the financial fairs from the standpoint of markets such as Genoa.

86 On the Parisian money market, see R. de Roover, "Le marché monétaire à Paris du règne de Philippe le Bel au début du xve siècle," and Jean Favier, "Une ville entre deux vocations: la place d'affaires de Paris au xve siècle," *Annales: ESC*, 28:2 (1973), 1245-1279.

87 See Reyerson, "Commerce and Society in Montpellier," 2, Appendix 5, pp. 261-267.

88 A. D. Hérault, II E 95/375, P. de Pena, f. 4r for example.

89 A. D. Hérault, II E 95/371, J. Holanie, f. 62v

90 A. D. Hérault, II E 95/372, J. Holanie et al., f. 144r.

91 J. Favier, "Une ville entre deux vocations," p. 1249, discerned a decline in Parisian operations by the period 1410-1440.

92 See Tables 2 and 3 and the discussion below.

93 My most sincere thanks are due Guy Romestan, of the Faculté des Lettres et des Sciences Humaines de Montpellier, who lent me his lengthy notes from research in the ACA of Barcelona, the ARV of Valencia and in the Archives Départementales des Pyrénées-Orientales. Without this information, the study of this most intriguing aspect of foreign exchange in Montpellier would have been more fragmentary than ever.

Among the multiple articles of Guy Romestan regarding Roussillonnais and Spanish economic history, particularly useful for this study is "Les relations commerciales entre Montpellier et Valence dans la première moitié du xive siècle," *Acta de VIII Congresso de historia de la Corona de Aragon* (1967), t. 2, v. 3 (Valencia, 1973), pp. 243-253.

94 Of the Montpellier records, a total of thirty-two of the sixty-nine references extant from 1293-1347 fall in the category of Spanish foreign exchange. Twenty-one of these occurred in the years 1327-1333. The data of these tables are summarized from the article and notes of Mr. Romestan.

lier with these Spanish centers included merchants of Narbonne, Perpignan, Barcelona, Tarrega, Lerida, Gerona, Majorca, Minorca, Valencia, Montpellier, Lucca and Montolieu.[95]

TABLE 2: PLACES OF REPAYMENT IN VALENCIAN CONTRACTS OF EXCHANGE

	1316-1325	1326-1335	1336-1345
Montpellier	52	42	4
Narbonne	22	38	3
Perpignan	4	19	49

TABLE 3: PARTICIPANTS IN VALENCIAN EXCHANGE CONTRACTS REPAID IN MONTPELLIER

	1316-1325	1326-1335	1336-1345
Narbonnais creditors	35	26	
Valencian debtors	38	23	3

Within the context of Spanish financial connections Montpellier was most frequently employed as a site of recovery of funds by creditors of Narbonne.[96] Most of the sums lent by the Narbonnais were reimbursable in Montpellier within fifteen to twenty-five days. In Barcelona merchants of Narbonne acted as creditors in ten of the twenty exchange contracts recorded with repayment in Montpellier in the years 1314-1316.[97] They extended credit to merchants of Valencia, Barcelona, Gerona, Lerida and Montpellier.[98] The sums involved in the exchanges of Valencia ranged in general from 50 *l.* to 250 *l.* of Valencian *reales* to be reimbursed in 50 to 250 *agneaux* (46.9 *l. t.* to 234.4 *l. t.*). From Barcelona reimbursements were often in the range of 50 *l.* to 250 *l. t.*[99] The Spanish debtors habitually designated associates in Montpellier to effect the repayments. The Narbonnais were present in person to recover their funds.

The financial operations of merchants of Narbonne were directly related to their international trade. Guy Romestan has calculated that over ninety percent of all cloth sales in Valencia in the years 1317-1340 were made by merchants of

[95] Synopsis of the extant exchange contracts of Montpellier can be found in Reyerson, "Commerce and Society in Montpellier," 2, Appendix 6, pp. 269-278.

[96] ARV, *Protocolos*, nos. 2071, 2627, 2757, 2791, 2792, 2801, 2812, 2855, 2873, 2876, 2880, 2946.

[97] ACA, manual of P. de Torre.

[98] In this fashion the Narbonnais Antonius Picot furnished credit in seven contracts of exchange over the years 1325-1327 to merchants of Barcelona, Gerona, Valencia and Lerida. These sums were reimbursed to Picot or an associate in person in Montpellier. See ARV, *Protocolos*, nos. 2855 and 2873.

[99] See n. 21 above for the mention of the *littera pagamenti* in this context.

Narbonne.[100] Their recovery of exchange credits in Montpellier represented a transfer of cloth profits. On the market place of Montpellier the Narbonnais were in need of capital to invest in *comanda* partnerships exporting woolen cloths to the Levant.[101]

Sources in Montpellier testify to the involvement of the Narbonnais in this network of Spanish exchange.[102] Moreover, merchants of Narbonne such as Jacobus Arquiayre, a creditor in the Valencian contracts, appeared as a debtor in contracts drawn on merchants of Majorca, Tarrega, Ampurias and Roussillon in Montpellier.[103] These contacts diminished in number in the mid 1330s as the growing competition from indigenous Spanish cloth industries reduced the volume of cloth sales by the Narbonnais in Spain and hence their transfers of profits from Spain to Montpellier.[104]

Also active in foreign exchange between Montpellier and Spain were merchants of Perpignan. From the money market in Barcelona in 1316 they lent sums of 60 *l.* to 238 *l.* in Barcelonese currency to merchants of Barcelona who promised reimbursement in amounts of 50 *l. t.* to 200 *l. t.* in Montpellier.[105] From Valencia in 1325-1326 they were the creditors of merchants such as Petrus and Pontius Salati of Lerida who acted on occasion as papal financiers.[106] An acquittal surviving in Montpellier recorded the acknowledgment by the representative of a Perpignannais of his receipt from Petrus Salati of 300 gold *agneaux* (281.3 *l. t.*).[107] After the mid 1330s the Perpignannais, like the Narbonnais, ceased to employ Montpellier as a place of repayment in their Spanish exchanges. As a site of fourteenth-century commercial expansion, Perpignan had by then become a major focus of this financial network.[108]

Catalan merchants also participated in foreign exchange between Spain and Montpellier prior to the mid 1330s. For example, in local evidence of 1327 the Salati of Lerida were recorded in three acquittals for repayment of exchange contracts established in Lerida; they borrowed three times in the same year in Montpellier with reimbursements scheduled for Valencia.[109] As papal financiers, the Salati used the monetary market of Montpellier in their transfers of funds

[100] G. Romestan, "À propos du commerce des draps dans la Péninsule Ibérique au moyen âge, les marchands languedociens dans le royaume de Valence pendant la première moitié du XIVe siècle," *Bulletin philologique et historique* (1969), 1 (Paris, 1972), 126.

[101] See, for example, A. D. Hérault, II E 95/368, J. Holanie, ff. 12r, 15v, 35r and 35v for Narbonnais partnership contracts.

[102] A. D. Hérault, II E 95/368, J. Holanie, f. 93v, for an acquittal of a contract of exchange recorded in Valencia. The Narbonnais received payment for the sum of 158 gold *agneaux*.

[103] A. D. Hérault, II E 95/368, J. Holanie, ff. 11v and 21r; II E 95/369, J. Holanie, f. 61v.

[104] See n. 100 above.

[105] ACA, manual of P. de Torre for 13, 17, 21 August 1316 and for 10 March 1316.

[106] ARC, *Protocolos*, nos. 2855 and 2873.

[107] A. D. Hérault, II E 95/368, J. Holanie, f. 55r.

[108] See Table 2. On economic expansion in Perpignan, see Guy Romestan, "Draperie roussillonnaise et draperie languedocienne dans la première moitié du XIVe siècle," *Fédération historique* (Perpignan, 1969), pp. 31-60.

[109] A. D. Hérault, II E 95/368, J. Holanie, ff. 18v (3 acts), 55r, 81v and 93v.

from the diocese of Lerida to Avignon.[110] Their involvement in currents of exchange to and from Spain suggests that they were engaged in financial speculation in exchange rates.

The activities of other Catalans, merchants of Barcelona and Tarrega, and of Roussillon followed a similar pattern. For these groups as for merchants of Perpignan and Narbonne, Perpignan replaced Montpellier as the site of reimbursement in exchanges contracted in Barcelona and Valencia. Of these groups, merchants of Barcelona were the most active. They were recorded as debtors in twenty contracts of exchange in Barcelona with repayment in Montpellier in the years 1314-1316. The Narbonnais were their creditors ten times; the remaining creditors came from Perpignan and Montolieu. Merchants of Barcelona arranged repayment through relatives or correspondents. Occasionally, they stipulated that repayment would be made upon the presentation of a *littera pagamenti*.[111] After 1316 the next evidence of exchange in Barcelona comes from the years 1329-1331 when merchants of Barcelona, Collioure, Perpignan and Tarrega obtained funds which they were to reimburse in Perpignan. The overwhelming choice of Perpignan over Montpellier as a place of repayment from Valencia in 1336-1345 is shown in Tables 2 and 3.[112] Reimbursements from Spain went increasingly to Perpignan, but Spaniards continued to contract exchanges in Montpellier.

In the years 1327-1333 merchants of Barcelona and Tarrega frequently availed themselves of the monetary market of Montpellier, borrowing and lending funds by exchange. They scheduled both repayments and recoveries of funds in Barcelona, Valencia, Lerida and Majorca in this period.[113] For Barcelona as for Perpignan, the first half of the fourteenth century was an era of economic expansion reflected in intense financial activities. The increasing independence of the Aragonese-Catalan world with regard to centers such as Montpellier did not completely eliminate their use of the Languedocian monetary market. Raymond de Roover noted that, about 1400, foreign exchange was relayed from Paris to Barcelona via Montpellier.[114]

A further phase of exchange operations in the first half of the fourteenth century involves the activities of Valencian merchants. They joined southern French merchants and Catalans in the exploitation of financial contacts between Montpellier and Spain. The commercial basis of the participation of the

[110] A. D. Hérault, II E 95/368, J. Holanie, f. 22r, for their appointment to transfer papal funds.

[111] ACA, manual of P. de Torre, 15 July 1316.

[112] The choice of Perpignan over Montpellier as a place of repayment in Valencia in 1316-1345 emerges from the data drawn from documents described in n. 93 above.

[113] A. D. Hérault, II E 95/368, J. Holanie, ff. 18v, 21r, 39r, 73r, 84r, 146v; II E 95/369, J. Holanie, ff. 47r, 55r.

[114] R. de Roover, "Le marché monétaire à Paris du règne de Philippe le Bel au début du XVe siècle," *Académie des Inscriptions et Belles-Lettres, comptes rendus* (1968), p. 558.

On the expansion of Barcelona, see for example, A.-E. Sayous, "Les méthodes commerciales de Barcelone au XIVe siècle, surtout d'après des protocoles inédits de ses archives notariales," *Estudis universitaris catalans* 18 (1933), 209-235, et "Notes sur l'origine de la lettre de change et les débuts de son emploi à Barcelone (XIVe siècle)," *Revue d'histoire du droit* 13 (1934), 315-322.

Valencians was their leather industry, the products of which were exported to northern Europe.[115] In Valencia such merchants borrowed funds through exchange to be repaid from leather sale profits in Montpellier. For them, too, the money market of Perpignan gradually replaced Montpellier as Table 3 shows. From Montpellier itself, Valencians borrowed twice for reimbursement in Valencia, lending once for repayment in Montpellier.[116]

Merchants of Majorca and Minorca were engaged in a somewhat different pattern of exchange operations from those observed above. There is little trace of their use of the monetary market of Valencia. In contrast, contracts extant in Montpellier recorded considerable exchange activity. Merchants of Majorca and Minorca furnished exchange credit to merchants of Narbonne, Tarrega, Barcelona and Montpellier and recovered their capital in Majorca and Barcelona.[117] Majorcans and Minorcans also contracted exchange debts with creditors from Barcelona, Lerida, Perpignan and Montpellier for reimbursement in Majorca, Minorca and Montpellier.[118] After the mid 1330s, records in Montpellier of the islanders' financial activities decline. The persistence of political ties between the Languedocian center and the kingdom of Majorca until 1349 may account for the fact that these contacts do not entirely disappear in the period under study.[119]

Merchants of Montpellier occasionally availed themselves of this network of Spanish foreign exchange. They drew up exchange contracts in Valencia scheduling repayment in Montpellier.[120] Although the Montpelliérains like the Narbonnais, engaged in sales of northern cloths in Spain, funds obtained through exchange on Spanish markets were probably necessary to finance purchases of Spanish leather and saffron.[121] Italian use of the monetary market of Montpellier included members of the Peruzzi Society of Florence who had business in

[115] Valencian merchants were debtors thirty-eight times with repayment in Montpellier in 1317-1325 as Table 3 reveals. They acted alone twenty-two times, and in association with Barcelonese four times, with merchants of Barcelona and Gerona five times, with merchants of Xativa five times, and with Stephanus Rotgerii, merchant of Aurillac and of Montpellier, twice.

The Ginestar brothers, *blanquerii* (bleachers) in the Valencian leather industry, were the most frequent borrowers, often designating themselves as agents for reimbursement in Montpellier.

See Reyerson, "Commerce and Society in Montpellier," 2, Appendix 5, pp. 261-267 for transport contracts detailing the shipment of leather to northern France.

On the leather trade of Valencia, see G. Romestan, "Les relations commerciales entre Montpellier et Valence," pp. 243-253.

[116] A. D. Hérault, II E 95/368, J. Holanie, f. 81v; II E 95/370, J. Holanie, f. 80r; II E 95/374, G. Nogareti, f. 60vR.

[117] A. D. Hérault, II E 95/368, J. Holanie, ff. 11v, 39v, 146v; II E 95/369, J. Holanie, ff. 32v, 61v.

[118] A. D. Hérault, II E 95/368, J. Holanie, f. 73r; II E 95/369, J. Holanie, ff. 70r, 83r, 84r, 91r.

[119] A. D. Hérault, II E 95/375, P. de Pena, f. 75v; II E 95/372, J. Holanie et al., f. 36r, for additional exchange contracts.

[120] A. D. Hérault, II E 95/368, J. Holanie, f. 18v, as creditors.

[121] In Valencia they appeared ten times as debtors, scheduling repayment in Montpellier. ARV, *Protocolos*, nos. 2791, 2873, 2855. On commercial activities of the Montpelliérains in Valencia, see G. Romestan, "Les relations commerciales entre Montpellier et Valence."

Valencia.[122] The convenient location of Montpellier made it an ideal intermediate market for commerce and finance between northern Italy and Spain.

Guy Romestan has argued that transformations of the Spanish cloth market and the economic expansion of Perpignan may account for the decline in foreign exchange operations between Montpellier and Spanish money markets.[123] Although hypotheses involving cause and effect arguments are difficult to sustain statistically in the medieval period, Romestan's explanation is reasonable. Between Montpellier and the Iberian peninsula, two commercial sectors appear to have maintained their vitality, with the likelihood of effects on foreign exchange. The Catalan trade in saffron which experienced a take-off in the mid 1330s stimulated exchange operations between Spaniards and Parisians on the monetary market of Montpellier.[124] Secondly, Montpellier, served as an intermediary for Italian merchants, particularly the Lucchese, in their business affairs in Catalonia and in Valencia.[125] The Lucchese undoubtedly repatriated profits from sales of silks in Spain. This commerce was flourishing with an important Spanish clientele in Montpellier in the 1330s and 1340s.[126]

The expansion of international trade brought increasing numbers of merchants from different localities into contact. The numbers of coinages in use in western Europe complicated payments between these merchants. In France alone in the thirteenth century, between thirty and forty separate coinages existed.[127] It was only with the efforts of the French monarchy in the fourteenth century that order in the form of dominance of the royal coinages of the mints of Paris and Tours emerged from the chaos of a monetary tower of Babel.[128] Problems of exchange persisted on an international level among the coinages of different regions and countries outside France.

The exchange operation facilitated the practice of international trade in several ways. In addition to furnishing the foreign merchant with the means of trafficking in local coinage on a local market, much as the operation of manual exchange had done, the exchange contract permitted a foreign merchant to make

[122] ARV, *Protocolos*, no. 2971.

[123] See n. 100 above.

[124] Catalans shipping saffron to Paris engaged in foreign exchange in Montpellier. See A. D. Hérault, II E 95/375, P. de Pena, f. 123v for the exchange and f. 99r for a saffron shipment.

[125] A. D. Hérault, II E 95/370, J. Holanie, ff. 27r and 49r. In the contracts of Valencia the Lucchese were mentioned six times as creditors for repayment in Montpellier in 1325-1326. Their debtors were Valencians such as the Ginestar. These exchanges involved sums ranging from 96.5 *reales* of Valencia to over 400 *reales* to be reimbursed in 100 to 450 *agneaux*. ARV, *Protocolos*, nos. 2873 and 2855.

[126] See my study "Medieval Silks in Montpellier: The Silk Market ca. 1250-ca. 1350," *The Journal of European Economic History* 11 (1982), 117-140.

[127] On the proliferation of baronial coinages in France, see Étienne Fournial, *Histoire monétaire de l'Occident médiéval* (Paris, 1970), pp. 65 and 83. See also Thomas N. Bisson, *Conservation of Coinage* (Oxford, 1979), for the history of coinages in southern France, Catalonia and Aragon in the eleventh and twelfth centuries.

[128] On the restrictions on coinage imposed by the kings of France, see E. Fournial, *Histoire monétaire*, pp. 151-157.

local purchases and defer the regulation of accounts to a later date and another place. The transport of specie was dangerous due to the risks of robbery and cumbersome given the limitations of overland transport on pack animals. Inherent in the exchange operation was the extension of short-term credit which financed the purchases in one locale. The goods obtained in this fashion might be shipped to the place of repayment and sold for a profit before the reimbursement had to be made. Exchange operations provided merchants with flexible means of cancelling debits and recovering credits. Finally, these financial transactions contained a speculative dimension since the exchange rates of coinages in the Middle Ages fluctuated just as the rates between the dollar and foreign currencies change today in the international money market.[129] The creditor's losses and/or gains depended on whether the rate of exchange agreed upon with the debtor reflected the actual relationship between the two coinages involved at the time of reimbursement. The vicissitudes of the monetary market might eliminate the favorable ratio envisioned by the creditor at the outset to cover the costs of extension of credit through the initial exchange contract and erase any profits. Any profits earned through exchange operations could be utilized in the town of repayment or repatriated through additional exchange contracts to the home market.[130]

The financial role of Montpellier within the European context can be demonstrated in local and foreign evidence. A north-south axis of exchange operations linked Montpellier with the Champagne fair towns and the growing commercial and financial markets of Paris and Bruges. Merchants of southern Europe (Italy and Spain), used the monetary market of Montpellier as an intermediary in their contacts with more northerly centers. An east-west axis, again paralleling commercial routes, resulted in the employment of Montpellier as a fulcrum of foreign exchange between the Iberian peninsula and the islands of Majorca and Minorca on the one hand and Provence and northern Italy on the other. The financial vocation of Montpelliérains was fully affirmed by the mid-fourteenth century.

The technical development of exchange in Montpellier did not in this period reflect the growth of that new financial instrument, the bill of exchange, already

[129] On exchange rates, see R. de Roover, *L'Évolution de la lettre de change*, pp. 58ff., and *Money, Banking and Credit in Mediaeval Bruges*, p. 66. The medieval merchant bankers learned to recognize cycles in the monetary market. According to de Roover, "Le marché monétaire au Moyen Âge et au début des temps modernes. Problèmes et méthodes." *Revue historique* 495 (1970), 26: "À Montpellier, l'argent était toujours cher pendant les foires de Pézenas et de Montagnac qui se tenaient dans le voisinage, sauf pour Paris, parce que les drapiers de Toulouse et de Montpellier, à ces moments-là, étaient *datori* ou donneurs pour cette dernière place. Signalons pourtant qu'on ne peut pas toujours se fier aux manuels et que le rythme des variations saisonnières changeait parfois avec les revirements de la conjoncture." It should be noted that de Roover's information came from fifteenth-century evidence.

[130] For a description of the exchange operation in actual practice, using the mature form of the bill of exchange, see Raymond de Roover, *The Rise and Decline of the Medici Bank, 1397-1494* (Cambridge, Mass., 1963), pp. 108-141. See also R. de Roover, *Money, Banking and Foreign Exchange in Mediaeval Bruges*, pp. 61-62.

used by some Italian merchants. However, a possible precursor of the bill, the *littera pagamenti*, left its trace in the local documents. In the period under study, the notarial contract of exchange provided a flexible instrument for the needs of international trade in Montpellier.

The operations of foreign exchange were closely linked to contemporary commercial endeavors. Credit extended through the exchange contract provided convenient capital for the advancement of trading activities. Financial speculation went hand in hand with the extension of credit. Exchange contracts offered opportunities for speculative investment of which Montpelliérains and foreigners alike availed themselves.

Conclusion

Because of its overland and maritime connections as a gateway to northern Europe for the Mediterranean world, Montpellier in the High and Late Middle Ages provides a unique context in which to examine banking and finance. Proximity to the sea opened possibilities of Italian, and especially Genoese, influence on business techniques. These contacts were important from the mid-twelfth century, if not earlier, when the Genoese sought out Montpellier as a *pied-à-terre* on the Mediterranean coast of what would become French territory.

Financial operations evolved in Montpellier in the course of the twelfth and thirteenth centuries. The Genoese example affected the development of commercial partnerships and foreign exchange transactions. By the early thirteenth century Montpelliérains had emancipated themselves from Genoese hegemony. They perfected their commercial and financial techniques in Marseille, trading in woolen cloths to Syria and in silks to North Africa. Though commercial markets in the Levant shifted to Cyprus and Byzantium in the fourteenth century, business techniques remained relatively stable. At home, other operations emerged. Deposit banking, a specialty of Montpellier changers, served multiple purposes: safe-keeping, investment and debt liquidation. Recognitions of debt stimulated medieval trade, helping to compensate for the problems of the velocity of circulation of coins and low medieval coinage stocks.[1] Lending contracts with land as collateral characterized the eleventh- and twelfth-century operations while the *mutuum* loan, a more versatile instrument adaptable to commercial investment and to consumer credit needs, predominated in the late thirteenth and fourteenth centuries.

Montpellier was a fulcrum of foreign exchange between northern and southern Europe in the twelfth, thirteenth and fourteenth centuries. In accordance with commercial conditions, the correspondent exchange markets varied. This type of

[1] Modern economic historians pinpoint problems of velocity of circulation of coins which affected the volume of transactions in the medieval economy according to the Fisher equivalance $MV \approx PT$ where M was the supply of money in the economy, V, the velocity of circulation of that money, P, the level of prices, and T, the volume of transactions. Harry A. Miskimin has argued recently that the use of credit operations was one of the means by which early modern England overcame difficulties of bullion supply and circulation in the economy. Although the volume of economic transactions was lower in the Late Middle Ages, credit served a similar function. See H. A. Miskimin, "Credit in Sixteenth Century England," in *The Dawn of Modern Banking* (New Haven and London, 1979), pp. 275-289.

Use of cash revealed in the extant notarial documents would belie the exaggeration of shortages of coinage in the Montpellier region. The presence of minting operations may have helped to keep the circulation of coins higher than in areas where mints were not present.

evolution is most visible in the shift of repayment operations arranged in Spanish centers away from Montpellier to Perpignan in the 1330s and 1340s. Exchange ties with Champagne remained strong long after the decline of financial markets there. Paris and Bruges were increasingly important sites of repayment at the mid-fourteenth century. Merchants from Spain, Italy and southern France availed themselves of the Montpellier market in exchange as did Parisians in search of Mediterranean luxury products in the south.

The pervasive role of credit in the Montpellier economy is clearly visible in the foregoing study. It is not surprising that the specialists of medieval finance – the merchant-bankers, deposit bankers, changers, the pawnbrokers, Lombards, Jews and businessmen of the retail/wholesale trades – were thoroughly familiar with credit practices. The use of credit was much wider spread, however. Every social and occupational group in Montpellier has left traces of credit use, often to a substantial degree. Agricultural workers, artisans, members of the service trades, women of all walks of life availed themselves freely of credit techniques.

The utilization of credit operations in international trade in Montpellier was demonstrated through the surviving maritime *comanda* and *societas* contracts. Merchants and foreigners dominated this phase of economic activity although the occasional participation of changers and members of the retail/wholesale trades, such as mercers, drapers and *canabasserii*, in these partnerships has been noted. Contracts of foreign exchange which underpinned long-distance commerce revealed a similar specialization of the local and foreign commercial elite.

The extension of credit in land-based *comanda* and *societas* partnerships was the activity of a broader cross-section of the urban population, including artisans and agricultural workers alongside merchants and members of the retail/wholesale trades. Land-based *comanda* and *societas* partnerships infused investment credit into overland international trade and into local commercial and industrial activities.

The traffic in luxury goods belonged to an international commercial network which functioned on a foundation of commercial credit. Foreigners and merchants dominated the trade in spices, silks and mercery. Drapers participated along with merchants and foreigners in the cloth trade. While the retail trade in cloth in years of prosperity may have been primarily a cash undertaking, in years of economic distress, small retail credit transactions in cloth were recorded in the extant notarial registers. Spices and pharmaceutical goods from the Levant and saffron from Spain were traded among merchants and foreigners on credit in Montpellier and shipped to northern markets in Champagne and Paris, to England, and to Avignon. The silk trade counted as principal participants merchants, mercers and silk merchants. Foreign merchants constituted the majority of the clientele, buying silks and mercery on credit, while at a local level, the silk merchants, acquiring inventory stock on credit, assumed an expanding share of the retail trade in silks and mercery.

Artisans of local industries which refined the goods of international trade obtained raw materials on credit, promising at times to repay the debt obligation with the fruits of their own specialized labor. Evidence of these practices was found in the silk finishing industry, the cloth industry and in the dyeing trade.

The commerce in leather, furs and skins had regional and international aspects as did the trade in wool and the traffic in animals of burden and transport. These economic sectors were tied to local industrial activities, but they also had connections with international trade. Most of the extant notarial acts record credit transactions in these spheres. Artisans of local industry procured raw materials on credit from regional and international suppliers.

The market in agricultural products, in grapes and grain, reflected a greater percentage of cash transactions than did the trade in luxury goods, spices, silks, cloths, skins and furs. In years of economic distress such as 1327-1328, 1333 and 1347-1348, the infusion of consumer credit into this rural economic agricultural system was necessary to permit the acquisition of the means of survival on the part of the inhabitants of Montpellier and the immediate region. The use of credit techniques such as futures appeared in these years. The trade in grain presented a local profile in years of good harvest, while during agricultural crises, foreign grain imports involved merchants and specialized grain merchants in large credit transactions with foreigners.

The grain trade provided a significant link between the rural and commercial economies, as the purchasing strategy of merchants would seem to have been directly affected by the need for imported grain in years of poor harvest. The majority of acts relating to grain involved retail sales by *ordearii* or grain merchants of Montpellier. These specialists were supplied in turn by international merchants. One of these, Jacobus de Magalassio, whose exploits in commerce have been referred to earlier, acted on behalf of another Montpellier merchant in 1333 to make a sale of 4000 *setiers* of wheat to local grain merchants.[2] In the same year representatives of the Bardi Society sold 10,000 *setiers* of grain to a group of local grain merchants.[3] In 1334 merchants of Montpellier, Béziers and Narbonne were robbed of a cargo of wheat, alum, wax and leather goods on a return trip from Constantinople to Aigues-Mortes.[4] Here, the diversification of commercial investment by merchants is evident.

Record of some of the same versatility of merchant investment survives in 1327-1328, again a bad agricultural year. Boninus de Meldeo, immigrant from Novara, and a specialist in cloth and in financial affairs, dealt in grain on several occasions in those years.[5] Some of the merchant capital, which in years of good harvest would have been invested in the luxury trade, found its way into the grain trade in bad times when the necessity of feeding a large urban population presented potential for profit in the international grain trade.

[2] A. D. Hérault, II E 95/369, J. Holanie, f. 80v.
[3] A. D. Hérault, II E 95/369, J. Holanie, ff. 52v and 84v.
[4] See A. Germain, *Histoire du commerce de Montpellier*, 1: 150-152 and Pièce justificative n°. 109.
[5] A. D. Hérault, II E 95/368, J. Holanie, ff. 39r, 41r, 44v, 70v and 145v.

The use of credit and the participants in credit transactions varied according to the economic sector under examination. A closer look at specific sectors will permit a better understanding of business and economic change. The commercial economy, as reflected in *comanda* and *societas* partnerships, presented an economic profile of some fluctuation but basic adaptability to crisis. The 1330s and 1340s were decades when large investments were still being made. In this period the largest average *societas* investments – over 1600 *l. t.* – were recorded. Maritime *comanda* and *societas* partnerships maintained a high average per individual transaction with peaks of almost 600 *l. t.* recurring over fifty-five years. Land *comanda* investments preserved a certain buoyancy during the 1330s and 1340s.

The graph depicting the average value of loan credit transactions showed peaks of investment at the beginning of the fourteenth century with a gradually rising level of investment in the decades of the 1330s and 1340s. The pattern within loan credit is difficult to interpret because of the presence of both commercial and consumer credit functions within these practices. However, the growth of loan credit in the late 1340s in both the consumer and commercial spheres is consistent with the accentuation of general economic problems in the mid-fourteenth century. Distress loans were necessary for the procurement of the means of existence. Business loans may have complemented investments in commercial and industrial partnerships in an era of shrinking economic opportunities for profit. The broad base of participation of the urban population in loan credit rendered this type of credit operation responsive to a wide variety of needs.

Luxury goods and agricultural commodities also admit of scrutiny. Average values of silk transactions were rising over the years 1293-1342 but evidenced some decline in 1343, the last year of record.[6] Mercery of Lucca, damasks and brocades of the Lucchese silk finishing industry, sold on the Montpellier market, rose in price through 1339 with lower levels in 1341-1343.[7] Spice transactions held up throughout the period under study.[8] The average values of transactions in cloth declined steadily from 1293 through the 1340s, with the lowest level recorded in 1344.[9] Cloth transactions, comprising as they did both the retail and the wholesale market, were more vulnerable perhaps to the effects of economic crisis. Overall, luxury goods seem to have maintained relatively high average values of transactions. In contrast, average values in grain sales were down in years of record from 1327 to 1347 with two exceptions in 1333 and 1344, each a year of difficult harvest. Animal transactions reached their highest level in the 1330s with lower records in the late thirteenth century and again in the 1340s.[10]

[6] See Reyerson, "Medieval Silks in Montpellier."

[7] *Ibid.*

[8] A synopsis of spice transactions was given in Reyerson, "Commerce and Society in Montpellier," 2: 145-150.

[9] See Reyerson, "Le rôle de Montpellier dans le commerce des draps de laine avant 1350."

[10] A synopsis of animal transactions was given in Reyerson, "Commerce and Society in Montpellier," 2: 216-234.

It would seem possible to distinguish the responses to fourteenth-century crises of the commodities market and of consumer loan credit from that of the wholesale luxury trade and of commercial partnership investments. Products more closely tied to subsistence displayed a downward trend in prosperity in the years of extant notarial evidence, 1293-1348. In contrast, the wholesale commercial and speculative economy revealed ups and downs but overall greater resilience.

Movements of the average values of transactions can also be examined in light of factors such as monetary debasements and revaluations. Appendix 2 on "Monetary Problems" gives a chart of monetary changes. Comparisons of periods of debased *tournois* coinage, identified by the dates of changes in the *pied de monnaie* at coinage, and the average values provide certain coincidences which reinforce the distinctions between the behavior of the commodities market and consumer credit on the one hand and the commercial economy on the other. A low *pied de monnaie* signified a coinage of high silver content; the *pied de monnaie* of the good coinage of 1330, the standard used in this study, was 12. A *pied* of 24 indicated coins with one-half the silver content.

Highest average values in new loans and in grain sales occurred when the *pied* was at 12, although in the case of grain, it must be said that the high prices of 1333 were attributable in all likelihood to the bad agricultural conditions. The highest values of the cloth trade, influenced by the numbers of retail transactions of 1327-1328, occurred at low *pieds* of 12 and 15.

When consideration is shifted to the behavior of the luxury market, highest average values tended to come at times of debased coinage, that is, with high *pieds de monnaie*. Mercery of Lucca highs occurred at a *pied* of 24 in 1339 and in 1341 with *pieds*, first of 42 and then of 48. Silk sales obeyed the same pattern with the highest average transactions in 1342 when the *pied* was at 60. The spice trade did not lend itself to a study of average values of transactions for specific spices because of the lumping of items in some sales; spices overall present a mixed picture with sales over 300 *l. t.* occurring at *pieds* of 12, 24 and 48.

A third type of response is evident in the area of commercial investment in business partnerships. Average values reached heights in years when the *pied* was 12 or 24, but average levels were almost as high in 1341 when the *pied* was 48.

The response of consumer credit, retail cloth sales and grain transactions can be clearly distinguished from that of the wholesale luxury trade. The former reflected the highest level of investment when the silver content of coinage was high. In contrast, the wholesale commercial sector showed high levels of average transactions in periods of weak coinage. It may have been that the presence of a large foreign clientele with probable foreign coin resources favored a rash of purchases of luxury products under conditions of debased *tournois* coinage. The behavior of the luxury market, visible in credit recognitions of debt, must be differentiated, in turn, from commercial investments since the latter were more speculative in that they were based on estimates of future market activity.

Further operation of monetary factors in the behavior of sectors of the Montpellier economy is more difficult to assess. No coincidence between large coinage emissions and price levels has been observed.[11] There does seem to be a relationship between the silver content of coins and the face value (as opposed to converted value) of prices in the notarial registers; however, the differences in prices in years of good coinage and bad did not fluctuate on a scale of one to five as did the silver content of the coins.

The reaction of the Montpellier population to coinage debasement is yet another level upon which to evaluate the effects of monetary factors upon the economy. One reaction was observed in the cloth trade data of 1327-1328, prior to the revaluation of the currency in 1330. Cloth transactions were of a retail nature in these years and price quotations were often in real coins as opposed to money of account. Again in the early 1340s when the coinage was being progressively debased by the king of France, greater numbers of quotations in "current money" and in real coins appeared. While the rapidity with which coinage changes were instituted in Montpellier cannot be estimated, local awareness governed the adjustment of indebtedness. Coinage variations were taken into account on 5 July 1343, when an immigrant merchant from Huesca, one Thomas Hugonis, made a cession of debts through the intermediary of his procurator against two men of Marseillan near Agde to two of their fellow citizens.[12] The debt was 80 *l. t.* in 1338 money owed by an act established by a notary of Marseillan on 5 July 1338. According to the table of conversion of Appendix 2, "Monetary Problems," money of 5 July 1338 was governed by the minting of 1 January 1337 when the *pied de monnaie* was at 18. In return for the cession, Hugonis received 263 *l.* in current money. This latter sum was governed by the emission of 26 June 1342 at a *pied* of 60. The ratio of 18/60 equalling 0.3 closely resembles that of 80/263 equalling 0.304. Here, changes in a theoretical unit, the *pied de monnaie*, corresponded to currency variations on the local market place. This was not the only instance when coinage variations were taken into account in the settlement of debts.[13]

Finally, the fact that the consuls of Montpellier voiced concerns about the economic effects of variations in coinage is further proof of local awareness of monetary factors. Included in a litany of excuses to justify a refusal of fiscal contributions to the king of France in 1328 was the consuls' observation that monetary mutations of recent years had absorbed one-half of all monetary wealth.[14] The *pied de monnaie* was, in fact, at 24 in 1327, reflecting debasement of

[11] On coinage emissions of the Montpellier mint, see Marc Bompaire, "L'Atelier monétaire royal de Montpellier et la circulation monétaire en Bas Languedoc jusqu'au milieu du XVe siècle," Thèse, École des Chartes, 1980, Deuxième Partie, Chapitre II.

[12] A. D. Hérault, II E 95/372, J. Holanie *et al.*, f. 51r.

[13] A. M. Montpellier, II 3, J. Laurentii, f. 95v.

[14] Jean Combes, "Finances municipales et oppositions sociales à Montpellier au commencement du XIVe siècle," *Fédération historique* (1971), see p. 109. See also John Bell Henneman, *Royal Taxation in Fourteenth Century France. The Development of War Financing. 1322-1356* (Princeton, N.J., 1971); he examined in great detail the growth of French fiscality. On the 1328 negotiations, see p. 71. On public finance and fiscality in Montpellier, see Jacques Ellul, "Notes sur les impôts municipaux à Montpellier aux XIIIe et XIVe siècles," *Revue historique de droit français et étranger* (1938), 365-403.

July 1326.[15] The consuls complained further of French tax levies, of piracy by the Genoese and the Aragonese, and of the infertility of the soil which occasioned bad harvests. In such a business climate, the consuls stated that merchants were afraid to undertake commercial ventures.

From the distant perspective of the late twentieth century, the outlines of a pattern of business practice still emerge as the economic activities of the inhabitants of Montpellier and foreigners are passed in review. Two economic systems are visible in the remaining evidence, the one, agricultural and subsistence oriented, the other urban and international with links to the trade and finance of medieval Europe.[16] These two economic systems had many interlocking features but they can be distinguished on several levels: variations in the participation of Montpelliérains and foreigners; differing credit operations; divergent trends in the average values of transactions over the years of notarial evidence, 1293-1348; and distinct responses to economic crisis.

It remains, in conclusion, to place the development of banking and finance in Montpellier in broader European perspective. The similarities, and to a lesser degree, the contrasts between the Montpellier evidence and that of other towns of southern France such as Toulouse, Grasse and Marseille have been pointed out on numerous occasions throughout this study. The case of Montpellier is an unusual one, however, in that the town, while not a port, was sufficiently close to the sea to assume the attributes of a port in the sphere of international trade. Sale credits represented an important, if inestimable, portion of transactions in the international trade of Montpellier, while investments in business partnerships attracted a large amount of local capital.

Credit and finance in Montpellier did not attain the technical sophistication of the great Italian ports and the large Flemish towns. The bill of exchange would not be in use in Montpellier, nor for that matter in Marseille, Toulouse or Barcelona, until the late fourteenth century. However, the notarial contract of exchange permitted the evolution of an intricate financial network linking Italy and Spain and connecting Mediterranean lands with northern France through the foreign exchange market of Montpellier. Complex administrative organization of merchant-banking companies was not characteristic of business partnership in Montpellier. Smaller scale family partnerships and one-venture commercial engagements recalling those of Genoa were representative of commercial structures in Montpellier. In an era of growing commercial risks and shrinking profits, such organization may well have permitted a quicker and more flexible response to economic exigencies. Deposit banking activities left only fragmentary records in the extant notarial registers, yet a whole range of operations is present in the surviving evidence. The Montpellier changers were of long-standing

[15] John Bell Henneman, *Royal Taxation in Fourteenth Century France*, p. 339.

[16] My study of land ownership and property rights suggests that the real estate economy behaved like the commodities market and consumer credit. See the Preface, n. 20 above. The use of cash transactions in real estate was much more prevalent than in commerce.

reputation within the town; their business interests and contacts were diversified. They may well, like their counterparts in Bruges and in Italy, have performed transfer banking functions.

The adaptability of business techniques to the needs of the local economic situation in Montpellier is perhaps best demonstrated through the negotiability of credit obligations. Cessions of credits in one economic sector permitted the creditor to cover debt obligations in another sector. Cessions of rights to specific credits enabled creditors to recover some portion of their original investment in cases where debt collection was inconvenient or protracted.

The financial techniques of Montpellier were responsive to economic needs. An expansion of consumer credit occurred in times of economic distress. Short-term business partnerships permitted the exploitation of immediate financial options. Merchants shifted their investment focuses from the luxury trade to the commodity trade in grain in eras of subsistence crisis. The negotiability of credit obligations smoothed transitions from one investment to another. Local business practice was imitative of Italian models from the time of earliest commercial expansion in Montpellier. These methods were successfully adapted by local inhabitants to the economic needs of a center of regional and local activities and of an entrepot of international trade and finance on the Mediterranean frontier of medieval France.

Appendix 1

Documents

COMANDA PARTNERSHIP
A. D. Hérault, II E 95/372, folio 52v.

7 July 1343.

Anno et die predictis.
Ego, Bernardus Cadoleti, mercator Narbonensis etc. confiteor etc. vobis Jacobo de Magalassio Montepessulano [sic] et Petro Goti de Narbonense, mercatoribus presentibus etc., me a vobis habere et tenere causa comande etc. scilicet: mille noningentas quadraginta et quinque libras et decem solidos monete nunc currente, vestros comunes implicatos ad meam voluntatem, in bonis pannis laneis hujus terre et Francie, tam bene valentibus, in quibus renuncio etc.

Cum qua comanda predicta promito, pro vobis et vestro nomine, ire et viatgiare, duce Deo, in partibus Cicilie, et ipso in aliis partibus, in navi que nunc est in portu Aquarum-Mortuarum cujus est patronus Columbaris Lartani de Janua. Et de dicto viatgio recte reddere in dicta navi, vel in alio navili in quo mihi utilius videbitur, ad portum Aquarum-Mortuarum vel ad alium portum ad quem volueritis et prout mihi mandabitis, eundo tamen et reddeundo ad periculum et ad resegne vestrum et ad fortunam Dei, ignis, maris, et malarum gentium. Et in dicto viatgio mercari, lucrari et negociari licite, bene et legaliter, et ut melius et utilius mihi videbitur, et in bonis rebus et mercaturis licitis. Et inde, in dicto viatgio scilicet: eundo et reddeundo, facere et procurare, pro posse meo, totum lucrum, comodum et emolumentum quod licite facere et adquirere potero cum dicta comanda. Ita tamen quod de meo salario et labore predictorum vos mihi satisfaciatis ad voluntatem vestram.

Promito etc., et convenio, dictis Jacobo de Magalassio et Petro Goti stipulantibus, et vestris per vos, quod dictam comandam in predictis partibus Cicilie, in bonis mercaturis et rebus non prohibitis, in quibus mihi utilius videbitur, pro vobis implicabo bene et legaliter et ut melius potero. Et ipsam dictam comandam per me sit implicatam vobis stipulantibus, seu vestris, reddam et solvam et in posse vestrum redducam. Et de omnibus predictis, vobis et vestris, bonum et legale computum, ac plenam, claram et districtam rationem reddam, absque fraude, incontinenti facto et completo dicto viatgio, et me et dicta comanda ad partes ipsas regressus de eodem.

Pro quibus etc., et pro omni restitutione dampni etc., obligo etc. me et omnia bona mea presentia et futura, volens etc. quod Curia Regis Montispessulani et alia quelibet etc., secundum formam statuti novi Montispessulani incipientis: "si per Christianum," et etiam juxta et secundum consuetudines et statuta Montispessulani super societatibus et comandis. Renuncio etc. Et predicta etc. attendere etc. promito et juro etc.

Actum in Montepessulano. Horum sunt testes: Johannes Naturalis, piperarius, Raymundus de Capite-Vilari, filius quondam magistri Raymundi de Capite-Vilari, jurisperiti Montispessulani et Ego ....

Post hec, anno domini M CCC XLVII et die vicesima mensis augusti, hec nota sunt cancellata, ut debitum hinc inde solutum, de partium voluntate, quantitate altera alterum de predictis.

Testes: Bremundus Buxer, clericus, magister Johannes Augerii, notarius regis et Ego, Johannes Holanie, notarius etc.

Loan

A. D. Hérault, II E 95/368, f. 98r.

2 January 1328.

Anno et die predictis. Ego Petrus de Coiano, mercerius Montispessulani, etc. confiteor etc. me debere vobis Guillelmo Borcati, cultori Montispessulani, presenti etc. scilicet: septuaginta et duos solidos turonensium parvorum etc. causa mutui etc. Solvere promito etc. in proximo festo pascali domini etc. Sub viribus etc. sigilli etc. Promito et juro etc.

Actum in Montepessulano. Horum sunt testes: Jacobus Petri, cultor, Stephanus Salvestri, esparerius Montispessulani, et Ego etc.

Extractum est instrumentum.

Downpayment Sale - Future in Grapes

A. D. Hérault, II E 95/368, f. 34v.

25 August 1327.

Anno et die predictis. Nos Guillelmus Andree, sartor Montispessulani, et Gaudiosa coniuges etc. vendimus vobis Arnaudo Marialis, sartori dicti loci presenti etc. scilicet: sexdecim saumatas fruthe racemorum etc. de tribus vineis nostris quorum una sita est apud Negacatz; alia sita est apud Coconem et ista confrontatur cum possessione Guillelmi de Podio, notarii; alia vero sita est in loco vocato Terrauba etc. pro pretio cuiuslibet saumate duodecim solidos et quatuor denarios turonensium de quarum universali pretio habemus a vobis sexaginta solidos turonensium. In quibus renunciamus etc. Residuum vero dicti universalis pretii vobis dabitis et soluetis nobis in continenti recepta per vos dicta frutha quod ego dictus Arnaudus facere promito etc. Solvere promitimus etc. Et apportare etc. in proximis vendemiis tempore opportuno etc. Sub viribus etc. sigilli etc. promitimus et juramus etc.

Actum in Montepessulano. Testes: Jacobus Taruesta, Jacobus Teralh, cultores dicti loci, et Ego etc.

Foreign Exchange Contract
A. D. Hérault, II E 95/372, f. 56v.

19 July 1343.

Anno quo supra et die decima octava mensis julii, domino Philippo etc. Ego, Durantus Vitalis, mercator, habitator Montispessulani, nomine meo proprio, et etiam ut procurator, cum instrumento inde subscripto et signato per magistrum Petrum de Pena, notarium regis, habitatorem Montispessulani, sub anno domini M CCC XXXIX et die XV mensis aprilis, et nomine procuratorio Johannis Janerii et Bernardi Cazalis, mercatorum de Orlhaco, et utroque nomine insolidum, confiteor me debere vobis, Petro de Ferreriis, mercatori Montispessulani presenti etc. scilicet: novingentas libras monete nunc currente pro cambio alterius bone monete, tam bene valente, quam a vobis, in Montepessulano, habui, nominibus quibus supra etc.

Solvere promito, nominibus quibus supra etc., in Montepessulano, per totum proximum mensum augusti, cum omni restitutione dampni etc.

Obligans etc. me et dictos Johannem et Bernardum, et nostrum quemlibet insolidum, et omnia bona mea, omniaque bona dictorum Johannis et Bernardi, et cujuslibet nostrum insolidum, presentia et futura. Renuncio etc. per fidem meam et dictorum Johannis et Bernardi etc.

Actum in Montepessulano. Horum sunt testes: Raymundus de Fonte, notarius regis, Guillelmus Jordani, ligator, et Ego etc.

Post hec, anno quo supra et die XXI octobris, hec nota sunt cancellata ut debitum solutum, de voluntate dicti Duranti Vitalis et de mandato Johannis Deleuze, mercerii, procuratoris dicti Petri de Ferreriis, prout de sua procuratione constat per instrumentum inde factum per me Johannem Holanie, notarium regis, sub anno quo supra et die XXVIII martii. Testes: Raymundus de Fonte, notarius regis, Johannes et Guiraudus Naturalis, fratres, piperarii Montispessulani, et Ego, etc.

Appendix 2

Monetary Problems

The monetary history of the Mediterranean world in the Middle Ages has yet to be explored fully. On a smaller scale, the same may be said of Montpellier, although this situation has been remedied in part through a study of the Montpellier mint in the late Middle Ages by a student of the École des Chartes.[1] At the center of every study of medieval economic history lies the problem of medieval currencies.[2] Questions regarding the movement of prices and the volume of trade and manufacture remain unanswerable in the absence of reliable price series and of import/export statistics. At a less ambitious level, comparison of the activities in various economic sectors of Montpellier has been attempted. Given the lack of sound data, comparisons of average transactions and of variations in transaction size from year to year have been used as a guide to the discussion of the importance of local and international sectors. Such comparisons are dependent upon the establishment of a standard of conversion for the multiple currencies cited in the notarial acts.[3] A brief historical perspective on coinage traditions in the region of Montpellier will provide an introduction to the problems of monetary conversion.

Silver coinage traditions were well established in the region of Montpellier long before the Capetian entry into southern French affairs.[4] The financial vocation of

[1] Marc Bompaire, "L'Atelier monétaire royal de Montpellier et la circulation monétaire en Bas Languedoc jusqu'au milieu du xve siècle," Thèse, École des Chartes, 1980. Thomas N. Bisson, *Conservation of Coinage. Monetary Exploitation and its Restraint in France, Catalonia, and Aragon (c. A.D. 1000-c. 1225)* (Oxford, 1979), has provided a useful study of the earlier period.

I am grateful to Dr. Alan M. Stahl, Curator of Medieval Coins at the American Numismatic Society, for his reading of this appendix on monetary problems. All the errors herein are entirely my own.

[2] The medieval merchant had to be a master of calculation in the matter of medieval currencies, as the manual of Francesco di Balduccio Pegolotti, *La pratica della mercatura*, ed. Allen Evans (Cambridge, Mass., 1936), illustrates.

[3] John Bell Henneman, *Royal Taxation in Fourteenth Century France. The Development of War Financing, 1322-1356* (Princeton, N. J. 1971), p. 333, was pessimistic regarding the possibility of comparisons: "Since most financial documents expressed figures in money of account, it should, in theory, be possible to convert these to marks and have a standard basis for comparing figures from periods of debasement with those from periods of sounder currency. So few financial documents have survived, however, that we cannot rely on this computation with complete assurance." Henneman gives a concise and clear presentation of monetary problems in his Appendix 1, pp. 331-353.

[4] The best treatment of local coinages remains Alexandre Germain, "Mémoire sur les anciennes monnaies seigneuriales de Melgueil et de Montpellier," *Mem. soc. arch. Mplr.*, 3 (1850-1854), 133-257. Also useful is the brief synthesis by Mireille Castaing-Sicard, *Monnaies féodales et circulation monétaire en Languedoc (x^e^-xiiie siècles)* (Toulouse, 1961).

medieval Montpellier was related to the proximity of the mint of Melgueil which can be traced first in the tenth century.[5] The local seigneurial family, the Guilhem, benefited from a share of mint profits from as early as 1125 when Count Bernard IV of Melgueil conceded six of the twelve *deniers* of seignoriage to Guilhem VI as a guarantee for a loan. In 1130, in return for another loan, the count gave Guilhem VI three *deniers* of every twenty *sous* in fief.[6] The Guilhem were one of the few noble families of southern France to possess important financial resources. Guilhem VII (1146-1172) and Guilhem VIII (1172-1202) were able to purchase lands in order to extend the boundaries of their seigneury in the second half of the twelfth century.[7] Guilhem VIII invested over 100,000 *sous melgoriens* in territorial expansion.[8]

With the replacement of the Guilhem family by the kings of Aragon as local lords in 1204, the establishment of the Montpellier consulate, and the transfer of the county of Melgueil to the bishop of Maguelone in 1215, a new division of seignoriage of silver coinage emerged; to the bishop-count went two *deniers* per *livre*, to the king-lord, two *deniers* and to the consulate, one *denier*.[9] The success of *melgorien* money in the south of France furnished a solid base for commercial and financial expansion.

Melgorien coinage was of low face value but of impressive stability. Evaluated at forty-eight *sous* to the mark in 1130, it remained essentially unchanged until 1175 when a devaluation lowered its value to sixty *sous* to the mark.[10] From 1175-1261 this equivalence persisted, permitting *melgorien* coinage to replace most of the baronial moneys in circulation in Lower Languedoc.[11] The range of circulation of *melgorien* coins stretched as far as Marseille in the east and Orange in the northeast. According to a bishop of Maguelone in the thirteenth century, it was used "in the *sénéchaussées* of Carcassonne and Beaucaire, in the Albigeois and in the county of Millau." [12]

The triumph of French money over *melgorien* coinage was a lengthy process. After papal infeudation of the county of Melgueil to the bishop of Maguelone, the French position regarding *melgorien* money was cautious. Saint Louis formally recognized the coinage rights of the bishop over which the papacy had ultimate surveillance.[13] Following the French acquisition of Montpelliéret, Philip IV decreed the transfer of the royal mint from Sommières to Montpellier, a move

[5] M. Castaing-Sicard, *Monnaies féodales*, p. 29.

[6] *Ibid.*, pp. 30-31. See also *LIM*, acts LXVII and LXVIII, pp. 119-123.

[7] Martine Dépinay, "Un aspect de l'activité des seigneurs de Montpellier," pp. 63-70.

[8] *Ibid.*, pp. 84-91.

[9] M. Castaing-Sicard, *Monnaies féodales*, p. 30.

[10] *Ibid.*, p. 31.

[11] *Ibid.*, pp. 10, 34.

[12] *Ibid.*, p. 33.

[13] A. Germain, "Mémoire sur les anciennes monnaies seigneuriales," p. 162. See also Thomas N. Bisson, "Coinage and Royal Monetary Policy in Languedoc during the Reign of Saint Louis," *Speculum* 32 (1957), 443-469, and "À propos d'un registre municipal de Narbonne. Notes sur la chronologie des ordonnances monétaires de Louis IX (1263-1265)," *Annales du Midi* 72 (1960), 83-88.

which took almost fifty years to execute.[14] Although Philip recognized the bishop of Maguelone's continuing right to coin *melgorien* money, he attempted to restrict the legitimate range of these coins to the diocese of Maguelone.[15] The bishop retorted by referring to the wide geographic use of his coinage. The bishop's jurisdiction over *melgorien* moneyers was acknowledged by Philip IV in letters of January 1298 to the seneschal of Beaucaire.[16] This jurisdiction was confirmed in 1329 by Philip VI and in 1355 by John. From 1293 on, however, conflicts of jurisdiction over these moneyers were numerous.[17].

The gradual ascendancy of *tournois* currency over *melgorien* coins was evident in the first half of the fourteenth century. In their 1328 assessment of economic conditions in Montpellier, the consuls revealed the dependence of commercial affairs upon the prosperity of *tournois* coinage.[18] The notarial registers of 1327-1348 corroborate the dominance of the latter in commercial and financial affairs. With the exception of property dues, sums were quoted characteristically in *tournois* money or in French gold coins.[19] In some transactions, such as exchange contracts, foreign currencies were used. The striking of *melgorien* coins was noted as late as 1316 and the habit of keeping accounts in *melgorien* coinage persisted into the seventeenth century, but a substantial decline in this currency was evident by the mid-fourteenth century.[20]

In the late thirteenth century the king of France assumed a more aggressive stance with regard to the coinage of the kings of Aragon-Majorca in Montpellier. In 1273 Jacme I had created his own coinage on the grounds that *melgorien* currency, despite recent encouragement, was not sufficient in quantity for the commercial needs of merchants of Montpellier.[21] Jacme coined silver in several denominations: a *gros* worth twelve *deniers* of Melgueil and an *obole* equal to six *deniers*. Sixty *gros deniers* were coined from a *marc* of Montpellier (239.1263 gm).[22] The Aragonese mint was installed at Castelnau-le-Lez, just north of Montpellier. On 4 February 1273, Jacme I prohibited the circulation of all coins with the exception of *melgorien* money and his new *gros* and *oboles* in the

[14] A. Germain, "Mémoire sur les anciennes monnaies seigneuriales," p. 156.

[15] *Ibid.*, p. 163.

[16] *Ibid.*, p. 165.

[17] *Ibid.*, p. 167.

[18] J. Combes, "Finances municipales et oppositions sociales," p. 108.

[19] A. D. Hérault, II E 95/368-377, *passim*.

[20] M. Castaing-Sicard, *Monnaies féodales*, pp. 81-82.

[21] A. Germain, "Mémoire sur les anciennes monnaies seigneuriales," pp. 151-152. This testimony suggests that the economy of Montpellier was still enjoying expansion in the 1270s. It is in this context that the controversial issue of *millarès*, a coinage imitation of Arab money by the bishop of Maguelone with the help of some inhabitants of Montpellier, must be set. On the *millarès*, see A. Germain, "De la monnaie Mahométane attribuée à un évêque de Maguelonne," *Mem. soc. arch. Mplr.* 3 (1850-1854), 683ff. See also Louis Blancard, "Le *millarès*, étude sur une monnaie du XIIIe siècle imitée de l'arabe par les chrétiens pour les besoins de leur commerce en pays maure," (Marseille, 1876), pp. 428-441. See the more recent discussion of the *millarès* in Andrew M. Watson, "Back to Gold- and Silver," *Economic History Review*, 2nd ser., 20 (1967), 12-14.

[22] This figure for the marc of Montpellier is drawn from Étienne Fournial, *Histoire monétaire de l'Occident médiéval* (Paris, 1970), p. 166.

seigneury of Montpellier.[23] This policy of exclusion met with resistance on the part of the French. Although Jacme II of Majorca confirmed Jacme I's position in 1278 and the existence of the Castelnau mint in 1277, the agreement of 1282 between the kings of France and Majorca extended the same recognition to French coins within Montpellier as that enjoyed by Majorcan money.[24]

The destruction of Majorcan currency was pursued by the French kings after the purchase of Montpelliéret; French and *melgorien* coinages predominated. It is significant that the earliest extant notarial registers of 1293-1294 and 1301-1302 contain no mention of the use of Majorcan coins.[25] In a letter of 1317 to the seneschal of Beaucaire, Philip V responded to complaints about the abuses of royal officials with regard to Majorcan money by emphasizing that the king of France alone had the right to strike coins in Montpellier and in the barony of Montpellier in keeping with his direct domain as the lord of Montpelliéret.[26] The assertion of such French prerogatives was rendered all the more feasible by the weakness of Jacme I's successors as kings of Majorca. The insertion of French money into the economic system of Montpellier led to the vulnerability of the latter to monetary manipulations practiced with frequency by the last Capetians and the first Valois kings.[27] In spite of the ensuing problems of monetary debasements, the long history of mint activity in the region of Montpellier contributed to the position which Montpellier occupied in the world of European finance in the Middle Ages.

A variety of currencies were quoted in the notarial acts of Montpellier over the period 1293-1348. In 1293-1294 *melgorien* currency predominated in all manner of transactions.[28] By 1301-1302 *tournois* coins were in ascendance.[29] In the notarial evidence of 1327-1348, sums were cited most frequently in *deniers tournois*, real coins of French royal issue which the documents term *turonensium parvorum* and in *tournois* of account.[30] However, examples of numerous other methods of quotation exist in these years. Gold coins, French *agneaux* and *réaux*, *écus*, florins, silver and gold *marcs* as well as multiple foreign currencies, especially in contracts of exchange, can be found.[31] In the years 1342-1343 money termed simply "current" became increasingly common, reflecting the unstable monetary climate preceding the currency reform of 26 October 1343.[32]

[23] A. Germain, "Mémoire sur les anciennes monnaies seigneuriales," p. 157.

[24] *Ibid.*, pp. 150 and 155.

[25] P. Wolff, *Commerces et marchands de Toulouse (vers 1350-vers 1450)*, pp. 303-354, provides an excellent discussion of medieval monetary problems with reflections on the period before 1350 as well as the century following 1350.

[26] A. Germain, "Mémoire sur les anciennes monnaies seigneuriales," p. 157.

[27] On the monetary mutations in question, see E. Fournial, *Histoire monétaire*, Chapters 4 and 5, pp. 78-125.

[28] A. M. Montpellier, II 1, J. Grimaudi.

[29] A. M. Montpellier, II 2, J. Grimaudi.

[30] A. M. Montpellier, II 3, J. Laurentii and A. D. Hérault, II E 95/368-377.

[31] The variety of medieval French coins has been described by Jean Lafaurie, *Les monnaies des rois de France de Hugues Capet à Louis XII*, 2 vols. (Paris, 1951-1956).

[32] A. D. Hérault, II E 95/372, J. Holanie *et al.*, f. 51r.

The development of a standard of currency conversion, even within *tournois* coinage to say nothing of conversions between currencies, is fraught with pitfalls. With the exception of the conversion of *melgorien* currency into *livres tournois*, the development of equivalences between *livres tournois* and baronial French and foreign currencies has not been attempted.[33] The currency manipulations of the Capetian and Valois kings resulted in devaluations and revaluations of the *livre tournois* over the period under study.[34] Underlying the following method of conversion is the assumption that the relative silver content of coins was a reasonable guide to their relative worth. The coinage issued as a result of the monetary reform of Philip VI on 8 April 1330, was selected as the norm to which weaker coinage issues were converted.[35] This conversion was accomplished by assessing the level of debasement according to changes in the *pied de monnaie*, a figure which resulted from a fractional formula expressing in the numerator the *taille*, or number of coins minted from one *marc*, multiplied by the *prix* (or *cours*), the value of the coin established officially by the king in *deniers tournois*, and in the denominator the *titre*, or silver content of the coin, calculated in *deniers* and *grains* of the most refined silver of the era, *argent-le-roy*, multiplied by five:[36]

$$\frac{\text{Taille} \times \text{Cours}}{5 \times \text{Titre}}$$

The lower the *pied de monnaie*, the sounder the coinage.[37] Comparison of the *pieds* established at the recorded dates of French monetary mutations has permitted the development of a fractional multiplier relating less pure coins to the 1330 standard.

[33] A recent brief but useful examination of monetary history is that of E. Fournial, *Histoire monétaire*. See pp. 148-159 for a description of the efforts of French kings to suppress baronial coinages. On the baronial coinages in Languedoc, cf. M. Castaing-Sicard, *Monnaies féodales*.

[34] There exist numerous studies of the variations of French currency in the Late Middle Ages: A. Landry, *Essai économique sur les mutations des monnaies dans l'ancienne France de Philippe le Bel à Charles VII* (Paris, 1910); Raymond Cazelles, "Quelques réflexions à propos des mutations de la monnaie royale française (1295-1360)," *Le Moyen Âge* 72 (1966), 83-105, 251-278; A. Grunsweig, "Les incidences internationales des mutations monétaires de Philippe le Bel," *Le Moyen Âge* 59 (1953), 117-172; Harry A. Miskimin, *Money, Prices and Foreign Exchange* (New Haven, 1963); Natalis de Wailly, "Mémoire sur les variations de la livre tournois depuis le règne de Saint Louis jusqu'à l'établissement de la monnaie décimale," *Mémoires de l'Institut Impérial de France* 21 (1857), pt. 2, 177-427; P. Guilhiermoz, "Avis sur la question monétaire donnés aux rois Philippe le Hardi, Philippe le Bel, Louis X et Charles le Bel," *Revue Numismatique* 30, part 7 (1927), 96-110; Allan Evans, "Some Coinage Systems of the Fourteenth Century," *Journal of Economic and Business History* 3 (1931), 481-496; Carlo Cipolla, *Money, Prices and Civilization in the Mediterranean World, 5-17th Centuries* (Princeton, N.J., 1956) and *Studi di storia della moneta* (Pavia, 1948). On contemporary theory behind the monetary manipulations, see E. Bridrey, *La théorie de la monnaie au XIVe siècle, Nicole Oresme* (Paris, 1906).

[35] On this reform, see E. Fournial, *Histoire monétaire*, pp. 94-95.

[36] On the *pied de monnaie*, see John B. Henneman, *Royal Taxation in Fourteenth Century France*, pp. 332-333 and Harry A. Miskimin, *Money, Prices and Foreign Exchange*, pp. 32-36.

[37] In the eyes of contemporaries the coinage ideal was that of Saint Louis. See John B. Henneman, *Royal Taxation in Fourteenth Century France*, p. 339.

Dates of changes in the *pied de monnaie* of coins have been carefully respected in the currency conversions. Acts passed after such dates were computed under the supposed new conditions, in an effort to maintain a consistent approach, but several caveats deserve mention with regard to the inevitable errors of such a tactic. It is a certainty that the old coins did not disappear immediately from circulation even though royal legislation declared them invalid and ordered that they be recalled for the reminting of new issues.[38] How successfully old money was recalled and how quickly new coins entered circulation are questions which cannot be answered satisfactorily. Moreover, given the fact that Montpellier remained in principle a foreign market place until its purchase in 1349, it is impossible to ascertain at dates of royal mutation, when corresponding coinage records are lacking for the mint of Montpellier, whether any change in local coinage usage occurred.[39]

According to Étienne Fournial, as a result of the currency reform of 8 April 1330, the *gros tournois* had a *titre* of 0.958, a *poids* of 4.079 gm and a *cours* of 12 *d. t.* The black money *denier tournois* (*petit tournois*) had a *titre* of .305, a *poids* of 1.112 gm and a *cours* of 1 *d. t.*[40] The *d. t.* of the 1330 reform contained 0.3263 gm *argent de fin*, slightly less than the 0.3369 gm of the coinage of Saint Louis. This reform brought the currency back to a standard only 3.3 percent lower than that of the revered money of 1266-1270.[41] In the intervening years, *tournois* coinage had traversed a series of crises. From 1285 the price of silver was rising, a trend which resulted in instability in the *tournois* currency in the early 1290s. It would seem that black money remained unchanged, however, and as a result, the quotations in *tournois* coinage of 1293-1294 were assimilated with 1330 good money for the purposes of this study.[42] A series of measures in the late 1290s were unable to arrest the rising price of silver and the probable resulting debasement of black money. The confusion of contemporary legislation is such that its practical effects are impossible to estimate.[43] As a result, for the limited data of 1301-1302, the same assimilation with the money of 1330 has been utilized, although here the margin of error may be higher than for 1293-1294.

The local *melgorien* coinage has been converted into *tournois* coinage. The rate of exchange between these two currencies was set in 1315 by Philip v at 13 *deniers melgoriens* for 12 *deniers tournois*. The *denier melgorien* was thus worth .92 *d. t.*; its weight was 1.045 gm.[44] The *denier tournois* had been reformed in

[38] See the comments of Jean Favier, *Philippe le Bel* (Paris, 1978), p. 151.

[39] H. Miskimin, *Money, Prices and Foreign Exchange*, Appendix D, Table 2, pp. 161-169, gave dates of coinage issues at the mint of Montpellier during the period under study. The number of mentions is limited, and more general dates were chosen for the establishment of the table of conversion.

[40] E. Fournial, *Histoire monétaire*, p. 94.

[41] *Ibid.*, p. 95.

[42] *Ibid.*, p. 88.

[43] *Ibid.*, pp. 88-89. On supplies of silver and gold and their relative values, see Andrew M. Watson, "Back to Gold- and Silver," pp. 1-34.

[44] E. Fournial, *Histoire monétaire*, p. 153. The last recorded minting of the *melgorien* coinage was in 1316. I am grateful to Dr. Alan M. Stahl for this information.

1313 to the equivalent of 0.336 gm silver, slightly higher in silver content than that of 1330 (0.3263 gm).[45] Since the literature consulted did not indicate a radical reevaluation of *deniers melgoriens* between 1293 and 1315, the figure of .92 has been adopted as the fractional multiplier for the conversion of *deniers melgoriens* to the good money of 1330.

From 1327 to 1348 the following table of conversion was established using data provided by the works of John Bell Henneman, Étienne Fournial and Harry A. Miskimin regarding the variations in silver coinage.[46]

Tournois of account were interpreted as *deniers tournois* unless otherwise indicated.[47] The local notaries on occasion specified that payment was to be made in *gros tournois*.[48] With regard to French gold coins (real money), the silver coin equivalences were drawn from the tables of Natalis de Wailly.[49] The silver equivalences were then adjusted according to the table of currency conversion.

The method of currency conversion just outlined was first utilized in a study of the silk trade of Montpellier from 1293-1348.[50] A common standard of currency permitted comparisons in trade from year to year and the study of the evolution of this economic sector. In the present monograph the method has been extended to permit exploration of changes in loans and commercial partnerships. Because of the use of multiple foreign currencies in exchange contract quotations, conversions were not attempted here. It may be possible, after further research in international monetary history on the part of specialists, to proceed with such conversions.[51]

[45] E. Fournial, *Histoire monétaire*, p. 91.

[46] For the years 1327-1328 the *pied*/4 was at 6 according to J. B. Henneman, *Royal Taxation in Fourteenth Century France*, p. 339. H. A. Miskimin, *Money, Prices and Foreign Exchange*, p. 166, provided an alternative quotation of 6.31 for the period 8 January-7 November 1328. Miskimin also cited the use of 6 for this value, and 6 has been retained for the purposes of the conversion table. The value of the silver marc established by the king was 1/4 of the *pied*.

For the purposes of calculation all transaction quotations were based on the closest full *livre*, rounding upwards from 1/2 to the higher figure and downwards from 1/2 to the next lowest *livre*.

According to E. Fournial, *Histoire monétaire*, p. 100, the good money of 1330 lasted until at least 1 January 1337. However, J. B. Henneman, p. 339, and H. A. Miskimin, p. 166, show issues of weaker currency in 1333 and 1334 with a *pied* of 16.6 and 18. I have followed Fournial in the table.

[47] It has not been possible on the basis of the Montpellier evidence to determine whether there was one unchangeable system of account in operation or multiple systems, as P. Wolff, *Commerces et marchands de Toulouse*, pp. 310-311, discerned for the later period.

[48] See, for example, A. D. Hérault, II E 95/377, B. Egidii, f. 284v where it was specifically stated that the silver *tournois* were worth 15 *d. t.* each.

[49] See n. 34 above. P. Wolff, *Commerces et marchands de Toulouse*, p. 305, n. 5 has termed these tables justly criticized but never replaced. These tables should be used with the corrections of A. Dieudonné, *Manuel de numismatique française*, 2 *Monnaies royales depuis Hugues Capet* (Paris, 1916).

[50] Reyerson, "Medieval Silks in Montpellier: The Silk Market ca. 1250-ca. 1350," *The Journal of European Economic History* 11 (1982), 117-140.

[51] It may be possible as the work of Peter Spufford and Wendy Wilkinson proceeds for me to perform some of these conversions in contracts of foreign exchange. I am grateful to Dr. Alan M. Stahl for having sent me a Xerox copy of P. Spufford and W. Wilkinson, "Interim Listing of the Exchange Rates of Medieval Europe" (The University, Keele, Staffordshire, 1977), ms.

TABLE OF CURRENCY CONVERSION

Date of Mutation	Pied de Monnaie	Fractional Multiplier
1327 (from July 1326)	24	1/2
1330 (April 8)	12 (index)	1
1337 January 1	18	2/3
1338 October 1	24	1/2
1340 January 29	30	2/5
1340 April 6	36	1/3
1341 January 27	42	2/7
1341 February 17	48	1/4
1342 June 26	60	1/5
1343 October 26	15	4/5
1346 April 27	24	1/2
1347 July	36	1/3
1348 January	22	6/11

Sources: Étienne Fournial, *Histoire monétaire de l'occident médiéval* (Paris, 1970); John Bell Henneman, *Royal Taxation in Fourteenth Century France: The Development of War Financing. 1322-1356* (Princeton, 1971); Harry A. Miskimin, *Money, Prices and Foreign Exchange in Fourteenth-Century France* (New Haven, 1963).

Bibliography

A. Archives

France:

1. *Archives Départementales de l'Hérault.*
   The following notarial registers have been exploited exhaustively (act by act):
   in: *II E 95/ Répertoire numérique des registres de notaires acquis par le clergé de Montpellier entre 1690 et 1704* by Marcel Gouron et Yvette Le Brigand. Montpellier, 1968 (MS)

		No. folios	No. legible acts
II E 95/368 Holanie, J.	7 Jul. 1327-3 Apr. 1328	151	825
II E 95/369 Holanie, J.	26 Mar. 1333-20 Dec. 1333	115	654
II E 95/370 Holanie, J.	16 Apr. 1336-7 Sept. 1336	131	356
II E 95/371 Holanie, J.	26 Mar. 1342-18 Oct. 1342	159	386
II E 95/372 Holanie, J. *et al.*	26 Mar. 1343-24 Feb. 1344	177	392
II E 95/373 Podio, G. de	1333	28	70
II E 95/374 Nogareti, G.	10 Oct. 1337-12 Nov. 1342	94	325
II E 95/375 Pena, P. de	31 Mar. 1339-22 Nov. 1339	139	309
II E 95/376 Laurentii, J.	1343-1346	12	
II E 95/377 Egidii, B.	17 Jan. 1347-23 Jun. 1348	318*	564

In addition, certain acts suggested by the published and manuscript inventories were examined in the following *fonds*:

* There is a misnumbering of II E 95/377, B. Egidii with a skip of 100 folios between f. 123v and f. 224v.

in: *Archives ecclésiastiques de l'Hérault, série G, clergé séculier. Répertoire numérique détaillé*, by Marcel Gouron, Montpellier, 1970.
Particularly: G 1244 reg. of the notary, Jean de Sala (1342).
Reception in doctorates of canon law and civil law.
in: *Série S, travaux publics et transports. Répertoire numérique détaillé*, by Pierre Jouve, Montpellier, 1968.
S 2539: *répertoire du Service Vicinal sur les Drailles* (XIXe s.)
in: *Répertoire numérique détaillé des parchemins de Cournonterral*, by Danièle Neirinck, Montpellier, 1969 (ms).
References have been made in the footnotes to specific acts.

2. *Archives Départementales des Pyrénées-Orientales.*
Information from the following registers was communicated by Mr. Guy Romestan and by Mr. R. W. Emery.
Série E notaries: reg. 11, 27, 29, 30, 32, 33, 35, 37, 38, 39, 40, 43, 46, 47, 49, 51, 54, 68 et 69.

3. *Archives Municipales de Montpellier*
The following registers have been exploited exhaustively:

	No. folios	No. legible acts
fonds des notaires acquis par le Consulat.[1]		
II 1 Grimaudi, Jean 7 Sept. 1293-22 Mar. 1294	94	434
II 2 Grimaudi, Jean 15 Apr. 1301-23 Jun. 1302	144	166
II 3 Laurentii, Jean 24 Mar. 1342-12 Apr. 1343	123	110

In addition, hundreds of parchments were examined after a study of the following inventories. Reference has been made in the footnotes to specific acts.

Volume 1: *Archives communales de Montpellier antérieures à 1790. Inventaires et documents: I. Notice sur les anciens inventaires, inventaire du Grand Chartrier*, by Joseph Berthelé, Montpellier, 1895.
Volume 2: *Documents omis dans l'inventaire du Grand Chartrier*, by Maurice Oudot de Dainville, Montpellier, 1955.
Volume 3: *Inventaire des cartulaires, suivi d'éclaircissements topographiques et de documents complémentaires concernant la ville et les environs de Montpellier*, by J. Berthelé, Montpellier, 1901-1904, 2 v.
Volume 4: *La viguerie de Montpellier au XIIIe siècle; Montpellier en 1697, en 1760, en 1768 et en 1836; les biens nobles du diocèse de Montpellier aux XVIIe et XVIIIe siècles; le premier jardin des plantes français 1593-1632*, by J. Berthelé, Montpellier, 1920.

[1] The notation II has been substituted for the old classification BB, on the advice of the late municipal archivist, Mr. Marcel Gouron.

Volume 5: *Éclaircissements topographiques, 2e série*, by J. Berthelé, Montpellier, 1928.

Volume 6: *Inventaire de Joffre, Archives du greffe de la Maison consulaire, armoires A et B*, by M. Oudot de Dainville, Montpellier, 1934.

Volume 7: *Inventaire de Joffre, armoire C*, by M. Oudot de Dainville, Montpellier, 1939.

Volume 8: *Inventaire de Joffre, armoire D et autres documents*, by M. Oudot de Dainville, Montpellier, 1943-1949, 2 v.

Volume 9: *Inventaire de Joffre, armoire D (suite)*, by M. Oudot de Dainville, Montpellier, 1949.

Volume 10: *Inventaire des sceaux des archives de la ville de Montpellier*, by M. Oudot de Dainville, Montpellier, 1952.

Volume 11: *Documents comptables*, by M. Oudot de Dainville, Montpellier, 1959.

Volume 12: *Fonds de la commune clôture et affaires militaires. Série EE*, by Maurice Oudot de Dainville et Marcel Gouron, Montpellier, 1974.

Spain:

1. *Archivo de la Corona de Aragon*.
Information from the following notarial registers was communicated by Mr. Guy Romestan.

Manual de Lor. Canals.
Manual de Petro de Torre.
Reg. 482 and 483.

2. *Archivo del Reino de Valencia*.
Information from the following notarial registers was communicated by Mr. Guy Romestan.

Fonds: Protocolos: 2071, 2627, 2757, 2791, 2792, 2801, 2812, 2837, 2855, 2873, 2876, 2880, 2946.

3. *Archivo Historico de Mallorca*.
During two weeks in Palma, a brief examination was made in the following *fonds*.
Archivo de Protocolos: notaries.
Archivo privados: a – Lletres communes.
b – Cartas Reales.
References to specific acts were communicated by the late archivist Fr. Sevillano Colom and are listed in the footnotes.

B. Primary Sources

Blancard, Louis, ed. *Documents inédits sur le commerce de Marseille au Moyen-Âge*, 2 vols. Marseille, 1885.

Bullaire de l'Église de Maguelone. Ed. by J. Rouquette. 2 vols. Montpellier, 1911-1914.

Cartulaire d'Aniane. Ed. by Abbé Cassan and E. Meynial. (Vol. 2 of *Cartulaires des abbayes d'Aniane et de Gellone*). Montpellier, 1900.

Cartulaire de Gellone. Ed. by Paul Alaus, Abbé Cassan and E. Meynial. (Vol. 1 of *Cartulaires des abbayes d'Aniane et de Gellone*). Montpellier, 1898.

Cartulaire de l'Université de Montpellier, 1181-1400: vol. 1. Montpellier, 1890. Vol. 2, *Inventaire des archives anciennes de la Faculté de medecine et supplément au tome 1*, par Joseph Calmette. Montpellier, 1912.

Cartulaire de Maguelone. Ed. by J. Rouquette and A. Villemagne. 5 vols. Montpellier, 1912-1925.

Cartularium Studii Bononiensis, documenti per la storia della università de Bologna dalle origine fino al secolo xv, 13 vols. Imola, 1907, Bologna, 1913-1936.

Chiaudano, Mario, ed. *Oberto Scriba de Mercato (1186)*. Turin, 1940.

Chiaudano, Mario and Moresco, Mattia, eds. *Il Cartolare di Giovanni Scriba*, 2 vols. Turin, 1935.

Chiaudano, Mario and Morozzo Della Rocca, R., eds. *Oberto Scriba de Mercato (1190)*. Turin, 1938.

Dom Devic et Dom Vaissète. *Histoire générale de Languedoc*, 14 vols. Toulouse, 1872-1904.

Doehaerd, Renée. *Les Relations commerciales entre Gênes, la Belgique et l'Outremont d'après les archives notariales génoises aux* XIIIe *et* XIVe *siècles*, vol. 3. Brussels/Rome, 1941.

Eierman, J. E., Krueger, H. G. and Reynolds, R. L., eds. *Bonvillano (1198)*. Turin, 1939.

Ferretto, Arturo. "Codice diplomatico delle relazioni fra la Liguria, la Toscana e la Lunigiana ai tempi di Dante, 1265-1321." *Atti della società ligure di storia patria*, 31 (1901).

Germain, A. *Histoire de la commune de Montpellier depuis ses origines jusqu'à son incorporation définitive à la monarchie française*, 3 vols. Montpellier, 1851. *Pièces justificatives*.

——. *Histoire du commerce de Montpellier antérieurement à l'ouverture du port de Cette*, 2 vols. Montpellier, 1861. *Pièces justificatives*.

Hall, M. W., Krueger, H. G. and Reynolds, R. L., eds. *Guglielmo Cassinese (1190-1192)*, 2 vols. Genoa/Turin, 1938.

Hall-Cole, M. W., Krueger, H. G., Reinest, R. G. and Reynolds, R. L., eds. *Giovanni di Guiberto (1200-1211)*, 2 vols. Turin, 1939-1940.

Jacobi, Petrus. *Subtilissimi et acutissimi legum interpretii Domini Petri Jacobi aurea famosissima practica*. Lyon, 1527.

Kahn, Salomon. "Documents inédits sur les juifs de Montpellier au Moyen Âge." *Revue des études juives* 19 (1889), 259-281; 22 (1891), 264-279; and 28 (1894), 118-141.

Liber Instrumentorum Memorialium, Cartulaire des Guilhems de Montpellier. Ed. by C. Chabaneau and A. Germain. Montpellier, 1884-1886.

Lopez, R. S. and Raymond, I. W. *Medieval Trade in the Mediterranean World*. New York/London, 1955.

Martin-Chabot, Eugène. *Les archives de la cour des comptes, aides et finances de Montpellier. Avec un essai de restitution des premiers registres de la sénéchaussée*. Bibliothèque de la Faculté des Lettres de l'Université de Paris, 22 (Paris, 1907).

Montel, Achille. "Le catalogue des chapellenies." *Revue des Langues romanes* 3 (1872), 292-310; 4 (1873), 5-43.

——, ed. "Le Livre des privilèges de la commune clôture." *Revue des Langues romanes* 2 (1871), 85-108.

Ordonnances des Roys de France de la troisième race, 23 vols. in folio. Paris, 1723-1849.

Pegolotti, Francesco di Balduccio. *La pratica della mercatura*. Ed. by Allan Evans. Cambridge, Mass., 1936.

Le Petit Thalamus de Montpellier. Ed. by F. Pégat, E. Thomas and Desmazes. Montpellier, 1840.

Petrarch, Franciscus. *Francisci Petrarchae Florentini Philosophi Oratoris et Poeta clarissimi ... Opera omnia*. Ed. by Henrichus Petri. Basel, 1554.

Sturler, L. L. de. *Les relations commerciales entre Gènes, la Belgique et l'Outremont d'après les archives notariales génoises, 1200-1400*. 2 vols. 1962.

Teulet, A. *Layettes du Trésor des Chartes*, 5 vols. Paris, 1863-1909.

Villani, Giovanni, *Cronica de Giovanni Villani*. 6 vols. Florence, 1823.

Wolff, Philippe, ed. *Documents de l'histoire du Languedoc*. Toulouse, 1969.

C. Secondary Sources

Ashtor, E. *Les métaux précieux et la balance des paiements du Proche-Orient à la basse époque*. Paris, 1971.

Aubenas, Roger. *Cours d'histoire du droit privé des anciens pays de droit écrit (XIIIe-XIVe siècles)*. Vol. 1. *Contrats et obligations d'après les actes de la pratique*. Aix-en-Provence, 1956.

——. *Étude sur le notariat provençal au moyen-âge et sous l'ancien régime*. Aix-en-Provence, 1931.

——. "La famille de l'ancienne Provence." *Annales d'histoire économique et sociale* 8 (1936), 523-541.

Babelan, Ernest. "La théorie féodale de la monnaie." *Mémoires de l'Académie des Inscriptions et Belles-Lettres* 4th ser., 38, Part 1 (1908).

Baldwin, John W. *Masters, Princes, and Merchants: The Social Views of Peter the Chanter and His Circle*. 2 vols. Princeton, 1970.

——. "The Medieval Merchant Before the Bar of Canon Law." *Papers of the Michigan Academy of Science, Arts and Letters* 44 (1959), 287-299.

——. *The Medieval Theories of the Just Price. Romanists, Canonists, and Theologians in the Twelfth and Thirteenth Centuries. Transactions of the American Philosophical Society*, new ser., 49, pt. 4. Philadelphia, 1959.

Baratier, Édouard, "Marseille et Narbonne au XIVe siècle d'après les sources marseillaises." *Fédération historique* (Montpellier, 1973), 85-92.

Baratier, Édouard and Reynaud, Félix. *Histoire du commerce de Marseille*. Vol. 2. Paris, 1951.

——. "La lettre de change à Marseille et à Avignon aux XIVe et XVe siècles." In *Recueil de travaux offerts à M. Clovis Brunel*, pp. 83-92. Paris, 1955.

Barro, Robert J. and Fischer, Stanley. "Recent Developments in Monetary Theory." *Journal of Monetary Economics* 2 (1976), 133-167.

Baumel, Jean. *Histoire d'une seigneurie du Midi de la France*. Vol. 1: *Naissance de Montpellier (985-1213)*. Montpellier, 1969. Vol. 2: *Montpellier sous la seigneurie de Jacques le Conquérant et des rois de Majorque. Rattachement de Montpelliéret et de Montpellier à la France (1213-1349)*. Montpellier, 1971.

Bautier, Anne-Marie. "Contribution d'un vocabulaire économique du Midi de la France." *Bulletin du Cange* 25 (1955), 5-74; 27 (1956), 241-286.

Bautier, Robert-Henri. "Les foires de Champagne. Recherches sur une évolution historique." *Recueils de la Société Jean Bodin*, 5: *La foire*. (Brussels, 1953) 97-148.

——. "L'Or et l'argent en Occident de la fin du XIIIe siècle au début du XIVe siècle." *Académie des Inscriptions et Belles Lettres, Comptes rendus* (1951), 169-174.

——. "Les registres des foires de Champagne. À propos d'un feuillet récemment découvert." *Bulletin philologique et historique* (1942-1943), 157-185.

——. "Un usurier siennois à Auxerre au début du XIVe siècle." *Annales de Bourgogne* (1951), 282-285.

Becker, Marvin B. "Gualtieri di Brienne e la regolamentazione dell 'usura a Firenze." *Archivio storico italiano* 114 (1956), 734-740.

——. "Nota dei processi reguardanti prestatori di denaro nei tribunali fiorentini dal 1343 al 1379." *Archivio storico italiano* 114 (1956), 741-748.

——. "Three Cases Concerning the Restitution of Usury in Florence." *Journal of Economic History* 17 (1957), 445-450.

Bensa, Enrico. *Francesco di Marco da Prato: Notizie e documenti sulla mercatura italiana del secolo XIV*. Milan, 1928.

Berger, Adolf. *Encyclopedic Dictionary of Roman Law. Transactions of the American Philosophical Association*. New Series, 43, part 2, 333-809. Philadelphia, 1953.

Berlow, Rosalind K. "The Development of Business Techniques Used at the Fairs of Champagne from the End of the Twelfth to the Middle of the Thirteenth Century." *Studies in Medieval and Renaissance History* 8 (1971), 3-32.

——. "The Sailing of the 'Saint-Esprit'." *Journal of Economic History* 39 (1979), 345-362.

Bernard, Jacques. "Trade and Finance in the Middle Ages, 900-1500." In *The Fontana Economic History of Europe*, ed. Carlo M. Cippola. 1: *The Middle Ages*, pp. 274-329. London and Glasgow, 1972.

Berne, Albert. *Consuls sur mer et d'outremer de Montpellier au moyen-âge (XIIIe et XIVe siècles)*. Carcassonne, 1904.

Besta, Enrico. *Le obligazioni nella storia del diritto italiano*. Padua, 1937.

Bigwood, Georges. "Les financiers d'Arras: contribution à l'étude des origines du capitalisme moderne." *Revue belge de philologie et d'histoire* 3 (1924), 465-508, 769-819; 4 (1925), 109-119, 379-421.

——. "La politique de la laine en France sous les règnes de Philippe le Bel et de ses fils." *Revue belge de philologie et d'histoire* 15 (1937), 79-103, 429-457; 16 (1938), 95-239.

——. *Le régime juridique et économique du commerce de l'argent dans la Belgique du moyen âge*. 2 vols. Brussels, 1921-1922.

Bisson, Thomas N. "Coinage and Royal Monetary Policy in Languedoc during the Reign of Saint Louis." *Speculum* 32 (1957), 443-469.

——. *Conservation of Coinage. Monetary Exploitation and its Restraint in France, Catalonia, and Aragon (c. A.D. 1000-c. 1225)*. Oxford, 1979.

——. "À propos d'un registre municipal de Narbonne. Notes sur la chronologie des ordonnances monétaires de Louis IX (1263-1265)." *Annales du Midi* 72 (1960), 83-88.

——. "Sur les origines du monedatge: quelques textes inédits." *Annales du Midi* 85 (1973), 91-99.

Bizaguet, Armand. "Les origines des institutions et des mécanismes bancaires en Europe occidentale: de la banque romaine à l'empire napoléonien." *Revue internationale d'histoire de la banque* 9 (1974), 17-79.

Blanc, A. *Le livre de comptes de Jacme Olivier, marchand narbonnais du xive siècle*. Paris, 1899.

Blancard, Louis. *Le millarès, étude sur une monnaie du xiiie siècle imitée de l'arabe par les chrétiens pour les besoins de leur commerce en pays maure*. Marseille, 1876.

——. "Note sur la lettre de change à Marseille au xiiie siècle." *Bibliothèque de l'École des Chartes* 39 (1878), 110-128, 388.

Blanchet, Adrien and Dieudonné, A. *Manuel de numismatique française*. 4 vols. Paris, 1912-1936.

Bloch, Marc. *Les caractères originaux de l'histoire rurale française*. New ed. Paris, 1964.

——. *Esquisse d'une histoire monétaire de l'Europe*. Paris, 1954.

——. *Feudal Society*. Tr. L. A. Manyon. 2 vols. Chicago, 1964.

——. "Le problème de l'or au moyen âge." *Annales d'histoire économique et sociale* 5 (1933), 1-34.

Blomquist, Thomas. "Administration of a Thirteenth-Century Mercantile Banking Partnership: An Episode in the History of the Ricciardi of Lucca." *Revue internationale d'histoire de la banque* 7 (1973), 1-9.

——. "The Castracani Family of Thirteenth-Century Lucca." *Speculum* 46 (1971), 459-476.

——. "Commercial Association in Thirteenth-Century Lucca." *Business History Review* 45 (1971), 157-177.

——. "De Roover on Business, Banking and Economic Thought." *Journal of Economic History* 35 (1975), 821-830.

——. "Trade and Commerce in Thirteenth-Century Lucca." Diss. University of Minnesota, 1966.

Bompaire, Marc. "L'Atelier monétaire royal de Montpellier et la circulation monétaire en Bas Languedoc jusqu'au milieu du xve siècle." Thèse, École des Chartes, 1980, 2 vols.

Bonnet, Émile. "Les séjours à Montpellier de Jacques le Conquérant, roi d'Aragon." *Mém. soc. arch. Mplr.*, 2nd ser., 9 (1927), 153-232.

Bonnet, Michèle. "Les changeurs lyonnais au moyen âge (1350-1450)." *Revue historique* 249 (1973), 325-352.

Borlandi, Franco, ed. *Libro di mercantantie et usanze de 'paesi*. Turin, 1936.

Borrelli de Serres, L. "Trois hypothèses sur les variations monétaires au xive siècle." *Recherches sur divers services publics, du xiiie au xviie siècle*. Vol. 3 (Paris, 1909), 437-545.

——. "Les variations monétaires sous Philippe le Bel." *Gazette numismatique française* 5 (1901), 245-367; 6 (1902), 9-67.

Boüard, Alain de. *Manuel de diplomatique française et pontificale*. 2 vols. Paris, 1948.

Boudet, M. "Les marchands d'Aurillac et de Saint-Flour aux foires de Champagne et à Montpellier (xiiie-xive siècles)." *Revue de la Haute-Auvergne* 15 (1913), 326-341.

Bouges, Philippe. "La pratique contractuelle à Montpellier de la fin du xiiie siècle à la fin du xve." Thèse d'État, Faculté de Droit et des Sciences Économiques – Université de Montpellier – I, 1972, 2 vols.

Bourquelot, Félix. *Étude sur les foires de Champagne*. 2 vols. Paris, 1865.

Boutruche, Robert. *Seigneurie et féodalité: le premier âge des liens d'homme à homme*. Paris, 1959, 1968.

——. *Une société provinciale en lutte contre le régime féodal; l'alleu en Bordelais et en Bazadais du xie au xviiie siècle*. Paris, 1947.

Braudel, Fernand. "Monnaies et civilisations: de l'or du Soudan à l'argent d'Amérique." *Annales: ESC* 1 (1946), 9-22.

Bresc, Henri. "Marchands de Narbonne et du Midi en Sicile (1300-1460)." *Fédération historique, Narbonne au moyen âge* (Montpellier, 1973), 93-99.

Bridrey, E. *La théorie de la monnaie au* XIVe *siècle, Nicole Oresme*. Paris, 1906.

Brown, Elizabeth A. R. "Royal Salvation and Needs of State in Late Capetian France." In *Order and Innovation in the Middle Ages: Essays in Honor of Joseph R. Strayer*, eds. William C. Jordan, Bruce McNab and Teofilo F. Ruiz, pp. 365-383, 541-561. Princeton, 1976.

——. "Taxation and Morality in the Thirteenth and Fourteenth Centuries: Conscience and Political Power and the Kings of France." *French Historical Studies* 13 (1973), 1-28.

——. "The Tyranny of a Construct: Feudalism and Historians of Medieval Europe." *American Historical Review* 79 (1974), 1063-1088.

Brun, Robert. "A Fourteenth-Century Merchant of Italy: Francesco Datini, Prato." *Journal of Economic and Business History* 2 (1930), 451-466.

Buckland, W. W. *A Manual of Roman Private Law*. 2nd ed. Cambridge, 1953.

Burns, Robert I. *The Crusader Kingdom of Valencia*. 2 vols. Cambridge, Mass., 1967.

Byrne, Eugene H. *Genoese Shipping in the Twelfth and Thirteenth Centuries*. Cambridge, Mass., 1930.

Cahn, Kenneth S. "The Roman and Frankish Roots of the Just Price of Medieval Canon Law." *Studies in Medieval and Renaissance History* 6 (Lincoln, Neb., 1969), 3-52.

Caramel, Alfred. *Bibliographie du Languedoc*. Montpellier, 1963.

Carbasse, Jean-Marie. "Consulats méridionaux et justice criminelle au Moyen Âge." Thèse d'État, Faculté de Droit et des Sciences Économiques – Université de Montpellier, I, 1974.

Carpentier, Elizabeth. "Autour de la peste noire: famines et épidémies dans l'histoire du XIVe siècle." *Annales: ESC* 18 (1962), 1062-1092.

Carrère, Claude. *Barcelone, centre économique à l'époque des difficultés (1380-1462)*. 2 vols. Paris, The Hague, 1967.

Castaing-Sicard, Mireille. *Les contrats dans le très ancien droit toulousain,* Xe-XIIIe *siècles*. Toulouse, 1959.

——. *Monnaies féodales et circulation monétaire en Languedoc (*Xe-XIIIe *siècles)*. Toulouse, 1961.

——. "Le prêt à intérêt à Toulouse aux XIIe et XIIIe siècles." *Bulletin philologique et historique* (1953-1954), 273-278.

Castellani, Christian. "Le rôle économique de la communauté juive de Carpentras au début du XVe siècle." *Annales: ESC* 27 (1972), 583-611.

Cazelles, Raymond. "Quelques réflexions à propos des mutations de la monnaie royale française (1295-1360)." *Le Moyen Âge* 72 (1966), 83-105, 251-278.

Cessi, R. *Note per la storia delle società di commercio nel Medio Evo in Italia*. Rome, 1917.

——, ed. *Problemi monetari veneziani (fino a tutto il secolo* XIV.) Padua, 1939.

Chenon, E. *Étude sur l'histoire des alleux*. Paris, 1888.

Chiaudano, Mario. *Contratti commerciali genovesi del secolo* XII *(Contributo alla storia dell'accomandatio et della societas)*. Turin, 1925.

——. "I Rotchild del Duecento: la Gran Tavola di Orlando Bonsignori." *Bulletino Senese di Storia Patria*, new ser., 6 (1935), 103-142.

Cholvy, Gérard, ed. *Le diocèse de Montpellier*. Paris, 1976.

Cippola, Carlo M. "Currency Depreciation in Medieval Europe." *Economic History Review*, 2nd ser., 15 (1963), 413-422.

——. *Money, Prices and Civilization in the Mediterranean World, Fifth to Seventeenth Centuries*. Princeton, 1956.

——. *Studi de storia della monetà*. 1: *I movimenti dei cambi in Italia dal secolo XIII al XV*. Pavia, 1948.

Combes, Jean. "La constitution de rente à Montpellier au commencement du XVe siècle." *Annales de l'Université de Montpellier et du Languedoc-Roussillon* 2, nos. 3-4 (1944), 216-223.

——. "Une famille de négociants quercynols à Montpellier et à Marseille au XIIIe siècle." *Fédération historique*, 27e congrès, (Perpignan, 1953), 28e congrès, (Saint-Gilles, 1954), off-print, pp. 1-8. Montpellier, 1956.

——. "Finances municipales et oppositions sociales à Montpellier au commencement du XIVe siècle." *Fédération historique* 44e congrès (Privas, 1971), pp. 99-120. Montpellier, 1972.

——. "Les foires en Languedoc au moyen âge." *Annales: ESC* 13 (1958), 231-259.

——. "Les investissements immobiliers à Montpellier au commencement du XVe siècle." *Recueil*, fasc. 2 (1951), 21-28.

——. "La monnaie de Montpellier et les gisements d'or et d'argent dans les Cévennes méridionales au XVe siècle." *Fédération historique* 5 (Montpellier, 1977), 145-155.

——. "Montpellier et les foires de Champagne." *Actes du 96e congrès national des sciences savantes* (Toulouse, 1971), *Philologique et historique*, 1 (Paris, 1978), 381-428.

——. "Origine et passé d'Aigues-Mortes." *Revue d'histoire économique et sociale* 50 (1972), 304-326.

——. "Quelques remarques sur les bourgeois de Montpellier au moyen âge." *Recueil*, fasc. 7, *Mélanges Pierre Tisset* (Montpellier, 1970), 93-132.

——. "Les relations commerciales entre Marseille et Montpellier au XIIIe siècle." In *Congrès de civilisation et culture provençales*, pp. 42-46. Avignon, 1961.

——. "Transports terrestres à travers la France centrale à la fin du XIVe siècle et au commencement du XVe." *Fédération historique*, 29e congrès (Mende, 1955), pp. 3-7. Montpellier, 1955.

Copeland, Morris A. "Concerning the Origin of a Money Economy." *American Journal of Economics and Sociology* 33 (1974), 1-17.

D'Achéry, Luc. *Spicilegium*. Vol. 3. Paris, 1723.

Delisle, Léopold. *Les opérations financières des Templiers*. Paris, 1889.

De la Ronnière, Charles M. *Un changeur florentin du Trecento: Lippo di Fede del Sega (1285 environ-1363 environ)*. Paris, 1973.

Denholm-Young, N. "The merchants of Cahors." *Medievalia et Humanistica* 4 (1946), 37-44.

Dépinay, Martine. "Un aspect de l'activité des seigneurs de Montpellier: l'extension territoriale de la seigneurie des origines à la mort de Guilhem VIII (985-1202)." Thèse de Maîtrise, Faculté des Lettres et des Sciences Humaines – Université de Montpellier – III, 1971.

Desportes, Pierre. *Reims et les Rémois aux XIIIe et XIVe siècles*. Paris, 1979.

Di Tucci, Raffaele. *Studi sull'economia genovese del secolo XII: La nave e i contratti marittimi, la banca privata*. Turin, 1933.

Dieudonné, A. "L'Actualité d'hier: changes et monnaies au moyen âge." *Revue des Deux Mondes*, 7e période, 37 (1927), 927-937.

Dion, Roger. *Histoire de la vigne et du vin en France des origines au XIXe siècle*. Paris, 1959.

Doehaerd, Renée. *Les relations commerciales entre Gènes, la Belgique et l'Outremont*. 3 vols. Brussels, Rome, 1941.

Dognon, Paul. *Les institutions politiques et administratives du pays de Languedoc du XIIe siècle aux guerres de religion*. Toulouse, 1895.

——. "De quelques mots employés au moyen âge dans le Midi pour désigner des classes d'hommes: *platerii, platearii*." *Annales du Midi* 11 (1899), 348-358.

Duby, Georges. *L'Économie rurale et la vie des campagnes dans l'Occident médiéval*. 2 vols. Paris, 1962.

——. *Guerriers et paysans, VIIe-XIIe siècle: Premier essor de l'économie européenne*. Paris, 1973.

——. *Histoire de la France rurale*. Vol. 1. Paris, 1975.

Dufourcq, Charles E. *La vie quotidienne dans les ports méditerranéens au moyen âge. Provence-Languedoc-Catalogne*. Paris, 1975.

Dugrand, R. "La garrigue montpelliéraine." *Bulletin de la société languedocienne de géographie* 2nd. ser., 34 (1963), 3-266.

Dumas, Auguste. "Dieu nous garde de l'*et cetera* du notaire." In *Mélanges Paul Fournier*, pp. 153-169. Paris, 1929.

Dunbar, Charles F. "The Bank of Venice." *Quarterly Journal of Economics* 5 (1892), 308-335; appendix, 371-397.

Dupont, André. *Les relations commerciales entre les cités maritimes de Languedoc et les cités méditerranéennes d'Europe et d'Italie du Xe au XIIIe siècle*. Nîmes, 1942.

Einaudi, Luigi. "The Medieval Practice of Managed Currency." In *The Lessons of Monetary Experience: Essays in Honor of Irving Fisher*, pp. 259-268. New York, 1937.

Ellul, Jacques. *Histoire des institutions. Le Moyen Âge*. Vol. 3. Paris, 1962.

——. "Notes sur les impôts municipaux à Montpellier aux XIIIe et XIVe siècles." *Revue historique de droit français et étranger* 17 (1938), 365-403.

Emery, Richard W. *The Jews of Perpignan in the Thirteenth Century: An Economic Study Based on Notarial Records*. New York, 1959.

——. "Le prêt d'argent juif en Languedoc et Roussillon." In *Cahiers de Fanjeaux*, 12: *Juifs et judaïsme de Languedoc*, pp. 85-96. Toulouse, 1977.

Erickson, Carolly and Kathleen Casey, "Women in the Middle Ages: A Working Bibliography." *Medieval Studies* 37 (1975), 340-359.

Estrup, H. "Oresme and Monetary Theory." *Scandinavian Economic History Review* 14 (1966), 97-116.

Evans, Allan. "Some Coinage Systems of the Fourteenth Century." *Journal of Economic and Business History* 3 (1931), 481-496.

Fabre de Morlhon, Jacques. *Le Montpellier des Guilhem et des rois d'Aragon*. Montpellier, 1966.

Fabrège, Frédéric. *Histoire de Maguelone*. 3 vols. Paris, Montpellier, 1893-1911.

Face, R. D. "The Techniques of Business in the Trade between the Fairs of Champagne and the South of Europe in the Twelfth and Thirteenth Centuries." *Economic History Review* 10 (1957-1958), 427-438.

Fanfani, Amintore. *Le origine dello spirito capitalistico in Italia*. Milan, 1933.

——. *Un mercante del Trecento*. Milan, 1935.
Favier, Jean. *Philippe le Bel*. Paris, 1978.
——. "Une ville entre deux vocations: la place d'affaires de Paris au xve siècle." *Annales: ESC* 28 (1973), 1245-1279.
Favreau, R. "Les changeurs du royaume de France sous le règne de Louis xi." *Bibliothèque de l'École des Chartes* 122 (1964), 216-251.
Finances et comptabilité urbaines du xiiie au xvie siècle. Colloque internationale. (Blankenberghe, 1962). Brussels, 1964.
Fisher, Irving. *The Purchasing Power of Money*. New York, 1913.
Fiumi, Enrico. "L'Attività usuraria dei mercanti sangimignanesi nell' età communale." *Archivio storico italiano* 119 (1961), 145-162.
——. "Fioritura et decadenza dell'economia fiorentina." *Archivio storico italiano* 115 (1957), 385-439; 116 (1958), 443-510; 117 (1959), 427-506.
——. *Storia economica et sociale di San Gimignano*. Florence, 1961.
Forestié, E., ed. *Les livres de comptes des frères Bonis, marchands montalbanais du xive siècle*. 2 vols. Paris, Auch, 1893.
Fournial, Étienne. *Histoire monétaire de l'Occident médiéval*. Paris, 1970.
——. *Les villes et l'économie d'échange en Forez aux xiiie et xive siècles*. Paris, 1967.
Fourquin, Guy. *"Raymond de Roover, historien de la pensée économique." Revue historique* 507 (1973), 19-34.
Funk, Arthur L."Confiscation of Lombard Debts in France (1347-1358)." *Medievalia et Humanistica* 7 (1952), 51-55.

Gaillard, Bernardin. "Origines de la commune de Montpellier." *Bulletin de l'Académie des sciences et lettres de Montpellier* 6 (1914), 92-109.
Galtier, Gaston. "Les conditions géographiques de Montpellier." In *Mélanges Philippe Arbos*, pp. 237-246. Clermont-Ferrand, 1953.
——. *Le vignoble du Languedoc Méditerranéen et du Roussillon. Étude comparative d'un vignoble de masse*. 3 vols. Montpellier, 1960.
——. "Le vignoble et le vin dans le Languedoc oriental de la fin du xie siècle à la Guerre de Cent Ans." In *Études médiévales offertes à M. le Doyen Fliche de l'Institut*, offprint. Montpellier, 1951.
Ganshof, François L. *Feudalism*, foreward by F. M. Stenton, tr. Philip Grierson. London, 1952.
Germain, Alexandre. "De la monnaie Mahométane attribuée à un évêque de Maguelonne." *Mém. soc. arch. Mplr.* 3 (1850-1854), 683-719.
——. *Histoire de la commune de Montpellier*. 3 vols. Montpellier, 1851.
——. *Histoire du commerce de Montpellier antérieurement à l'ouverture du port de Cette*. 2 vols. Montpellier, 1861.
——. "Mémoire sur les anciennes monnaies seigneuriales de Melgueil et de Montpellier." *Mém. soc. arch. Mplr.* 3 (1850-1854), 133-257.
Gèze, J. B. *Les drailles de l'Hérault*. Montpellier, 1926.
Gilchrist, J. *The Church and Economic Activity in the Middle Ages*. London and New York, 1969.
Gilles, Henri. "Notes sur les bayles de Montpellier." *Bulletin philologique et historique* (1961) (Paris, 1963), 441-455.
Giraud, Charles. *Essai sur le droit français au moyen-âge*. Vol. 1. Paris, 1846.
Giry, Alfred. *Manuel de diplomatique*. Paris, 1896.

Glansdorff, M. "Les travaux d'André-E. Sayous sur l'histoire économique." *Revue économique internationale* 6 (1935), 393-412.

Goitein, S. D. *A Mediterranean Society*. 1: *Economic Foundations*. Berkeley, 1967.

——. *A Mediterranean Society*. 2: *The Community*. Berkeley, Los Angeles, London, 1971.

Gonnard, René. *Histoire des doctrines monétaires dans ses rapports avec l'histoire des monnaies*. 2 vols. Paris, 1935.

Gouron, André. "Les archives notariales des anciens pays de droit écrit au moyen âge." *Recueil*, fasc. 5 (Montpellier, 1966), 47-60.

——. "Diffusion des consulats méridionaux et expansion du droit romain aux XIIe et XIIIe siècles." *Bibliothèque de l'École des Chartes* 121 (1963), 26-76.

——. "Enseignement du droit, des légistes et canonistes dans le Midi de la France." *Recueil*, fasc. 5 (1966), 1-33.

——. "Les étapes de la pénétration du droit romain en Septimanie." *Annales du Midi* 69 (1957), 103-120.

——. "Les juristes de l'école de Montpellier." *Ius Romanum Medii Aevi*, pars IV, 3, a (Milan, 1971), 1-35.

——. "L'origine du Tribunal du Petit-Scel de Montpellier." *Fédération historique* (Mende, 1955), pp. 57-70. Montpellier, 1955.

——. "La potestas statuendi dans le droit coutumier montpelliérain du treizième siècle." *Diritto commune e diritti locali nella storia dell'Europa, Atti del convegno di Varenna* (June 12-15, 1979), pp. 95-118. Milan, 1980.

——. *La réglementation des métiers en Languedoc au moyen âge*. Paris, 1958.

——. "Le rôle social des juristes dans les villes méridionales au moyen âge." In *Villes de l'Europe méditerranéenne et de l'Europe occidentale du moyen âge au XIXe siècle. Annales de la Faculté des Lettres et des Sciences Humaines de Nice*, nos. 9-10 (1969), 55-67.

——, et Hilaire, Jean. "Les 'sceaux' rigoureux du Midi de la France." *Recueil*, fasc. 4 (1958), 41-77.

Grand, Roger et Delatouche, Robert. *L'Agriculture au moyen âge. De la fin de l'Empire Romain au XVIe siècle*. Paris, 1950.

Gras, N. S. B. "Bill of Exchange." *Encyclopedia of the Social Sciences*, 2: 539-540. New York, 1932.

——. *Business and Capitalism: An Introduction to Business History*. New York, 1939.

——. "Capitalism – Concepts and History." *Bulletin of the Business Historical Society* 16 (1942), 21-34.

——. "Economic Rationalism in the late Middle Ages." *Speculum* 8 (1933), 304-312.

——. "The Growth of Rigidity in Business during the Middle Ages." *American Economic Review* 30 (1940), suppl. 281-289.

Graus, P. "La crise monétaire du XIVe siècle." *Revue belge de philologie et d'histoire* 29 (1951), 445-454.

Grierson, Philip. *Monnaies du Moyen Âge*. Tr. Hélène Huvelin. Paris, 1976.

——. *Numismatics and History*. London, 1951.

Grunwald, Kurt. "Lombards, Cahorsins and Jews." *Journal of European Economic History* 4 (1975), 393-398.

Grunzweig, A. "Les incidences internationales des mutations monétaires de Philippe le Bel." *Le Moyen Âge* 59 (1953), 117-172.

Guerreau, Alain. "L'Atelier monétaire royal de Mâcon (1239-1421)." *Annales: ESC* 29 (1974), 369-392.

Guilhiermoz, P. "Avis sur la question monétaire donnée aux rois Philippe le Hardi, Philippe le Bel, Louis x and Charles le Bel." *Revue numismatique* 30, part 7 (1927), 96-110.

——. "De l'équivalence des anciennes mesures. À propos d'une publication récente." *Bibliothèque de l'École des Chartes* 74 (1913), 267-328.

Guillemain, Bernard. *La cour pontificale d'Avignon (1309-1376): étude d'une société*. Paris, 1962.

Guiraud, Louise. "Recherches topographiques sur Montpellier au moyen âge." *Mem. soc. arch. Mplr.* 2nd ser., 1 (1899), 89-335.

Hall, Margaret W. "Early Bankers in the Genoese Notarial Records." *Economic History Review* 1st ser., 6 (1935), 73-79.

Heers, Jacques. "The 'Feudal' Economy and Capitalism: Words, Ideas, and Reality." *Journal of European Economic History* 3 (1974), 609-653.

——. *Gênes au xve siècle. Activité économique et problèmes sociaux*. Paris, 1961.

——. *L'Occident aux xive et xve siècles. Aspects économiques et sociaux*. 3rd ed. Paris, 1970.

Henneman, John Bell. "The Black Death and Royal Taxation in France, 1347-1351." *Speculum* 43 (1968), 405-428.

——. *Royal Taxation in Fourteenth Century France. The Development of War Financing. 1322-1356*. Princeton, 1971.

——. "Taxation of Italians by the French Crown, 1311-1363." *Mediaeval Studies* 31 (1969), 15-43.

Henry, Louis. *Manuel de démographie historique*. Paris, 1967.

Herlihy, David. "Land, Family and Women in Continental Europe, 701-1200." *Traditio* 18 (1962), 89-120.

——. *Medieval and Renaissance Pistoia. The Social History of an Italian Town*. New Haven, 1967.

——. *Pisa in the Early Renaissance*. New Haven, 1958.

—— and Christiane Klapisch-Zuber. *Les Toscans et leurs familles. Une étude du catasto florentin de 1427*. Paris, 1978.

Heyd, Wilhelm. *Histoire du commerce du Levant au moyen âge*. 2 vols. Leipzig, 1885-1886, rev. ed. Amsterdam, 1959.

Hilaire, Jean. *Le régime des biens entre époux dans la région de Montpellier du début du xiiie siècle à la fin du xvie siècle*. Montpellier, 1957.

Hollander, Samuel. "On the Interpretation of the Just Price." *Kyklos* 18 (1965), 615-634.

Hoover, Calvin B. "The Sea Loan in Genoa in the Twelfth Century." *Quarterly Journal of Economics* 40 (1926), 495-529.

Huvelin, Paul. *Essai historique sur le droit des foires et des marchés*. Paris, 1897.

——. *L'Impôt dans le cadre de la ville et de l'État. Colloque internationale* (Spar, 1964). Brussels, 1966.

Jordan, William C. "Jews on Top: Women and the Availability of Consumption Loans in Northern France in the Mid-Thirteenth Century." *Journal of Jewish Studies* 29 (1978), 39-56.

Juifs et judaïsme en Languedoc. Cahiers de Fanjeaux 12 (Toulouse, 1977).

Kaeuper, Richard W. *Bankers to the Crown: The Riccardi of Lucca and Edward I*. Princeton, 1973.

Kahn, Salomon. "Documents inédits sur les Juifs de Montpellier au moyen âge." *Revue des études juives* 19 (1889), 259-281; 22 (1891), 264-279; 28 (1894), 118-141.

——. *Étude sur les Israëlites de Montpellier au moyen âge*. Nîmes, 1924.

Kedar, Benjamin. *Merchants in Crisis. Genoese and Venetian Men of Affairs and the Fourteenth-Century Depression*. New Haven, London, 1976.

Kirshner, Julius. "Les travaux de Raymond de Roover sur la pensée économique des Scholastiques." *Annales: ESC* 30 (1975), 318-338.

Kosminsky, E. A. *Studies in the Agrarian History of England in the Thirteenth Century*. Ed. R. H. Hilton. Oxford, 1956.

Krueger, Hilmar C. "Genoese Merchants, Their Associations and Investments, 1155 to 1230." In *Studi in onore di Amintore Fanfani*, 1: 423-426. Milan, 1962.

——. "Genoese Merchants, Their Partnerships and Investments, 1155 to 1164." In *Studi in onore di Armando Sapori*, 1: 255-272. Milan, 1957.

Kuznets, Solomon. "Pawnbroking." *Encyclopedia of Social Sciences*, 12: 32-40. New York, 1934.

Laborderie-Boulous, P. "La viguerie de Montpellier au XIIe siècle." *Archives de la ville de Montpellier, Inventaires et documents* 4 (Montpellier, 1920), v-xix.

Lacave, Michel. "Note sur une source de l'histoire monétaire méridionale, XVe-XVIe siècles." *Revue historique de droit français et étranger* 51 (1973), 418-424.

——. "Recherches sur la *cessio bonorum* dans le droit méridional à la fin du moyen âge." *Recueil*, fasc. 9, *Mélanges Roger Aubenas* (1974), 443-460.

Lafaurie, Jean. *Les monnaies des rois de France: Hugues Capet à Louis XII*. Paris, 1951.

Landry, Adolphe. *Essai économique sur les mutations des monnaies dans l'ancienne France de Philippe le Bel à Charles VII*. Paris, 1910.

Lane, Frederic C. *Andrea Barbarigo, Merchant of Venice, 1418-1449*. Baltimore, 1944.

——. "Family Partnerships and Joint Ventures." In *The Collected Papers of Frederic C. Lane, Venice and History*. pp. 36-55. Baltimore, 1966.

——. "Investment and Usury in Medieval Venice." *Explorations in Entrepreneurial History* 2nd ser., 2 (1964), 3-15.

——. "Ritmo e rapidità di giro d'affari nel commercio veneziano." In *Studi in onore di Gino Luzzato*, 1: 254-273. Milan, 1949.

——. "Venetian Bankers, 1496-1533: A Study in the Early Stages of Deposit Banking." *Journal of Political Economy* 45 (1937), 187-206.

——. *Venice and History. The Collected Papers of Frederic C. Lane*. Baltimore, 1966.

——. "Venture Accounting in Medieval Business Management." *Bulletin of the Business Historical Society* 19 (1945), 164-173.

Lapeyre, Henri. "Contribution à l'histoire de la lettre de change en Espagne du XIVe au XVIIIe siècle." *Annuario de Historia económica y social* 1 (1968), 107-125.

——. "Une lettre de change castillane du début du XVe siècle." *Revue internationale de l'histoire de la banque* 2 (1967), 245-246.

——. "Une lettre de change endossée en 1430." *Annales: ESC* 13 (1958), 260-264.

Larenaudie, Marie-Josèphe. "Les famines en Languedoc au XIVe siècle." *Annales du Midi* 64 (1952), 27-39.

Lattes, Alessandro. *Il diritto commerciale nella legislazione statutaria delle città italiane*. Milan, 1884.

Le Bras, Gabriel. "Conceptions of Economy and Society." *Cambridge Economic History* 3 (Cambridge, 1963), 554-575.

——. "L'Usure." *Dictionnaire de Théologie Catholique*, 15, 2nd part (1950), 2336-2372.

Lecoy de la Marche, A. *Les relations politiques de la France avec le royaume de Majorque (Iles Baléares, Roussillon, Montpellier, etc.)*, 2 vols. Paris, 1892.

Le Goff, Jacques. *Marchands et banquiers au moyen âge*. Paris, 1972.

——. "The Usurer and Purgatory." In *The Dawn of Modern Banking*, pp. 25-52. New Haven and London, 1979.

Le Roy Ladurie, Emmanuel. *Les paysans de Languedoc*. Vol. 1. Paris, 1966.

Lestoquoy, J. "Les usuriers du début du Moyen Age." In *Studi in onore di Gino Luzzato*. 1: 67-77. Milan, 1950.

Lewis, Archibald R. *The Development of Southern French and Catalan Society, 718-1050*. Austin, 1965.

——. "The Development of Town Government in Twelfth-Century Montpellier." *Speculum* 22 (1947), 51-57.

——. "The Guilhems of Montpellier: A Sociological Appraisal." *Viator* 2 (1971), 159-169.

——. "Seigneurial Administration in Twelfth-Century Montpellier." *Speculum* 22 (1947), 562-577.

Lopez, Robert S. "An Aristocracy of Money in the Early Middle Ages." *Speculum* 28 (1953), 1-43.

——. "Back to Gold, 1252." *Economic History Review* 2nd ser., 9 (1956), 219-240.

——. *The Commercial Revolution of the Middle Ages*. New York, 1971.

——. "Continuità e adattamento nel medio evo: un millennio di storia delle associazioni di monetieri." *Studi in onore di Gino Luzzatto*. 1: 74-117. Milan, 1950.

——. "The Dawn of Medieval Banking." In *The Dawn of Modern Banking*, pp. 1-24. New Haven and London, 1979.

——. "The Evolution of Land Transport in the Middle Ages." *Past and Present* 9 (1956), 17-29.

——. "L'Extrême frontière du commerce de l'Europe médiévale." *Le Moyen Âge* 69 (4th ser., 18) (1963), 479-490.

——. *Genova marinara nel Duecento, Benedetto Zaccaria*. Messina, 1933.

——. "Hard Times and Investment in Culture." In *The Renaissance. A Symposium*, pp. 19-32. New York, 1953.

——. "Italian Leadership in the Medieval Business World." *Journal of Economic History* 7 (1948), 63-68.

——. "Nouveaux documents sur les marchands italiens en Chine à l'époque mongole." *Comptes rendus, Académie des Inscriptions et Belles-Lettres* (1977), 445-458.

——. *La prima crisi della banca di Genova, 1250-1259*. Genoa, 1956.

——. *Studi sull'economia genovese nel medio evo*. Turin, 1936.

——. "The Unexplored Wealth of the Notarial Archives in Pisa and Lucca." In *Mélanges Louis Halphen*, pp. 417-432. Paris, 1951.

Lopez, Robert S. and Irving W. Raymond. *Medieval Trade in the Mediterranean World*. New York, 1955, 1961.

Luzzatto, Gino. "Les activités économiques du patriciat vénitien (xe-xive siècles)." *Annales d'histoire économique et sociale* 9 (1937), 25-57.

——. "L'Oro et l'argento nella politica monetaria veneziana dei secoli xiii e xiv." *Studi di storia economica veneziana* (Padua, 1954), 259-270.

——. *Studi di storia economica veneziana*. Padua, 1954.

——. "Tasso d'interesse e usura a Venezia nei secoli xiii-xiv." In *Miscellanea in onore di Roberto Cessi*, 1: 191-202. Rome, 1958.

Magnou-Nortier, Elisabeth. "Fidélité et féodalité méridionale d'après les serments de fidélité (xe siècle-début xiie siècle)." *Annales du Midi* 80 (1968), 457-484.

Malafosse, J. "Contribution à l'étude du crédit dans le Midi aux xe et xie siècles: les sûretés réelles." *Annales du Midi* 63 (1951), 105-148.

Malausséna, Paul-Louis. *La vie en Provence orientale aux xive et xve siècles. Un exemple: Grasse à travers les actes notariés*. Paris, 1969.

Malowist, Marian. "Quelques observations sur le commerce de l'or dans le Soudan occidental au Moyen Âge." *Annales: ESC* 25 (1970), 1630-1636.

Marin, Anne Catherine. "Montpellier à la fin du moyen âge d'après les compoix (1380-1450)." Thèse, École des Chartes, 1980.

Martinès, Lauro. "Early Effects of Credit Mechanisms in Italy." *Journal of Interdisciplinary History* 4 (1974), 603-609.

Mäschke, Erich. "La mentalité des marchands européens au moyen âge." *Revue d'histoire économique et sociale* 42 (1964), 457-484.

Mate, Mavis. "A Mint of Trouble, 1279 to 1307." *Speculum* 44 (1969), 201-212.

Mayer, P. "Le livre journal de Maître Ugo Teralh, notaire et drapier à Fourcalquier." *Notices et extraits des manuscrits de la Bibliothèque Nationale* 36 (1899), 129-170.

Mayhew, N. J. "Numismatic Evidence and Falling Prices in the Fourteenth Century." *Economic History Review* 2nd ser. 27 (1974), 1-15.

McLaughlin, Terrence P. "The Teaching of the Canonists on Usury (xii, xiii and xiv Centuries)." *Mediaeval Studies* 1 (1939), 81-147 and 2 (1940), 1-22.

Melis, Federigo. "Ancora sulle origini della partita doppia. In riposta ad un articolo del professore R. L. Reynolds." *Bollettino linguistico per la storia e la cultura regionale* 6 (1954), 1-12.

——. *Aspetti della vita economica medievale. Studi nell' Archivio Datini di Prato*. Siena, 1962.

——. *Note di storia della banca pisana nel Trecento*. Pisa, 1955.

Meynial, Edmondo. "De l'application du droit romain dans la région de Montpellier aux xiie et xiiie siècles." *Atti del Congresso internazionale di scienze storiche* 9 (Rome, 1904), 147-169.

——. "Des renunciations au moyen âge et dans notre ancien droit." *Nouvelle revue de droit français et étranger* 24 (1900), 108-142; 25 (1901), 241-277.

——. "Notes sur la formation de la théorie du domaine divisé du xiiie au xive siècle dans les romanistes; Étude de dogmatique juridique." In *Mélanges Fitting*, pp. 409-461. Montpellier, 1908.

Michel, Robert. *L'Administration royale dans la sénéchaussée de Beaucaire au temps de Saint Louis*. Paris, 1910.

——. "Les chevaliers du château des Arênes de Nîmes aux xiie et xiiie siècles." *Revue historique* 102 (1909), 45-61.

Miskimin, Harry A. *The Economy of Early Renaissance Europe*. New York, 1969.

——. "The Impact of Credit on Sixteenth-Century English Industry." In *The Dawn of Modern Banking*, pp. 275-289. New Haven and London, 1979.

——. *Money, Prices and Foreign Exchange in Fourteenth-Century France*, New Haven, 1963.

——. "Le problème de l'argent au Moyen Âge." *Annales: ESC* 17 (1962), 1125-1130.

Molho, A. *Florentine Public Finances in the Early Renaissance, 1400-1433*. Cambridge, Mass., 1971.

Morize, J. "Aigues-Mortes au xiiie siècle." *Annales du Midi* 26 (1914), 313-348.

Mueller, Reinhold C. "Les prêteurs juifs de Venise au moyen âge." *Annales: ESC* 30 (1975), 1277-1300.

——. *The Procuratori di San Marco and the Venetian Credit Market: A Study of the Development of Credit and Banking in the Trecento*. New York, 1977.

——. "The Role of Bank Money in Venice, 1300-1500." *Studi Veneziani*, new series, 3 (1979), 47-96.

Mundy, John H. "Un usurier malheureux." In *Hommage à M. François Galabert*, special ed. *Annales du Midi* (1956), 117-127.

Munro, John H. "Billon – billoen – billio. From Bullion to Base Coinage. An Essay in Numismatic Philology." *Revue belge de philologie et d'histoire* 52 (1974), 293-305.

——. "Bullionism and the Bill of Exchange in England, 1272-1663. A Study in Monetary Management and Popular Prejudice." In *The Dawn of Modern Banking*, pp. 169-239. New Haven and London, 1979.

——. *Wool, Cloth and Gold: The Struggle for Bullion in Anglo-Burgundian Trade. 1340-1478*. Toronto, 1973.

Muto, Giovanni. "Money and the European Economy from the XIIIth to the XVIIIth Centuries." *Journal of European Economic History* 4 (1975), 739-751.

Nahon, Gérard. "Condition fiscale et économique des Juifs." In *Cahiers de Fanjeaux* 12: *Juifs et judaïsme de Languedoc*, pp. 51-84. Toulouse, 1977.

——. "Le crédit et les Juifs dans la France du XIIIe siècle." *Annales: ESC* 24 (1969), 1121-1148.

Nef, John U. "Silver Production in Central Europe (1450-1618)." *Journal of Political Economy* 49 (1941), 575-591.

Nelson, Benjamin N. *The Idea of Usury*. Princeton, 1949.

——. "The Usurer and the Merchant Prince: Italian Businessmen and the Ecclesiastical Law of Restitution, 1100-1500." *The Journal of Economic History* 7 (1947), suppl., 104-122.

—— and Starr, J. "The Legend of the Divine Surety and the Jewish Moneylender." *Annuaire de l'Institut de philologie et d'histoire orientales et slaves* 7 (1939-1944), 289-338.

Nicholas, David. "Structures du peuplement, fonctions urbaines et formation du capital dans la Flandre médiévale." *Annales: ESC* 33 (1978), 501-527.

——. *Town and Countryside: Social, Economic and Political Tensions in Fourteenth-Century Flanders*. Bruges, 1971.

Noonan, John T. *The Scholastic Analysis of Usury*. Cambridge, Mass., 1957.

Origo, Iris. *The Merchant of Prato: Francesco di Marco Datini, 1335-1410*. New York, 1957.

Ourliac, Paul and Malafosse, J. *Histoire du droit privé*. 1: *Les obligations*. Paris, 1957, 1969. 2: *Les biens*. 2nd ed. Paris, 1971.

Pagézy, J. *Mémoires sur le port d'Aigues-Mortes*. 2 vols. Paris, 1879, 1886.

Patterson, C. C. "Silver Stocks and Losses in Ancient and Medieval Times." *Economic History Review* 2nd ser., 25 (1972), 205-233.

Pernoud, Régine. *Histoire du commerce de Marseille*, 1: 109-375. Paris, 1949.

Perroy, Édouard. "À l'origine d'une économie contractée: les crises du XIVe siècle." *Annales: ESC* 4 (1949), 167-182.

——. "Le 'décrochage' des monnaies au temps des mutations, le cas du viennois faible en 1304-1308." *Le Moyen Âge* 64 (1958), 437-448.

——. *The Hundred Years War*. New York, 1965.

Petot, P. *La constitution de rente aux* XII*e et* XIII*e siècles dans les pays coutumiers*. Dijon, 1928.

Peyron, Jacques. "Montpellier médiéval, urbanisme et architecture." *Annales du Midi* 91 (1979), 255-272.

Picheire, Joseph D. *Histoire d'Agde*. Lyon, 1960.

Piquet, Jules. *Les banquiers au moyen-âge: les Templiers*. Paris, 1939.

Piquet-Marchal, Marie-Odile. "Doctrines monétaires et conjoncture aux XIVe et XVe siècles." *Revue internationale de l'histoire de la banque* 4 (1971), 327-405.

Pirenne, Henri. *Histoire économique de l'Occident médiéval*. Bruges, 1951.

——. "The Stages in the Social History of Capitalism." *American Historical Review* 19 (1913), 494-515.

Pitou, C. *Les Lombards en France et à Paris, leurs marques, leurs poids de monnaies, leurs sceaux de plomb*. 2 vols. Paris, 1892, 1893.

Portal, Charles. *Lettres de change et quittances du* XIV*e siècle*. Marseille, 1901.

Postan, Michael M. "Credit in Medieval Trade." *Economic History Review* 1 (1928), 234-261.

——. *Essays in Medieval Agriculture. General Problems of the Medieval Economy*. Cambridge, 1973.

——. *Medieval Trade and Finance*. Cambridge, 1973.

——. "Partnership in English Medieval Commerce." Reprinted in *Medieval Trade and Finance*, pp. 65-92. Cambridge, 1973.

Pounds, N. J. G. *An Economic History of Medieval Europe*. New York, 1974.

Pryor, John H. *Business Contracts of Medieval Provence. Selected Notulae from the Cartulary of Giraud Amalric of Marseilles. 1248*. Toronto, 1981.

——. "The Origins of the *commenda* contract." *Speculum* 52 (1977), 5-37.

Pugh, R. B. "Some Medieval Moneylenders." *Speculum* 43 (1968), 274-289.

Racine, Pierre. "À Marseille en 1248: l'activité des hommes d'affaires de Plaisance." *Annales du Midi* 78 (1966), 221-233.

——. "I banchieri piacentini ed i campi sulle Fiere di Champagne alla fine del Duecento." In *Studi storici in onore di Emilio Nasalli Rocca*, pp. 475-504. Piacenza, 1971.

Recueils de la Société Jean Bodin. 3: *La tenure*. Brussels, 1938.

Relazioni del X Congresso internazionale de Scienze Storiche. Storia del Medioevo. Vol. 3. Florence, 1955.

Renouard, Yves. "Les Cahorsins hommes d'affaires français du XIIIe siècle." *Transactions of the Royal Historical Society* 5th ser., 2 (1961), 43-67.

——. *Les hommes d'affaires italiens du moyen âge*. Paris, 1949, rev. ed. Paris, 1968.

——. "Lumières nouvelles sur les hommes d'affaires italiens du moyen âge." *Annales: ESC* 10 (1955), 63-78.

——. *Les relations des papes d'Avignon et des compagnies commerciales et bancaires de 1316 à 1378*. Paris, 1941.

——. "Vignobles, vignes et vins de France au Moyen Âge." *Le Moyen Âge* 15 (1960), 337-349.

Renouvier, J. and Ricard, A. "Des maîtres de pierre et des autres artistes gothiques de Montpellier." *Mém. soc. arch. Mplr.* 3 (1854), 135-350.

Reyerson, Kathryn L. "Changes in Testamentary Practice at Montpellier on the Eve of the Black Death." *Church History* 47 (1978), 253-269.

——. "Commerce and Society in Montpellier: 1250-1350." 2 vols. Diss. Yale University, 1974.

——. "Commercial Fraud in the Middle Ages: The Case of the Dissembling Pepperer." *Journal of Medieval History* 8 (1982), 63-73.

——. "I lucchesi in Montpellier al tempo di Castruccio: il commercio e le finanze." *Castruccio Castracani e il suo tempo*, Convegno internazionale, Lucca, Italy. (papers forthcoming).

——. "Medieval Silks in Montpellier: The Silk Market ca. 1250-ca. 1350." *Journal of European Economic History* 11 (1982), 117-140.

——. "The Medieval Spice Trade before 1350: One Index of Mediterranean Commerce from the Perspective of Montpellier." October 1976 Northern Great Plains History Conference, University of Wisconsin, La Crosse, Wisconsin.

——. "Montpellier and the Byzantine Empire: Commercial Interaction in the Mediterranean World before 1350." *Byzantion, Revue internationale des études byzantines* 48 (1978), 456-476.

——. "Les opérations de crédit dans la coutume et dans la vie des affaires à Montpellier au moyen âge: le problème de l'usure." *Diritto comune e diritti locali nella storia dell'Europa. Atti del convegno di Varenna*, pp. 187-209. Milan, 1980.

——. "Patterns of Population Attraction and Mobility: The Case of Montpellier: 1293-1348." *Viator* 10 (1979), 257-281.

——. "Le rôle de Montpellier dans le commerce des draps de laine avant 1350." *Annales du Midi* 94 (1982), 17-40.

Reynolds, Robert L. "Bankers' Account in Double-Entry in Genoa, 1313 and 1316." *Bollettino linguistico per la Storia e la Cultura Regionale* 3 (1951), 104-107.

——. "A Business Affair in Genoa in the Year 1200: Banking, Bookkeeping, a Broker and a Lawsuit." In *Studi di storia e diritto in onore di Enrico Besta*. 2: 167-181. Milan, 1938.

——. "Gli studi americani sulla storia genovese." *Giornale storico e letterario della Liguria*, 3rd ser. 14 (1938), 1-24.

——. "Origins of Modern Business Entreprise: Medieval Italy." *Journal of Economic History* 12 (1952), 350-365.

Richardot, Hubert. "Le fief roturier à Toulouse aux XIIe et XIIIe siècles." *Revue historique du droit français et étranger* 4th ser. 14 (1935), 307-359, 495-569.

Riesenberg, Peter. "Roman Law, Renunciations and Business in the Twelfth and Thirteenth Centuries." In *Essays in Medieval Life and Thought Presented in Honor of Austin P. Evans*, pp. 207-225. New York, 1955.

Riu, Manuel. "Banking and Society in Late Medieval and Early Modern Aragon." In *The Dawn of Modern Banking*, pp. 131-168. New Haven and London, 1979.

Robinson, W. C. "Money, Population and Economic Change in Late Medieval Europe." *Economic History Review* 12 (1959), 63-76.

Rogozinski, Jan. "The Lawyers of Lower Languedoc. A Study of the Social Origins, Training, Career Patterns and Wealth of the Professionally Trained Lawyers and Judges Resident in the Sénéchaussée of Beaucaire and Nîmes and the Baronnie of Montpellier between circa 1270 and circa 1345." Diss. Princeton University, 1967.

——. "Notarial Archives in Southern France in the Fourteenth Century." *French Historical Studies* 7 (1971), 111-116.

——. *Power, Caste and Law. Social Conflict in Fourteenth-Century Montpellier*. Cambridge, Mass. 1982.

Romestan, Guy. "À propos du commerce des draps dans la Péninsule Ibérique au moyen âge. Les marchands languedociens dans le royaume de Valence pendant la première moitié du XIVe siècle." *Bulletin philologique et historique* (1969), 1 (Paris, 1972), 115-192.

——. "Draperie roussillonnaise et draperie languedocienne dans la première moitié du XIVe siècle." *Fédération historique* 42e congrès (Perpignan, 1969), pp. 31-59. Montpellier, 1970.

——. "Les relations commerciales entre Montpellier et Valence dans la première moitié du XIVe siècle." In *Acta de VIII Congresso de historia de la Corona de Aragon* (1967) II, 3: 243-253. Valencia, 1973.

de la Roncière, Charles. *Un changeur florentin du Trecento: Lippo di Fede del Sega (1285 env.-1363 env.)* Paris, 1973.

(de Roover), Florence Edler. "Éclaircissements à propos des considérations de R. Davidsohn sur la productivité de l'argent au moyen âge." *Vierteljahrschrift für Sozial- und Wirtschaftsgeschichte* 30 (1937), 375-380.

——. *Glossary of Mediaeval Terms of Business, Italian Series, 1200-1600*. Cambridge, Mass., 1934.

——. "Lucchese Silks." *Ciba Review* 80 (1950), 2902-2931.

——. "Partnership Accounts in Twelfth-Century Genoa." *Bulletin of Business Historical Society* 15: 92 (1941), 87-92.

——. "The Silk Trade of Lucca during the Thirteenth and Fourteenth Centuries." Diss. University of Chicago, 1930.

De Roover, Raymond. "Aux origines d'une technique intellectuelle: la formation et l'expansion de la comptabilité à partie double." *Annales d'histoire économique et sociale* 9 (1937), 171-193, 270-288.

——. "La balance commerciale entre les Pays Bas et l'Italie au quinzième siècle." *Revue belge de philologie et d'histoire* 37 (1959), 374-386.

——. *The Bruges Money Market around 1400 with a Statistical Supplement by Hyman Sardy*. Brussels, 1968.

——. *Business, Banking and Economic Thought in Late Medieval and Early Modern Europe: Selected Studies of Raymond de Roover*. Ed. Julius Kirshner. Chicago and London, 1974.

——. "Cambium ad Venetias: Contribution to the History of Foreign Exchange." In *Studi in onore di Armando Sapori*, 1: 631-648. Milan, 1957.

——. "The 'Cambium maritimum' Contract according to the Genoese Notarial Records of the Twelfth and Thirteenth Centuries." *Explorations in Economic History* 7 (1969-1970), 15-33.

——. "The Commercial Revolution of the Thirteenth Century." *Bulletin of the Business Historical Society* 16 (1942), 34-39.

——. "The Concept of the Just Price: Theory and Economic Policy." *Journal of Economic History* 18 (1958), 418-434.

——. "Le contrat de change depuis la fin du treizième siècle jusqu'au début du dixseptième." *Revue belge de philologie et d'histoire* 25 (1946-1947), 111-128.

——. "The Development of Accounting Prior to Luca Paccioli According to the Account-Books of Medieval Merchants." In *Studies in the History of Accounting*, ed. A. C. Littleton and B. S. Yamey, pp. 114-174. London and Homewood, Ill., 1956.

——. "La doctrine économique des scholastiques: à propos du traité sur l'usure d'Alexandre Lombard." *Revue d'histoire économique* 59 (1964), 854-866.

——. "La doctrine scholastique en matière de monopole et son application à la politique économique des communes italiennes." In *Studi in onore di Amintore Fanfani*, 1: 151-179. Milan, 1962.
——. "Early Accounting Problems of Foreign Exchange." *The Accounting Review* 19 (1944), 381-407.
——. "Early Banking before 1500 and the Development of Capitalism." *Revue internationale d'histoire de la banque* 4 (1971), 1-16.
——. *L'Évolution de la lettre de change (XIVe-XVIIIe siècles)*. Paris, 1953.
——. "Joseph A. Schumpeter and Scholastic Economics". *Kyklos* 10 (1957), 115-146.
——. "Le marché monétaire à Paris du règne de Philippe le Bel au début du XVe siècle." *Académie des Inscriptions et Belles Lettres, Comptes rendus* (1968), pp. 548-558. Paris, 1969.
——. "Le marché monétaire au Moyen Âge et au début des temps modernes. Problèmes et méthodes." *Revue historique* 495 (1970), 5-40.
——. *The Medici Bank*. New York, 1948.
——. *Money, Banking and Credit in Mediaeval Bruges: Italian Merchant-Bankers, Lombards and Money-Changers*. Cambridge, Mass., 1948.
——. "Monopoly Theory Prior to Adam Smith." *Quarterly Journal of Economics* 65 (1951), 492-524.
——. "New Interpretations in the History of Banking." *Journal of World History* 2 (1945), 38-76.
——. "New Perspectives on the History of Accounting." *The Accounting Review* 30 (1955), 405-420.
——. "The Organization of Trade." *Cambridge Economic History* 3 (Cambridge, 1963), 42-118.
——. *La pensée économique des scholastiques: doctrines et méthodes*. Montreal and Paris, 1971.
——. *The Rise and Decline of the Medici Bank, 1397-1494*. Cambridge, Mass., 1963.
——. "The Scholastic Attitude toward Trade and Entrepreneurship." *Explorations in Entrepreneurial History* 2nd ser., 1 (1963), 76-87.
——. "The Scholastics, Usury and Foreign Exchange." *Economic History Review* 41 (1967), 257-271.
——. "The Story of the Alberti Company of Florence, 1302-1348, as Revealed in Its Account Books." *Business History Review* 32 (1958), 14-59.
——. "The Three Golden Balls of the Pawnbrokers." *Bulletin of the Business History Society* 20 (1946), 117-124.
——. "What is Dry Exchange? A Contribution to the Study of English Mercantilism." *The Journal of Political Economy* 52 (1944), 250-266.
Roquebert, Michel. *L'Epopée cathare. 1198-1212: L'Invasion*. Toulouse, 1970.
——. *L'Epopée cathare. 1213-1216: Muret ou la dépossession*. Toulouse, 1977.
Rouquette, Jean. *Histoire du diocèse de Maguelone*. 2 vols. Montpellier, 1921-1927.
Russell, Josiah C. "L'Évolution démographique de Montpellier au moyen âge." *Annales du Midi* 74 (1962), 345-360.
——. *Medieval Regions and Their Cities*. Newton Abbot, 1972.

Saige, Gustave. *Les juifs de Languedoc antérieurement au XIVe siècle*. Paris, 1881.
Salvioli, G. "La dottrina dell'usura secondo i canonisti e i civilisti italiani nei secoli XIII e XIV." In *Studi guiridici in onore di Carlo Fadda*, pp. 259-278. Naples, 1906.

Sapori, Armando. *La crisi delle compagnie mercantili dei Bardiz e dei Peruzzi*. Florence, 1926.

——. *I libri di commercio dei Peruzzi*. Milan, 1934.

——. *Le marchand italien au moyen âge*. Paris, 1952.

——. *Studi di storia economica (secoli XIII-XIV-XV)*. 3 vols. Florence, 1926.

De Saulcy, F. *Recueil de documents relatifs à l'histoire des monnaies frappées par les rois de France depuis Philippe II jusqu'à François I. Documents inédits sur l'histoire de la France*. Vol. 2. Paris, 1888. Vol. 3. Paris, 1887.

Sautel, Gérard. "Une juridiction paroissiale dans le Midi de la France au moyen âge. La cour de Saint-Firmin à Montpellier." *Recueil*, fasc. 2 (1951), 47-65.

Sayous, André-E. "Une caisse de dépôts: la table des changes de Valence (1407 et 1418)." *Annales d'histoire économique et sociale* 6 (1934), 135-137.

——. "Le capitalisme commercial et financier dans les pays chrétiens de la Méditerranée occidentale, depuis la première Croisade jusqu'à la fin du moyen âge." *Vierteljahrschrift für Sozial- und Wirtschaftsgeschichte* 29 (1936), 270-295.

——. "Dans l'Italie à l'intérieur des terres: Sienne de 1221 à 1229." *Annales d'histoire économique et sociale* 3 (1931), 189-206.

——. "Les méthodes commerciales de Barcelone au XIIIe siècle." *Estudis universitaris catalans* 16 (1931), 155-199.

——. "Les méthodes commerciales de Barcelone au XIVe siècle, surtout d'après des protocoles inédits de ses archives notariales." *Estudis universitaris catalans* 18 (1933), 209-235.

——. "Les méthodes commerciales de Barcelone au XVe siècle, d'après des documents inédits de ses archives: la bourse, le prêt et l'assurance maritime, les sociétés commerciales, la lettre de change, une banque d'État." *Revue historique de droit français* 15 (1936), 255-301.

——. "Notes sur l'origine de la lettre de change et les débuts de son emploi à Barcelone (XIVe siècle)." *Revue historique du droit français et étranger* 4th ser., 13 (1934), 315-322.

——. "Les opérations des banquiers de Gênes à la fin du XIIe siècle." *Annales de droit commercial et industriel français, étranger et international* 43 (1934), 285-296.

——. "Les opérations des banquiers italiens en Italie et aux foires de Champagne pendant le XIIIe siècle." *Revue historique* 170 (1932), 1-31.

——. "L'Origine de la lettre de change: les procédés de crédit et de paiement dans les pays chrétiens de la Méditerranée occidentale entre le milieu du XIIe siècle et celui du XIIIe." *Revue historique de droit français et étranger* 4th ser., 12 (1933), 66-112.

——. "Les transferts de risques, les associations commerciales et la lettre de change à Marseille pendant le XIVe siècle." *Revue historique de droit français et étranger* 4th ser., 14 (1935), 469-494.

——. "Les transformations des méthodes commerciales dans l'Italie médiévale." *Annales d'histoire économique et sociale* 1 (1929), 161-176.

——, et Combes, Jean. "Les commerçants et les capitalistes de Montpellier aux XIIIe et XIVe siècles." *Revue historique* 65 (1940), 341-377.

Schaube, Adolf. *Handelsgeschichte der romanischen Völker des Mittelmeergebiets bis zum Ende der Kreuzzüge*. Munich and Berlin, 1906.

Schnapper, Bernard. "Les rentes chez les théologiens et les canonistes du XIIIe au XVIe siècle." In *Études d'histoire du droit canonique dédiées à Gabriel le Bras*. 2: 965-995. Paris, 1965.

——. "La répression de l'usure et l'évolution économique (XIIIe-XVIe siècles)." *Tijdschrift voor Rechtsgeschiedenis* 37 (1969), 47-75.

Schumpeter, Joseph. *History of Economic Analysis*. Ed. Elizabeth Boody Schumpeter. New York, 1954.

Shatzmiller, J. *Recherches sur la communauté juive de Manosque au Moyen Âge, 1240-1329*. Paris, 1973.

Sicard, G. *Le métayage dans le Midi toulousain à la fin du Moyen-Âge*. Toulouse, 1955.

Sivéry, G. "Les profits agricoles au Bas Moyen Âge." *Annales: ESC* 31 (1976), 604-630.

Slicher van Bath, B. H. *The Agrarian History of Western Europe, A. D. 500-1850*. London, 1963.

Sombart, Werner. *Der Moderne Capitalismus*. Vol. 1. 2nd ed. Munich, 1916.

Spengler, Joseph J. "Coin Shortage: Modern and Premodern." *The National Banking Review* 3 (1965), 201-216.

Stelling-Michaud, Sven. "Le transport international des manuscrits juridiques bolonais entre 1265-1320." In *Mélanges d'histoire économique et sociale en l'honneur du professeur Antony Babel*. 1: 95-127. Geneva, 1963.

Strayer, Joseph R. *The Albigensian Crusade*. New York, 1971.

——. *Les gens de justice du Languedoc sous Philippe le Bel*. Toulouse, 1970.

——. "Italian Bankers and Philip the Fair." In *Economy, Society and Government in Medieval Italy: Essays in Memory of Robert L. Reynolds*, pp. 239-247. Kent, Ohio, 1969.

——. *The Reign of Philip the Fair*. Princeton, 1980.

Les Structures sociales de l'Aquitaine, du Languedoc et de l'Espagne au premier âge féodal. Paris, 1969.

Thomas, Louis J. "Montpellier entre la France et l'Aragon pendant la première moitié du XIVe siècle." In *Monspeliensia, Mémoires et documents relatifs à Montpellier et à la région montpelliéraine*, 1, fasc. 1, pp. 1-56. Montpellier, 1928-1929.

——. *Montpellier, ville marchande: histoire économique et sociale de Montpellier des origines à 1870*. Montpellier, 1936.

Timbal, Pierre C. *Histoire des institutions et des faits sociaux*. 4th ed. Paris, 1970.

Tisset, Pierre. "Placentin et l'enseignement du droit à Montpellier. Droit romain et Coutume dans l'ancien pays de Septimanie." *Recueil*, fasc. 2, pp. 67-94. Montpellier, 1951.

Tourtoulon, Charles de. *Études sur la maison de Barcelone, Jacme Ier le Conquérant, roi d'Aragon, comte de Barcelone, seigneur de Montpellier, d'après les chroniques et les documents inédits*. 2 vols. Montpellier, 1863.

Trumble, Rufus. "The Law Merchant and the Letter of Credit." *Harvard Law Review* 61 (1948), 981-1008.

Udovitch, A. L. "At the Origin of the Western *Commenda*: Islam, Israel, Byzantium?" *Speculum* 37 (1962), 198-207.

——. "Credit as a Means of Investment in Medieval Islamic Trade." *Journal of the American Oriental Society* 87 (1967), 260-264.

——. *Partnership and Profit in Medieval Islam*. Princeton, 1970.

Usher, Abbott P. "Deposit Banking in Barcelona, 1300-1700." *Journal of Economic and Business History* 4 (1931), 121-155.

——. *The Early History of Deposit Banking in Mediterranean Europe*. Cambridge, Mass., 1943.

——. "The Origins of Banking: The Primitive Bank of Deposit." *Economic History Review* 4 (1934), 399-428.

Van der Wee, Herman. "Anvers et les innovations de la technique financière aux XVIe et XVIIe siècles." *Annales: ESC* 22 (1967), 1067-1089.

——. "Monetary Credit and Banking Systems." In *The Cambridge Economic History of Europe*, E. E. Rich and Charles Wilson, eds. 5: *The Economic Organization of Early Modern Europe*, pp. 290-393. Cambridge, 1975.

Van Houtte, Jean A. "Bruges et Anvers, marchés 'nationaux' ou 'internationaux' du XIVe au XVIe siècle?" *Revue du Nord* 34 (1952), 89-108.

Van Werveke, Hans. "Monnaie de compte et monnaie réelle." *Revue belge de philologie et d'histoire* 13 (1934), 123-152.

——. "Monnaie, lingots ou marchandises? Les instruments d'échange aux XIe et XIIe siècles." *Annales d'histoire économique et sociale* 4 (1932), 452-468.

——. "Le mortgage et son rôle économique en Flandre et en Lotharingie." *Revue belge de philologie et d'histoire* 8 (1929), 53-91.

——. "Les origines des bourses commerciales." *Revue belge de philologie et d'histoire* 15 (1936), 133-141.

Vigié, M. "Des enceintes successives de la ville de Montpellier et de ses fortifications." *Bulletin de la société languedocienne de géographie* 21 (1899), 123-172, 291-323, 459-481.

Violante, Cinzio. "Les prêts sur gage foncier dans la vie économique et sociale de Milan au XIe siècle." *Cahiers de civilisation médiévale* 5 (1962), 147-168, 437-459.

De Wailly, N. "Mémoire sur les variations de la livre tournois depuis le règne de Saint Louis jusqu'à l'établissement de la monnaie décimale." *Mémoires de l'Institut Impérial de France* 21 (1857), 177-427.

Wakefield, Walter L. *Heresy, Crusade and Inquisition in Southern France, 1100-1250*. London, 1974.

Ware, R. Dean. "Medieval Chronology: Theory and Practice." In *Medieval Studies, An Introduction*, ed. James M. Powell, pp. 213-238. Syracuse, 1976.

Watson, Andrew M. "Back to Gold – and Silver." *Economic History Review* 2nd ser., 20 (1967), 1-34.

Wolff, Philippe. "Les bouchers de Toulouse aux XIIe et XIIIe siècles." *Annales du Midi* 65 (1953), 375-395.

——. *Commerces et marchands de Toulouse (vers 1350-vers 1450)*. Paris, 1954.

——. "Esquisse d'une histoire de la draperie en Languedoc du XIIe au début XVIIe siècle." In *Produzione, commercio e consumo dei panni di lana (nei secoli XII-XVIII)*, a cura di Marco Spallanzani, pp. 435-462. Florence, 1976.

——. *Les "Estimes" toulousaines des XIVe et XVe siècles*. Toulouse, 1956.

——, ed. *Histoire du Languedoc*. Toulouse, 1967

——. "Le problème des Cahorsins." *Annales du Midi* 62 (1950), 229-238.

Index